Goin' O

THE STORY OF THE JUICE CREW & C

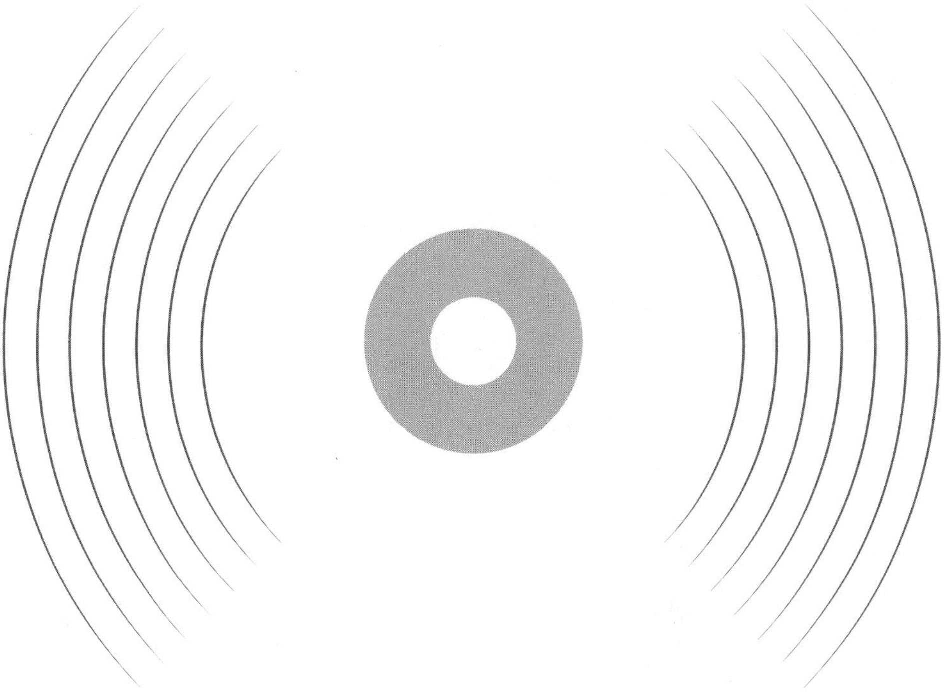

BEN MERLIS

BMG

RPM SERIES 3

Goin' Off
The Story of the Juice Crew & Cold Chillin' Records

Printed in the United States of America.

Cover Design by Patrick Crowley
Cover Photo by George DuBose

Library of Congress Cataloging-in-Publication Data available upon request.

ISBN: 9781947026322

Published by BMG
www.bmg.com

To Hugh Moore, Jr., architect
1920–2018

CONTENTS

FOREWORD
My World Premiere

For me, discovering popular music started in 1977 in 2nd grade. My teacher, Mr. Bowman, introduced me to disco, soul, and funk, and I was hooked. By 1979, I was saving lunch money and buying 45s from artists like Fatback, Cameo, and Zapp whenever I could. On holidays, I'd get a 12" single which was almost always rap. Grandmaster Flash and Sugarhill Gang had songs based around funk rhythms, but I also loved how they were rhyming on top rather than singing. It was totally different than anything I had ever heard and immediately drew me in. As a kid living in San Jose, California, I didn't really have an opportunity to witness rapping live or even on TV. Listening to these records was my only glimpse into this other world that was out there on the opposite side of the country.

By 1982, when I heard "Planet Rock" by Soulsonic Force, I started getting sucked into what we called "space jams." The sci-fi sound built around drum machines and synths really leant itself to a futuristic *Star Wars* type fantasy. These records generally didn't even have cover art so there was no telling what the artists looked like, which even made it more mysterious. Having an image was almost a distraction, and not knowing anything about the artists made the music more underground and cool. I loved watching people pop lock to songs like "Clear" by Cybotron or "Al-Naafiysh" by Hashim in the quad at my middle school or at Chuck E. Cheese.

Even as a pre-teen, I began to notice that most rap music just wasn't being represented by major labels—it was usually on smaller, lesser-known labels like Sleeping Bag, Tommy Boy, and Profile. I had an understanding that Hip-Hop started in New York and that the best stuff was still coming out of the East Coast, oftentimes on mixtapes my friends bragged about getting. A lot of this music was impossible to find in San Jose record stores.

Then Run-DMC came out and everything changed. They were considered *the new school*—their attitude and rhyme style were just what Hip-Hop needed to save it from this electro thing that had our attention but was starting to all sound the same. It was *Hardcore* rap. Run-DMC had uptempo electro songs like "It's Like That," but "Sucker MC's" is the one that had the most impact with everyone I knew, and that song pretty much reignited Hip-Hop. Soon after, a female answer version came out that caught my attention. "Sucker DJ's" by Dimples D was produced by someone named Marley Marl.

By the mid '80s, artists like the Fat Boys, Whodini, and LL Cool J had mainstream success, yet there were also underground rappers coming out that only a handful of my friends knew about. I was loving it all and making mixtapes for the high school basketball team instead of doing my homework. I was known as the kid "with all the jams."

"Roxanne, Roxanne," a b-side to a single called "Hanging Out" by UTFO was one of those organic hits that even the record label couldn't predict, and it became big enough for even casual fans of rap at my school to know. Kinda like "La-Di-Da-Di," another b-side (by Doug E Fresh & MC Ricky D) that was simple enough for everyone on the school bus to rap in unison a cappella on the way to a field trip. As the song was still reaching its peak, an answer version "Roxanne's Revenge" with rapper Roxanne Shanté surfaced. Like "Sucker DJ's," it was produced by Marley Marl. Right after that, UTFO endorsed an "official" female version by a girl they called The Real Roxanne. Ironically, Shanté sounded so much more "real" than The Real Roxanne. When I found out she was fourteen like me, it made me feel like if I found the right rapper, we could make our own record. My friend Miles lent me a Dr. Rhythm drum machine, and I recorded a song with my other friend Marcus who rapped about coming after UTFO because Roxanne was "his sister." I never made it into an actual studio until 1990, but I recorded lots of demos at the house with various rapping friends, and it basically defined my teenage years.

In 1985, Marley Marl, now a name in his own right, followed up "Roxanne's Revenge" with the "Marley Marl Scratch" featuring MC Shan. The beat hit hard, and the distorted vocals by this new rapper with a high-pitched voice who sounded like a total b-boy made it stand out. Every lyric could be easily memorized and would later be used for scratched-in choruses of countless other rap songs. The cool factor was there and I just wanted more of this. I still play it in my DJ sets today.

The year 1986 brought us The Biz. Marley's production of Biz Markie had the same raw, underground sound with lo-fi beats and lots of reverb, delay, and distortion on the vocals. "Make The Music With Your Mouth, Biz" wasn't as sonically refined as some of the other Hip-Hop stuff coming out like Heavy D, Fresh Prince, or Salt-N-Pepa, and that's part of what appealed to me. I had never heard that piano riff before (or sampling in general), and I had to find out where it came from. I still remember my amazement a few years later when I accidently came across the original sample on an Isaac Hayes album I bought for twenty-five cents. Biz's rapping was kinda off beat in a relaxed, sloppy-yet-confident way. "Nobody Beats the Biz" had that same eerie vibe to it. When I hear it today, I can't help but think of the routine a DJ named Rob Swift did with the record a decade later. Around the same time, I heard "Eric B Is President" by Eric B. & Rakim. I noticed that anything Marley Marl had a hand in, I wanted. This was the year Cold Chillin' was created, and I wrote a high school term paper that I still have (dated September 4, 1986) where I explain how I wanna start a Hip-Hop record label when I grow up. I'm a firm believer that the music you listened to in your teen years becomes some of the most significant, life changing music of your life. This was mine.

I was a high school senior in 1987 when I was introduced to *Down By Law*—the first album by MC Shan and also the first LP on Cold Chillin'. The singles from the album didn't make their way to me in San Jose, but songs like "Project Ho," "The Bridge," and "MC Space" all felt like singles to me. Shan was in the middle of a feud with another MC named KRS-One, and I refused to take sides.

By the time 1988 hit, I was already buying anything Marley Marl-related that I could find, starting with Biz Markie's long awaited debut LP *Goin' Off* in February. "Vapors" was the runaway hit off that album. It wasn't even a danceable or hard hitting song—it was just an interesting story (written by Big Daddy Kane) with a James Brown type sample that wasn't familiar to anyone my age. I later found out the sample *was* James Brown.

A few months after Biz's album, Marley's artist Big Daddy Kane hit with his debut album *Long Live the Kane*. "Ain't No Half-Steppin'" was a goosebump-inducing song and video. The mellow, ballad-y sounding music mixed so nicely with those eerie ESG sirens, hard lyrics, and delivery. Kane shared the summer of '88 with monumental albums by EPMD, Public Enemy, and Eric B. & Rakim, but he was arguably that year's biggest Hip-Hop superstar.

In the fall of that same year, Marley came out with his own album where he was both the producer *and* the artist. *In Control, Volume 1* exposed the rest of the world to this collective known as the Juice Crew, and is now a staple in the diet of any Hip-Hop fan over the age of thirty. That album was the first Hip-Hop compilation that really inspired me. Let me set this up: before *In Control,* I bought *every* Hip-Hop compilation album I could find that contained exclusive songs based around a theme (a studio, a posse, a producer) because there were so few available, and my hunger for Hip-Hop was insatiable. Albums like *Spyder D Presents Battle of the Raps* (1985), *This is Tuff City* (1985), *At the Fever! (1986), Uptown Is Kickin' It* (1986), *B. Girls Live and Kicking* (1987), and *Hurby's Machine—The House That Rap Built* (1987) had a song or two I liked by an artist I didn't previously know, but for the most part, none of them really stood up to the artist albums coming out. And none of them prepared me for *In Control*. What Marley did before any other Hip-Hop producer was prove that the DJ/producer could put together a cohesive album with nothing but heat.

I used *In Control* as the blueprint for an album I made in 1990 that never came out. I produced tracks and got rappers from San Jose to rhyme over them. I literally first got into the music industry through working on that Marley Marl-influenced project, which led me to meet Charizma. Just sixteen at the time, Charizma was a huge fan of Juice Crew rappers Masta Ace, Tragedy, Kane, and Craig G. *In Control* was a common point of interest for the two of us Northern California natives who preferred the "underground New York Hip-Hop" over the LA, Bay Area, Southern, and Miami styles of rap that were big where we lived. We worked on music together for four years until Charizma was killed in 1993 at the age of twenty.

After Charizma passed away, I took a break from creating music but remained a Hip-Hop fanatic. I noticed other crews gaining popularity who were influenced by Marley Marl and his Juice Crew "model." The crew would often be based around a single producer, but often there would be no chosen leader. There was RZA's Wu-Tang

Clan, 45 King's Flavor Unit, EPMD's Hit Squad, Gang Starr Foundation, Boot Camp Clik, Native Tongues, Hieroglyphics, and later on, Madlib's Crate Diggers Palace.

Almost exactly a decade after I wrote that high school term paper inspired by labels like Cold Chillin', I started my own "true school" Hip-Hop label, Stones Throw, in 1996. I had people (including family members) tell me for years and years that I'd never be able to make it in the music industry, but the inspiration I received from those Juice Crew records during my teen years was the impetus for my label creation. For my first release, I purposely chose a song that Charizma and I had made called "My World Premiere," which I happened to sample from "Roxanne's Revenge," signifying the world premiere of Stones Throw. Soon after, I finished my first producer-based album featuring different rappers over my beats, the Marley Marl-influenced *My Vinyl Weighs A Ton*.

Today I was on IG and noticed a photo DJ Premier posted that shows Eminem wearing an original Masta Ace T-shirt. Em was mentioning that he always wears old school Hip-Hop tees because he wants *his* fans to learn about what influenced him growing up. Life is full of coincidences, and this was one of them—that I would be looking at my favorite producer of all time, IG's, feed, and he's posting a picture from one of the most successful rappers of all time explaining the importance of Masta Ace. Thanks, Em, thanks, Preemo, and thanks, Juice Crew.

—Peanut Butter Wolf, April 2019

PROLOGUE
Set It Off

Why Cold Chillin'? There are plenty of other Hip-Hop labels that have been more commercially successful by at least a factor of ten. There is also no shortage of recording artists who have outsold any member of the Juice Crew—the collective of talent on which the label was based. The answer lies in one word: *influence*. There is a trope that the Ramones never sold many records, but everyone who bought a Ramones record started a band. In much the same way, Cold Chillin'—a label with only three gold albums and one platinum single to its name—inspired a wave of young fans to become artists themselves, propelling the Hip-Hop genre into the stratosphere at a crucial time in its development.

This story is really part of a greater narrative about the spreading of a culture that was in its adolescence by adolescents themselves. The teens and young adults in the Juice Crew/Cold Chillin' stable were at the epicenter, introducing innovations to the music that we now take for granted. It's difficult to imagine a time before Hip-Hop could be heard on commercial radio, and we have Mr. Magic, aka Sir Juice, to thank for that. Before a fourteen-year-old girl named Roxanne Shanté trashed rap group UTFO on vinyl, diss records weren't a part of the landscape. MC Shan's war on wax with Boogie Down Productions codified the practice. A Brooklyn MC named Big Daddy Kane and a Queens MC named Kool G Rap used complex rhyme structures with speed and precision, changing the way people rapped. The former was also an idol and sex symbol to a generation; the latter was among the first to be stamped with the "gangsta rap" label and singled out for corporate censorship. The Genius co-founded a dynasty called the Wu-Tang Clan. Masta Ace is the embodiment of survivalism in a cutthroat industry. These are bona fide rap MVPs in a game with constantly changing rules.

Musically, the story is roughly bookended by "super producer" Marley Marl's accidental discovery of new sampling techniques that pushed Hip-Hop out of its drum machine-dominated sound and into the *Golden Era*, and the gradual decline of sampling spearheaded by a landmark lawsuit against Biz Markie and his label Cold Chillin'. When the much more profitable Def Jam Recordings was putting out radio hits, Cold Chillin' was making what Marley calls "street classics." The southern soul music that the producer and his disciples used as sound beds, captured on primitive sampling equipment often made in home studios, made the music grittier and funkier than that of its cross-town counterpart. Cold Chillin' was Stax to Def Jam's Motown.

There is a dual nature to Cold Chillin'. During its ascent as one of the premier rap labels in the mid- to late-eighties, there was an aura of fun surrounding it, whether it was George DuBose's brightly colored record covers based on literal interpretations of album titles, or rapper Biz Markie's songs about bodily functions. Beneath the surface, there was also a lot of pain. The artists, who were almost exclusively African Americans from the greater New York metropolitan area, were largely brought up in public housing, oftentimes in single-parent households. The rise of the Juice Crew coincides precisely with the rise of the 1984–1990 crack epidemic, which decimated urban centers and broke apart families. Not everyone came out unscathed.

Where the 1980s was a time of growth and prosperity for the label, the 1990s saw the gradual decline and closure of Cold Chillin', ironically just as Hip-Hop was entering the mainstream and spreading outward to become a worldwide phenomenon. What went wrong? Why was the enormity of talent not reflected in sales? Hopefully this book will shed light on some of the possible reasons, but more importantly, it will help ensure that these pioneers get their due in the pantheon of Hip-Hop, and also music writ large. Respect the architects.

THE EIGHTIES

1

SIR JUICE & THE BIRTH OF RAP RADIO

DJs, MCs, b-boys and b-girls, fresh dressed and full of wonder, emerged from the South Bronx and spread into other boroughs, whose residents got a closer look at this strange new culture. Born between the mid 1960s and early 1970s in predominantly black working class neighborhoods, there emerged a generation, the first ever, to be raised on what came to be known as Hip-Hop.

They Used To Do It Out In the Park

Big Daddy Kane (MC, writer, producer, b. 1968): I'm from 158 Lewis Avenue [Bedford Stuyvesant, Brooklyn]. Going out to park jams, they have the block parties they set up in the projects over there. It was like the Roosevelt projects, Tompkins projects, Bushwick projects. As a b-boy, those were the main ones we'd go to. You go out there and listen to cats playing music outside, and I want say around '75, that was my first time hearing Hip-Hop like DJ Master D and I think Frankie D. There were certain DJs who would cut up disco breaks like "Love Is the Message" [by MFSB] and you had cats get on the mic and rhyme.

Grand Daddy I.U. (MC, writer, producer, b. 1968): I started out in Queens, but I moved to Hempstead, Long Island when I was maybe eight or nine. Shit, in '78, '79 the older cats used to go in the boroughs and come back with the tapes and shit. Back in the day, you go to the clubs and you would bring your fucking box in the spot, and tape the shit right off the fucking speakers. Everybody had the tapes. That was before Hip-Hop was on record. It was rare, when the Cold Crush or whoever had the latest battle, whoever was the first muthafucka on the block with that tape was *the man*.

Kool G Rap (MC, writer, producer, b. 1968): I grew up in Corona, Queens. I lived a couple of different places in Corona, and one time even East Elmhurst. That's like a neighboring section of Queens. When I was born, my family lived in Jamaica, Queens. Going into my early teenage years, I lived in LeFrak City. I lived in a few different places throughout Queens, but most of my growing up was in Corona. About nine or ten years old, there was what they call a jam in the park. I had never heard of that until this particular time. I just followed the crowd on my block that was going to this jam at the park, which was maybe a block and across an avenue from where I resided at. It was at a drug rehabilitation center. They had this little area outside the center that was like a big yard. It was like outside activities for recovering addicts and things of that nature. When I first got introduced to Hip-Hop, DJs would go in there and set up speakers, turntables, and they would start playing music. It was my first time ever being introduced to Hip-Hop not only live, but at all, period. From then on, I fell in love with it. First time hearing it, first time seeing it. It was an automatic addiction. Some of the names I would become aware of from my area a few years later was Phase, Disco Twins, CC Boys, DJ Smalls. I believe DJ Smalls was from Astoria. A DJ from Astoria might come to Corona to jam and vice versa. There was a time when it was like that. It was more unity back then. It didn't really matter. Hip-Hop united everybody on top of the unity that already existed.

TJ Swan (Hip-Hop singer, b. 1968): I was born in the South Bronx, but I was raised in Suffolk County. Central Islip, Long Island. As a young DJ I was the first in my town to play the Fatback Band. They put out the first rap record. They came out before the Sugarhill Gang. That's when I discovered Hip-Hop on wax. The record was called "King Tim III (Personality Jock)."

Masta Ace (MC, writer, producer, b. 1966): I grew up in Brownsville, Brooklyn, in the projects. Howard Houses. It was strictly black and Hispanic. Overwhelmingly black. It's a notoriously dangerous neighborhood, but I remember having a good time as a kid and getting into Hip-Hop real young. We didn't realize we were living in the hood. That was home. That's where we lived. We didn't have anything to compare it to. To me, it was a very cool upbringing and childhood—nothing but fond memories. It was definitely a time when we were learning ourselves, learning this culture. Hip-Hop was just starting out, in terms of DJ'ing in the parks. That was all pretty new. We were living the life of Hip-Hop at a very, very young age. I was raised as Hip-Hop started out in its infancy. I first heard "Rapper's Delight" at my best friend's sister's Sweet Sixteen party. Up to that point we were partying to disco records. That's what was the hot thing: records like "Good Times" by Chic, Donna Summer. When I heard "Rapper's Delight" at this Sweet Sixteen party, all I knew is that it was different. It didn't sound like anything else. It seemed like it was the first time anyone at that party heard that record. I was probably fourteen or maybe even thirteen. We just went crazy when that song came on and started dancing. They played the record three or four times back-to-back. That's how much it got the party jumping. That was the beginning.

Glamorous (MC, b. 1967): I grew up in Long Island. Freeport and Roosevelt border my mom's house. I went to both school districts, but I graduated from Roosevelt High School. I discovered Hip-Hop when Sugarhill Gang dropped their track. But I was writing rhymes before that.

Easy Mo Bee (DJ, producer, b. 1965): I grew up in Brooklyn, in these housing projects called Lafayette Gardens. We would call it for short "LG." I grew up throughout the disco era. I witnessed them bringing the systems into the park. My first real experience of Hip-Hop was just watching the DJ going back and forth on the 1 and 2's thing, but at first I watched DJs rock records like Crown Heights Affair "Dreaming a Dream," stuff like that. This right here is as early as 1975. I was ten years old, standing behind the rope watching the DJs do their thing. To me they were all that I wanted to be. The DJ was the controller. He would basically control the crowd. Everybody go into a frenzy just because of this jam they played and the way they were mixing it. For me, that's my first real experience with the *DJ* thing, period. The disco era began to fade out somewhere like around 1980. Maybe about three or four years before that, I'm talking now like first witnessing Hip-Hop maybe somewhere around '77 to '78—that's when we started to hear the MC, the breakbeats, a certain part of a record being repeated by the DJ, and there was an MC on top. There was no real true rhyming back then. It was just kind of small talk on top of the beat. And they used the echo chamber. "Yes yes y'all *y'all* . . . to the beat y'all *y'all* . . . freak freak y'all *y'all!*"

Mister Cee (DJ, producer, b. 1966): Growing up in the Lafayette Gardens projects in Bed-Stuy, Brooklyn, and seeing the DJs outside in the park was my first exposure to Hip-Hop. There was the "back park" and the "fish park" and the "monkey bar park" around our projects where DJs would be. Then I saw the Cold Crush Brothers battling the Fantastic Romantic 5, and also the Force MCs a little later.

Craig G (MC, writer, producer, b. 1973): I was born and raised in Queensbridge. It's one of the biggest housing projects in the world. It was dangerous. People didn't really have any money. But when you were young, you didn't really notice all that. It was like its own little city. We had our own park jams and our own famous neighborhood MCs that never really made records, but they were big. I used to go to all of these park jams even though I had to be home when it got dark. I lived on the block near the park, where you could hear the music through the window. Hip-Hop was always around. They had the park jams. There was a lot of local DJs that would set up on the block or go to the park. And you had these big DJs from Queens that would go out to the park, because it was such a big park for a project. They would try to stack as much speakers as they can to see who was the loudest. It was pretty dope. Hip-Hop was always around.

WHBI

It was in this climate that tiny, independent record companies were able to capitalize on the general dismissal or wholesale ignorance of Hip-Hop by the major labels. The first success story came from Sylvia and Joe Robinson's Sugar Hill Records with "Rapper's Delight" by Sugarhill Gang. Purists dismissed the single, being that the group was pieced together by Sylvia herself, and many of the words came straight out of the lyric book of Grandmaster Caz, a highly respected MC from the Bronx. Nonetheless, "Rapper's Delight" exploded in 1979, igniting a wave of other attempts at capturing the energy of the new art form on vinyl. Labels like Bobby Robinson's Enjoy, Tom

Silverman's Tommy Boy, Aaron Fuchs' Tuff City, Arthur Baker's Streetwise/Partytime, and Cory Robbins and Steve Plotnicki's Profile Records all took stabs at it, but they needed radio airplay to promote their wares. There was initially one individual who held that key: John Rivas, aka Mr. Magic.

Fly Ty (co-owner of Cold Chillin', artist manager, radio producer): I produced the first Hip-Hop radio show ever. It was called the *Mr. Magic Rap Attack* [originally named *The Disco Showcase*]. It was the only place you could hear rap *at all, period*. That was it. We had a go on a station called WHBI we had to pay to be on—twenty-five dollars an hour—but we paid to be on it.

Tom Silverman (founder of Tommy Boy): He [Mr. Magic] broke my first record "Jazzy Sensation" [by Afrika Bambaataa & The Jazzy 5] on WHBI on his show when he got to like a one or two hour once a week show on this little station—the first rap radio show in the world in this time when there were only five or six labels making rap records. We're talking about 1981. He's sitting in Riverside Drive in an apartment building or an old hotel down in the basement where they have a little, tiny room that's the WHBI studios and I guess they're getting off the roof of the building with 1000 watts. They didn't hit Midtown. They just hit northern Manhattan and the Bronx, but that was a sweet spot. I guess they must have got into Brooklyn too because the show before them was definitely a Williamsburg kind of Hasidic Jew show. It was like *Talmud Time* or something like that. And then in the show after was deep Rasta reggae show. Neither of them you could understand what they were saying. So it was really interesting to see a Hip-Hop show between. But you have to also understand in 1981 that they didn't even start calling it "Hip-Hop" yet. It was "rap" or "b-boy music" or "break music." It's still the early days. Probably in '82 it started to become more comfortably known as "Hip-Hop."

Aaron Fuchs (founder of Tuff City): I met Mr. Magic because I put out my first Hip-Hop record in '82. You would make rounds if you had a record, and the rounds weren't very big or very long. Magic was one of the very, very few guys you would bring a record to.

Fly Ty: HBI was a station we would have to pay hourly. Tommy Boy would pick up the tab. Sugar Hill would pick up the tab. Profile would pick up the tab. Jive would pick up the tab. We never actually had to pay the station. They would pay it. They communicated with each other, and they would take turns. They would put money in our hands, but they would pay for the time on air. We had Brad's Record Bin, the Soul Shack, the Disco Fever—stuff like that. We would charge you twenty dollars a spot. You would buy blocks of five. We could do 12 minutes an hour, so we would get $240 an hour.

Monica Lynch (Former president of Tommy Boy): Oh, Magic was a sweetheart! It was such a teeny, tiny industry back then. Everybody knew everybody. He had a wife, he had a little baby. Him and Ty would come to the office. Let's put it this way—Tommy Boy among other labels, were sponsors of Mr. Magic's show. We had a great relationship with Mr. Magic.

Tom Silverman: I used to go to his house. He lived in Harlem, and I just always had a memory of his house having sofas that were all covered with clear plastic. I never saw that anywhere else. It was the kind of thing you thought your grandmother would have.

Fly Ty: We came on Tuesday night at 3:00 A.M., Thursday at 4:00 A.M., and Saturday was midnight. Kids would stay up or tape it at night. If they slept, they would wake up in time, press record, and fall back asleep. Or stay up to hear it. Parents started catching their kids up listening to this show. If you didn't have a tape of the *Mr. Magic Rap Attack* when you went to school, you were lame. You were a bum. We got spread by word of mouth. It was that day and time.

Kool G Rap: I was one of the "Super Listeners" that Magic would talk about. G Rap was a *Super* fucking Listener.

WBLS

Mr. Magic's star was on the ascent. Frankie Crocker, the smooth talking and rhyming jock who dominated black radio and created the urban contemporary format in the 1970s, had graduated to program director for WBLS 107.5 FM. Crocker brought Mr. Magic's show to BLS in 1982, making it the first ever Hip-Hop show on commercial radio.

Troy Shelton (Xpertz promotion company, Warner Bros. Records): John [Rivas] loved radio and he wanted to be the Hip-Hop Frankie Crocker.

Fly Ty: We didn't realize at the time why we got all this listenership. We got all these listeners because at this point in time there was no computers, so we the only ones that had it. Kids would run to the record stores looking for this record, this song they heard. The record stores never heard them. They would call the distributors. The distributors didn't know what the hell they were talking about. They would call the record companies. Then it finally came back to, "Where'd you hear this at?" "*Mr. Magic Rap Attack*." The radio station BLS thought it was good promotion if they snatched us up. The adults—I don't care what color they were—were resistant to it. They did not like it. They didn't want it.

Aaron Fuchs: It was a time when the commercial radio stations really took note of the following that he and a couple of others had had. They were graduating them. Magic was the closest to a personality of them all. You could see him doing radio during the Frankie Crocker era. He wasn't a creature of Hip-Hop. He was a radio personality that was hitting on the explosion that happened. The private Magic had his druthers about music, but the public Magic was totally about Hip-Hop. His theme was Grover Washington's "Mr. Magic" theme. If you knew him, if you met him, he wasn't b-boyish. He was someone who was looking to identify with a more status quo R&B.

Grand Daddy I.U.: Everybody that got on from that early era, they had to come through Mr. Magic, because he was the first DJ who played Hip-Hop on the radio.

Muthafuckas didn't know what Hip-Hop was. He was the man to go to. He could call up any label and say, "Yo, I'm sending in these two cats over there—sign them." Just because he said that, they could be signed. Because they know that he in turn is going to play their music, because Mr. Magic and Fly Ty had the radio.

Marley Marl

Contemporaneously, just across the East River from Manhattan in the Queensbridge Houses, a DJ named Marlon Williams (b. 1962) was coming up. Marvelous Marlon the Magical Mixer of Disco Sounds had a knack for blending records together—seamlessly transitioning from one song to the next. The middle child of seven, his parents had split up when he was a small child, and he was raised by his mother and disciplinarian stepfather. He would spend time in upstate New York every year with his "Fresh Air Fund family"—third-generation cattle ranchers who took in poor inner city kids during summers as part of the Fresh Air Fund, a not-for-profit agency that was established in 1877. Marlon's older brother, who went by Larry Larr, had been a DJ in a group called High Fidelity Crew before enlisting in the armed forces. Larry's younger brother in turn was left with a sizeable record collection.

Cagey and combative, Marlon valued what little alone time he was afforded in such a large household. While attending high school at one of New York's "600" schools—dumping grounds for disruptive students where teachers were paid an extra $600 per year for hazardous duty—Marlon got his first taste of Hip-Hop from cassettes being played on a classmate's boombox. He recalled in an October 1991 issue of *The Source,* "I was in 600 schools as far back as 5th grade. All boys. Crazy teachers who would hit you and stuff. Yo, it was mad! From P.S. 41 I went to Manhattan High School, and there I met a guy named Breakout." Marlon had first heard DJ Breakout's music on a cassette, years before the Bronx pioneer's group Funky 4 + 1 became the first Hip-Hop act on *Saturday Night Live*. Soon after, Marlon witnessed Afrika Bambaataa DJing at Queensbridge Center. Too young to gain admittance, he had to watch through a window, peering into his future. The teenager was hooked. He also began tinkering around with recording equipment, working with his friend Andre Booth.

Andre Booth (keyboardist, songwriter, producer): I'm his big brother. I'm the one that got him in all this. I'm from Brooklyn. Bed-Stuy. I moved here [Queensbridge] in '72. That's when we ran into a lot of talent that was out here—sports guys and everything. I started a band when I moved here. And we were playing around local places, playing little clubs. Back then we changed [names] like the weather. We was Visual Vibes in the beginning. Top 40. Whatever was popular at the time we played. That's when I ran into Marley. He was a quiet kid. He wanted to get in and learn how they make records and how they do things. That's how I am. If I see someone who has an ambition for something, I share that with them. In the park, they were DJing at the time. That was the transition from the bands to the Hip-Hop starting to come in. That was the early '80s, like '81, '82. We would play, they would do they little DJing, and we combined it in the park. So we used to jam *and* DJ. We used to plug in outside and play on the different blocks. Just plug into a light pole and the band would come out and we'd just play all morning and all night. And then I used to bring my whole band over to Marley's house, [his mother] Shirley's house on Vernon, and we used to get in there and we would play, and I used to tell him to hook the cassette up to the mixer and mix our music through the mixer and make it sound decent. We would play and we would track right in the house through the mixer. I would tell him, "Make it sound good." That was part of the start there. Trying to get him to hear how musicians track in the studio. I used to record at Unique Recording Studios in Manhattan. That's where everybody was going. I always used to hang around and say, "Does anybody need a keyboard player?" They said, "Yeah." That was it. They needed a keyboard player one day and they said, "Let's see what he can do." I went in there and I played, and the next thing I know, he said, "Can you be here tomorrow?" I started playing, doing that stuff with Arthur [Baker].

Arthur Baker (producer, DJ, founder of Streetwise and Partytime): I discovered Hip-Hop living in New York, before "Rapper's Delight" came out. So it would have been '77. I was doing a disco record with Joe Bataan. He said, "You gotta come up to the Bronx and check this stuff out. It's guys talking over records." I said, "Okay, let's go up there and check it out." It was in a park and guys had big bass machines and they were rapping over records. The records they were rapping over at that time were the current hits—"Got To Be Real" by Cheryl Lynn, "Good Times" by Chic. Joe Bataan said, "Someone's gonna make a million dollars outta that." The first rap record I did was Jazzy 5, which was the track "Jazzy Sensation." That's sort of how I met Marley and all that—through working with the guys I used as the band on the "Jazzy Sensation" record. I met them through Tee Scott, who was the DJ at Better Days. They had a group. They did a track with Vicky D—"This Beat Is Mine." They had a few disco records and they were Tee Scott's friends from Queens. Andre Booth, who was the keyboard player, he played on a North End track for me called "Happy Days," and I used his guitarist Charlie Street on it. So these were guys I was working with and I used them on "Jazzy Sensation." That was literally the only rap record I did with a live band. They were excellent players. It came out very well and did really well.

Andre Booth: I used to bring Marlon along with me into the studio so he could see how records were made. I would just put him in association with me. We started out doing dance music. I was doing dance music, and he would be there, and used to cut it and do remixes. That's how he really got into doing what we do. Then he started getting in with other cats in the industry. Marlon went on to start doing the stuff with the Hip-Hop.

Planet Rock

The genre of Hip-Hop music was defined by MCs rhyming over DJs juggling the instrumental breaks from other peoples' records between two turntables. Capturing this on vinyl was generally considered faux pas. How could you make a record of a record? With a handful of exceptions, the standard method of production was to record bands replaying the very pieces of songs that were being DJ'd at park jams. "Jazzy Sensation" was essentially five MCs rhyming over Andre Booth's group replaying Gwen McCrae's "Funky Sensation." Marlon, now going by DJ Marley, thought the majority of the first wave of Hip-Hop records missed the mark. Where were the breakbeats? Where was the scratching? Where were the echo effects on the vocals everyone used in the park jams? His sense was the genre could be pushed in a different direction by taking cues from his personal hero Giorgio Moroder—a pioneer in electronic music production who incorporated futuristic sounds in disco records by Donna Summer. What Moroder did for disco, Arthur Baker did for Hip-Hop a few years later, and Marley was fortunate enough to be interning for him when the seemingly disparate worlds of Hip-Hop and electronica collided. Baker had recently produced a record by Bronx group Afrika Bambaataa & the Soulsonic Force that spun both the Hip-Hop and dance music planets off their axes.

Arthur Baker: Marley would come to the studio and hang out when we were doing sessions. I would call that an intern. I was using electronics, bringing choruses in to kind of make it more of a song structure. Those are two things in "Planet Rock." We didn't really sample. The only thing we did was we used the sample of the orchestra, but that was already in the Fairlight [synthesizer/sampler]. That was maybe the first Hip-Hop record that used a sampler, but we used the existing sounds in the sampler. Tom [Silverman] was putting out "Planet Rock."

Monica Lynch: We [Tommy Boy] had the test pressings for "Planet Rock." Actually it wasn't even a test pressing, it was a plate that we had done at the mastering lab. Tom and I drove over to Mr. Magic's show when he was on WHBI. I remember going there with this plate of "Planet Rock" with Tom. This would have been around March or April of 1982. He played "Planet Rock" on the air while we were driving away in the car, and it was a very exciting moment to hear "Planet Rock" played by Mr. Magic on WHBI. That's how immediate things were back then.

Arthur Baker: You could make the case that we used the [Roland TR-] 808 first in that kind of music, triggering a genre.

The genre was christened *electro funk,* or *electro,* defined by its uptempo, 808-driven beat and space-age sounds. One of the main tools was the Fairlight CMI (Computer Musical Instrument), which was a prohibitively expensive sampler. Costing tens of thousands of dollars in 1982 money, they were out of reach for most individuals building home studios, which is what the living room of Marley's sister's Queensbridge apartment was quickly becoming. Marley began experimenting with his first sampler—a delay effect pedal intended for the electric guitar. Delay plays back a second or two of whatever signal is inputted, essentially making it a rudimentary sampler.

Sucker DJ's

Just as fast as "Planet Rock" changed the musical landscape in 1982, another record came out the following year that pushed things in another direction.

Fly Ty: Russell Simmons and [Uptown Records founder] Andre Harrell were my roommates—the three of us. Russell was a promoter and manager. He kind of walked into management. Kurtis Blow was our friend and he needed a road manager. Russell became his road manager, and Russell had connections with a band called the Orange Krush. The country didn't know about Hip-Hop, so if you went around the country to do a show with a DJ, the crowd would boo. They didn't understand what Hip-Hop was. They just thought they were playing a record. "Where's the band?" So Kurtis got the Orange Krush band. Kurtis Blow's songs were always live music too, initially. The three of us grew together. Russell's little brother Joey—Run—he was Kurtis Blow's DJ. Darryl McDaniels was a friend of ours, a young kid. They got together and became Run-DMC.

Craig G: That's when everything changed for me. I was already rapping, not really taking it seriously. But Run-DMC to me was the catalyst for me, because they looked like they just came off the block. They looked like my older brother.

Signed to Profile Records, the b-side of Hollis, Queens-based Run-DMC's first single "It's Like That" stood in stark contrast to both the disco-based rap and electro records that came before it. Produced by Orange Krush member Larry Smith, "Sucker MC's (Krush Groove 1)" consisted of Run and DMC (Darryl McDaniels) rapping over a drum machine programmed by Erol "Pumpkin" Bedward, and nothing else. The stripped down sound and look of the trio, filled out by DJ Jam Master Jay, took the city by storm. Meanwhile, on the other end of Queens, Marley had assembled a seven MC group called the Sure Shot Crew. He quickly figured out that most of his rappers were great live, but couldn't pull it off in the studio. Even Barshon, who had given the DJ his new name Marley Marl, had to go. There was only one who could hack it—Marley's girlfriend at the time, Crystal Smith, aka Dimples D. They recorded "Sucker DJ's (I Will Survive)"—playing on the theme of Run-DMC's new hit, with the aid of a machine called a LinnDrum. It wasn't intended to be a record, but rather a remix or "DJ tool"—not something for public consumption. While Marley was playing a cassette for Arthur Baker of electronic music he had produced, one accidental second of the Dimples D song caught Baker's ear. Marley was dragged into the world of Hip-Hop production when Baker paid him $6,000 for permission to release it.

Arthur Baker: Partytime was a Hip-Hop subsidiary of Streetwise. I started Streetwise right around the same time Tom started Tommy Boy. At the same time Tom [Silverman] was putting out "Planet Rock," my partners at the label were a little pissed off, and I wasn't looking very good to them at that point. Andre and Marley did a Dimples D record. They brought it to me and I put it out. That was Marley's first credit on record.

Andre Booth: We did that record "Sucker DJ's" over at my friend Paul Young's house in Astoria. He had an eight-track studio in his apartment. Paul was also my manager at the time with my band B.b.c.S. & A.

Craig G: That was like a big song for us in Queensbridge.

While "Sucker DJ's" was only a minor hit within the tiny universe of Hip-Hop, it generated waves. An eleven-year-old Angeleno named Lucas McFadden was listening to KDAY, a west coast R&B station that had just switched to a rap-centric format. He was inspired to become a DJ and producer as he entered his teens.

Cut Chemist (Lucas MacFadden, DJ, producer, Jurassic 5): I first heard Marley on "Sucker DJ's" by Dimples D as a DJ, and he was cutting up crazy patterns for '83. "Paddup padep pep paddup padep pep pep pep pep pep pep pep!" I mean, damn that was pretty quick cuts. And what was that noise? He always found these sounds that no one else had. He became one of my favorite DJs immediately, in the early days when I heard that record. I don't know if he was cutting that quick, or if the sound was such that it had a warble to it, where it sounded like it was double time. The sound could have been like, "Walelelelele," so when he cut it, it sounded like "Paddup padep pep paddup padep pep pep pep pep pep pep pep!" Still not sure.

Andre Booth: She [Dimples D] never had a manager. It happened so fast and she was shocked because after they got the deal, everybody vacated. She had a record out, people wanted to see her, [promoters] were trying to figure out who they could contact. They contacted me. They wanted her to play. One of the gigs was up in Boston. I had my own band, so I'm like, "I can't." But that one time I took her to Boston, and did the show, and turned it out. She was the first MC for Marlon.

Instead of squandering his first paycheck, Marley invested in a Roland TR-808 drum machine, which would prove invaluable to him in the near future. Word spread to Mr. Magic about this Marley Marl character. The two were introduced to each other through a mutual friend—another Queensbridge DJ named Bob Lee who attended the New York Institute of Technology. Magic wanted Marley to do mixes live on the air, but Marley was resistant. He didn't see the point in doing something for Magic that he was already being paid good money to do at Club Pegasus. When Magic offered Marley double what Pegasus was paying, the two were now a team. Marley's dream had been to have a record on the radio like his neighbor Darryl Payne, who had co-produced "Thanks To You" by Sinnamon. Now Marley himself was literally *on* the radio.

Fly Ty: Before Marley, Grandmaster Flash DJ'd on the *Rap Attack,* also June Bug, Starchild, and Brucey B. But they were not responsible. Marley was responsible. To Marley it was a dream. The first day Marley came in there, the board was intimidating. Marley said to BLS, "Show me what controls the turntable." That was it. Before Marley left there, Marley could take that board apart and put it back together. Since I was the FCC engineer on duty, I would let Marley do what he wanted to do. Marley would figure out how to unscrew the board, pull it up, and he would increase the bass on our show and kinda tweak the treble. Paul Sanchez was our chief engineer. He walked in one night unexpectedly. "How are you guys getting that sound? You guys are getting a sound the rest of our station never gets!" We showed him. He fell in love with Marley after that. He took Marley under his wing to teach him other things. Magic used to call Marley "the Engineer All Star." He would say, "Marley Marl, the Engineer All Star—is it live or is it Memorex?" It gave us more clout at studios, because when rap first started going to studios, the engineers would not let them touch the board. They would be very nice to us and Marley would teach *them* things. Marley is a genius. When Marley would buy a piece of electronic equipment, before he actually used it, he would unscrew the cabinet take it off, then turn it on and see what lights up. When we would go to buy something, he would ask for the schematics. I never saw that before. Before you knew it, Marley could make it. Marley Marl—I never saw anybody like him in my life. Ever.

Marley Marl was now in Mr. Magic's *Juice Crew*.

Juice Crew Law

Fly Ty: Mr. Magic's aka is "Sir Juice." [Owner of the Disco Fever nightclub] Sal Abbatiello—he started the Juice Crew. It was a celebration for the *Rap Attack* radio show being brought to WBLS—a commercial station. The original members of the Juice Crew were Sal and Magic, Grandmaster Flash, Kurtis Blow, Melle Mel, Sweet G, Mandingo, Whodini, and June Bug. The original Juice Crew all had these solid gold rings with a diamond "J" in the middle that Sal bought. Without going into detail, the Abbatiellos was a family in the Bronx.

Tom Silverman: There was a connection with Sal Abbatiello. He was buying ads for the Fever, so he was he was one of the people that supported the radio show with advertising. He [Magic] had to sell his ads himself, so he bought the time and sold ads, and Sal was one of the guys who ran ads. I think his father did an after-hours gambling . . . there was some other stuff. You know they were in that business. So they were well-connected.

Fly Ty: I'm not even original [Juice Crew]. I'm second [generation]. The Fearless Four, the Force MDs, the Fat Boys, Stetsasonic, Dimples D, me, Marley—that was that second crew.

Aaron Fuchs: That was the sort of Bronx edge of Hip-Hop posses. Sal formed his own label and those guys were around his club area. Fever Records.

Jay Quan (Hip-Hop historian, The Foundation): On the street "juice" meant power. Mr. Magic would always talk about juice. It had nothing to do with rap in the beginning. It was moguls. "We got power in the industry, we got fame."

Fly Ty: If somebody in the Juice Crew has a party and says, "Okay, the party's over, everybody go home," nobody from the Juice Crew moves. Because you not talking about *me*—you talking about those other people!

It was around this time that Dimples D and Marley Marl were booked to perform in Baltimore, and Marley asked the fast-talking Brooklynite Fly Ty to come down with them to *pretend* to be their manager. Marley figured it would make them seem more official and help prevent the club from stiffing them. Without asking permission, Ty brought Mr. Magic along. On the train ride back, Mr. Magic was so obnoxious that Dimples was soured on the whole experience. By the time she got to Queensbridge, she put a halt to her own career as an MC before it had a chance to blossom. Crystal Smith went off to college, and didn't put out another record for seven years—an eternity in a genre that was barely a decade old. The experience had the reverse effect on Fly Ty—it planted a seed in his head that he could be a *real* manager.

Tom Silverman: Fly Ty was out there. He was active in the scene. You'd see him around. Juice Crew was his thing. So he and Marley would hang around, as he was sort of the impresario who represented that group of talent. And he was also close with Magic. Magic was a magnet for talent, so some stuff came in. I signed my first acts from Magic. After Bambaataa, my next acts the Force MDs and Stetsasonic came through Mr. Magic.

Monica Lynch: The Force MDs, who also went to Warner Bros. later, were winners of a Mr. Magic talent contest. Back then, a DJ like Mr. Magic, him and Fly Ty together, had to have an entrepreneurial bent, because you had to sell advertising, pay your rent,

[and] be on the air. And then as he's developing this audience with this new Hip-Hop thing going on, how do you make money? You can have talent shows and make personal appearances.

Roxanne, Roxanne

R&B fanatic Charles Stettler moved to the U.S. in 1970 from his native Switzerland after quitting a professional soccer team because he refused to cut his hair. In 1981, he and and his partner Lynda West released a cassette consisting of field recordings of New York City sounds called *Tin Pan Apple (Take The City With You!)* which he hocked on street corners dressed as King Kong. It caused a sensation and the two branched out, organizing *The Tin Pan Apple After Dark Dance & Rap Contest,* to be held at Radio City Music Hall in May of 1983. WBLS promoted it, with Mr. Magic, decked out in matching white suit and top hat, serving as the host of the event. Coca-Cola signed on as a sponsor, kicking down $300,000—an unprecedented sum for a largely underground genre. Five days before the event was to take place, three local union employees told Stettler, "We don't want any niggers in Radio City Music Hall." Stettler threatened to hold a press conference where he would repeat exactly what he was told, and the venue caved. The contest went off without a hitch, but also without any venue employees; 5,655 people, mostly inner city teens, poured through the doors of the historic building, many for the first time in their lives. The winning groups were both from Brooklyn: Untouchable Force Organization (UTFO), and Disco 3, who soon thereafter became Fat Boys.

Fly Ty: UTFO won our contest. They were dancers. They won the dance part; Fat Boys won the rap part. The prize for the rap part was you got a deal with Morris Levy, one of his labels [Sutra Records]. The prize for the dancers is you got to be Whodini's dancers.

Just as quicky as Magic and Ty gained their *juice* on commercial radio, they lost it.

Fly Ty: It was hard to get on BLS. I was doing so well, it was time for a contract renegotiation. We got a lawyer to see Charles Warfield. "We got great news, Magic. We're gonna put you on every day." I did news also, and sports. They had AM/FM.

[W]LIB. "Ty, we'll give you a news show. And Marley, we'll put you on Mary Thomas every day, *but* no more rap." Magic said, "What about Kurtis Blow? What about the Fat Boys?" Charles Warfield said, "Listen, the majors don't know what to do with it. Magic, if you stop playing it, it'll go away." We were young, brash. We quit! We walk out the office and go back to HBI. That means we're going back to no money at first. It takes a minute to start getting payouts and all that. UTFO comes to HBI one night with a new manager Steve Salem. They got a song called "Hanging Out" where they're singing. Magic does not like it. None of us like it. We play the b-side with a song called "Roxanne, Roxanne" on it. Magic says, "Yo! This the one!" "No no no no no, regular radio is not playing rap anymore! We down to sing!" We play "Roxanne, Roxanne." It start hittin'.

Marley Marl remembered Mr. Magic getting fired from WBLS, not quitting. With Dimples D gone and WBLS in the past, Marley kept plugging away in his sister's living room in Queensbridge doing *remixes*. He had an idea to exploit UTFO's "Roxanne, Roxanne" hit, just as he had taken advantage of Run-DMC's breakout record the previous year. He just needed someone to rap over it. Marley peered out of the window at 41–14 12th Street, Apartment 2A. At that moment, fourteen-year-old neighbor Lolita Shanté Gooden was walking across the courtyard on the way to a laundry room at the behest of her mother.

2
ROXANNE'S REVENGE

Craig G: First of all, female MCs weren't that common back then. So not only that, but Shanté was already known around the neighborhood as a battle MC. She was already dope.

Shanté grew up on 12th Street in Queensbridge with her mother and three younger sisters. She was a "booster"—she would take down orders for specific items, usually clothing, steal said items and sell them for less than the sticker price. By her early teens, she had already developed a reputation in her neighborhood as a fierce battle rapper—she would face off against opponents and competitively boast, brag, and insult, in structured, rhyming verse. Her ability and compulsion to speak in rhyme is what she would retrospectively dub the "Nipsey Russell Syndrome," after the comedian who appeared on various TV programs since the 1950s, gifting the world his short poems, usually consisting of crass love advice.

In her first battle at the age of ten in the nearby Woodside Projects, Shanté had to stand on a milk crate just to be seen. The first place prize was fifty dollars. "I remember looking at my mom and saying, 'Can I say bad words?' She was like, 'Say whatever the fuck you got to to get that fifty dollars!'" Shanté recollected on *The Final Level* podcast. Her quick wit and foul mouth paid off.

Jay Quan: Before her, female MCs had the dainty voice, like the girls were "supposed to be." Dimples D had a very feminine voice. Even though Sha-Rock [of Funky 4 + 1] was fierce, she had a feminine voice. Shanté was very raw and street.

Masta Ace: She always be dangerous in a battle because she's witty. She's gonna come up with something. She's good at playing the dozens. We call it snapping, ranking, whatever. She gonna have something to say about you. I put her up against anybody, guy or girl. When it come to battling, she's a wildcard, because you don't know what she gonna come with.

On that day in late 1984, Shanté had just put a load of laundry in a communal washing machine when Marley Marl called her upstairs. He wanted her to rap over the instrumental version of UTFO's "Roxanne, Roxanne," found on the b-side of their debut single. Bowlegged Lou of R&B group-turned-production team Full Force explained on *The Combat Jack Show* in 2016 how the song was the brainchild of his brother/bandmate B-Fine. "B came up with the whole concept of Roxanne . . . The three of them [UTFO]—Educated Rapper, Dr. Ice, and Kangol [Kid] is fighting for this one girl, and at the end of the day nobody gets the girl." It proved to be the perfect set up for a response. For four minutes and twenty seconds, Shanté laid down one uninterrupted, unscripted verse, whereby she verbally tore apart each UTFO member, in the order of their original verses, moving on to trash DJ Mix Master Ice, all done from the perspective of the Roxanne character. Her payment came in the form of a pair of Sergio Valente jeans from the factory where Marley worked. Shanté walked out in time to retrieve the laundry and thought little of it.

That weekend, late at night, the phone in Shanté's apartment rang. She picked it up and heard friends screaming on the other end. "You're on the radio!" Not wanting to wake up her mother, she hung the phone up and disconnected the receiver. Marley must have been playing the cassette of this *remix*—"Roxanne's Revenge"—on *Rap Attack*. She wondered what she sounded like, but didn't dare turn on the radio. The next morning, when Lolita Shanté Gooden stepped out of her home and onto the street, she was now Roxanne Shanté. She had spoken herself into existence.

Queen of Rox

Masta Ace: She is definitely one of the dopest female rappers ever, just on the strength of her doing records off the top of her head. She had records, "Roxanne's Revenge" being one, but there are others, where there's nothing written down. There's nothing preplanned. She went in the booth, put the beat on, and just started rhyming. And just went with train of thought. There's no other girl that I know that's done that, ever.

"Roxanne's Revenge" was an *answer record*—a response to a previously existing song. The answer record tradition goes back almost as far as recorded music itself. In 1902, Arthur Collins answered his own record "(Won't You Come Home) Bill Bailey" by recording "I Wonder Why Bill Baily Don't Come Home." The practice continued through the middle of the century, perhaps most notably with Willie Mae "Big Mama" Thornton's version of the Lieber and Stoller-penned "Hound Dog" and its numerous responses. By the 1970s and '80s, answer records were still very much a part of the musical landscape.

Peanut Butter Wolf (DJ/producer, founder of Stones Throw record label): "Ring My Bell" [by Anita Ward, T.K. Disco, 1979] is an answer to "Pull My Strings" by Lakeside [Solar, 1978]. After Michael Jackson "Billie Jean" came out, there was the song "Superstar" by Lydia Murdoch [Tem Entertainment Records, 1983] and the song "I'm Billie Jean" by Bullet [Earwax, date unknown]. There's a guy and girl rap answer to "How Long (Betcha' Got a Chick On the Side)" by the Pointer Sisters [ABC Blue Thumb, 1975] called "Betcha Got a Dude On the Side" by Star Quality & Class [R & R Records] from 1982. Clarence Reid, aka Blowfly, wrote "Clean Up Woman" for Betty Wright [Alston Records, 1971] and then co-wrote and produced "Clean Up Man" by Jimmy "Bo" Horne [Alston Records, 1972] before he started the Blowfly persona.

Jay Quan: Mel Brooks had a record called "It's Good To Be the King" [WMOT, 1981] and Sylvia answered with "It's Good To Be the Queen" [Sugar Hill, 1982], but those aren't really rap records. Some people would say *The Showdown* between Furious Five and Sugarhill Gang [Sugar Hill, 1981], but that was a staged battle.

What was exceptional about "Roxanne's Revenge" is that it was a *diss record*—a recording that specifically called out others by name in a disrespectful (albeit playful in this case) fashion. This type of rhyming may have been de rigueur for battles in parks, projects, and clubs across the city, but not in a recording studio.

Aaron Fuchs: Before the Hip-Hop record business, tapes were being circulated, and there's this very legendary tape of Kool Moe Dee dissing Busy Bee Starski.

Pop Art

The diss still needed to be pressed onto vinyl, especially considering the demand for it from *Rap Attack* listeners. Hip-Hop had expanded outside of New York, and opportunity knocked in the form of two brothers, who were brothers, in the City of Brotherly Love.

Troy Shelton: Pop Art Records were two guys that had a deli at 52nd and Race Street in Philadelphia. That was the middle of West Philadelphia. That was the main hub. Dana and Lawrence [Goodman] were the first guys I ever knew to have a mobile phone in their car. This was around the time that cell phones was big as a fucking book.

Grand Dragon KD (DJ for Steady B/A&R for Pop Art Records): Lawrence Goodman became friends with Ron Aiken, who was from Galaxxy. Galaxxy was a band and they was making music. They linked up and started Pop Art Records. Galaxxy and Eddie "D" was like their first artists on the label.

Fly Ty: That same weekend [after "Roxanne's Revenge" was recorded] we go to Philly. We play it on WDAS, which is a commercial station with a large listenership. Dana Goodman says, "Whoa! Whose record is *that?*" We say, "It's not a record. It's just a tape we got." "You mean nobody has that?" He leaves and comes back with his brother Lawrence. By the time he went and got Lawrence, kids were talking about this record everywhere they go. "You know that girl saying that she's Roxanne?" Shanté's nickname was Shanté. I named her Roxanne Shanté, as though "Roxanne" was a title, like "Captain Shanté." We give Dana a copy of the air check. Listen, I can't sign her. She's fourteen. I don't know her parents. I don't know nothing about her. They took that air check, and pressed it, and put it out without asking anybody anything.

Grand Dragon KD: It was a tape from off of Mr. Magic's show with Marley. That tape went straight onto wax.

The original version of the "Roxanne's Revenge" 12" single is so clearly taped off the radio, that a piece of UTFO's song "Roxanne, Roxanne" can actually be heard at the very beginning, as the two songs had been played on air sequentially. Mr. Magic's pre-recorded voice declaring the Roxanne Shanté track "a world premiere!" is then played before the song itself kicks in.

Fly Ty: Now I got to her mother. Her mother had heard of me. Her mother listened to the AM station, to the news and sports. She had a whole different perspective of me other than rap. She looked at me totally different. She said, "My daughter could do it, but Tyrone Williams gotta manager her." I started managing her. Shanté hit like she was crack. All of a sudden, everywhere across the country she was just *hot*. In a month period! We didn't care about records. We weren't in the record business. We were trying to use that to syndicate the show. Every market we went to, every radio station they called us. We said, "We'll do it. We got to be on the radio." They were happy to oblige. It was because of the Roxanne record that our show was syndicated.

"Roxanne's Revenge" was an immediate hit in both Philadelphia and New York, and Pop Art profited mightily.

Fly Ty: If I told you how much I got paid for the Roxanne Shanté record, you would die laughing. They gave it to us Christmas Eve in Philly. A check. After 3:00 P.M.. We had a bank account with no money in it at Chemical in New York. We flying up the highway. It's snowing. We don't get back to New York until 7:30 P.M., but we get past the bank on Lexington Avenue in Manhattan anyway. We looked in and the manager is in there. We tap on the window with a coin. Tap tap tap tap. Me, Magic, and Marley. He opens the door, he takes the check. He says, "You guys don't have any money in your account." He looks it up and says, "You know what? It's Christmas Eve. I'm gonna take a chance." And he give us the $750. Me and Magic and Marley took $375, we gave Shanté $375, and we split the $375—$125 a piece. Shanté lives in the projects. I give the $375 to her mother. She kissed me and hugged me—$375 out of no place—that was a lot of money. We go up to 125th Street, and a guy is walking up the street selling leathers. I don't know if they're stolen or what. "I got these three leathers for girls." They happen to be in the size of our girls. He's selling them for $75 each. We bought 'em. We went and bought flowers for $10 and went home. "Merry Christmas, Honey!" But that $750 we got as an advance. I got, off the total sale of all those records, $1,200. Shanté might have got $4,000. Magic and Marley probably got about $1,200.

Marley remembered getting a $1,500 advance from Pop Art for "Roxanne's Revenge," and contends that it is the only money he ever saw from the production of a Roxanne Shanté record.

Bite This

When it got back to UTFO, their production team Full Force, and their label—Fred Munao's Select Records—action had to be taken. Instead of cutting an answer record directly from UTFO, they found another teenage girl, Elease Jack, to record a B-Fine/Bowlegged Lou-penned song called "The Real Roxanne" under the name "Roxanne (with UTFO)." Lou described it as "jumping on our own bandwagon." The record had the Roxanne character dissing UTFO, with no reference to the existence of a Roxanne Shanté. The only acknowledgement that there was another Roxanne out in the universe was the "Real" component in the song title—by contrast, Shanté must *not* be real. To complicate matters, UTFO and Full Force had a falling out with Elease, and replaced her with another Roxanne—a Puerto Rican-American waitress, who true to this brand new tradition, was not actually named Roxanne. Adelaida Martinez was a striking beauty who exuded femininity, in contrast to her tough-as-nails African-American rival Shanté. Adelaida adopted the moniker The Real Roxanne as her stage name.

Without realizing it, Roxanne Shanté made the first hole in a dam, setting off a flood. A dizzying number of Roxanne answer records came out over the course of the following year, largely by unknowns on tiny labels. There are so many that it's impossible to estimate the total number. Some of these include:

- "Roxanne's Doctor—The Real Man" by Dr. Freshh (Zakia Records, 1985)
- "Do the Roxanne" by Doctor Rocx and Co. (Slice Records, 1985)

- "The Parents of Roxanne" by Gigolo Tony, Lace Lacey (4 Sight Records, 1985)
- "Yo, My Little Sister (Roxanne's Brothers)" by Crush Groove (Singh Records, 1985)
- "Rappin' Roxy: Roxanne's Sister" by DW and the Party Crew featuring Roxy (Party Crew Records, 1985)
- "Roxanne's a Man (The Untold Story—Final Chapter)" by Ralph Rolle (Streetwise, 1985)
- "Roxanne Is a Man" by Anthony (Out-Rage-Us Records, 1985)
- "Rap Your Own Roxanne" by Doctor JR Kool (Compleat Records, 1985)
- "I'm Lil Roxanne" by Tanganyika (A-Side Records, 1985)
- "She Died" by Rocksann (Street Corner, 1985)
- "Roxanne's Man"/"Roxanne's Dis" by The Invasions (Specific Records, 1985)
- "Planet Detroit vs. The Roxanne Plague" by Maggotron (Jamron, 1985)
- "Do It Ricardo (Roxanne's Man)" by Ricardo & Chocolate Boogie (Singh Records, 1985)
- "Roxann'es Baby" [sic] by The Overnite Bandits (Fly by Nite, date unknown)
- "The Saga of Roxanne (It's Fresh)" by Korner Boyz (Renaissance Recording, 1985)
- "Roxanne (Is My Girl)" by G-Mann (Flashbeat Records, 1985)
- "Ice Roxanne" by Little Ice (G. Jaguar Records, 1985)
- "Blowfly Meets Roxanne" by Blowfly (from *Blowfly On Tour '86,* Oops! Records, 1986)
- "Roxann'es Real Fat" [sic] by Potato Chips (Double Duce, 1985)
- "No More Roxanne (Roxanne No More)" by Zelee Groove & Osé (Treasure, 1985)
- "The Final Word—No More Roxanne (Please)" by The East Coast Crew (Chit Records, 1985)

Monica Lynch: In terms of these answer records, the Roxanne legacy is sort of like a mini-catalog of various 12" singles.

Craig G: It was one of the first big gossip things with rap music. But when so many different versions of the song came out, it kind of got out of hand. I think maybe

UTFO's version, Shanté's version, The Real Roxanne, and maybe Sparky D [were good]. From there everything else was like, "Aight, enough."

Monica Lynch: Sparky D! Another Roxanne participant.

NIA

Doreen Broadnax was an MC who went by Sparky D (sometimes spelled Sparky Dee), and started her career with the answer record "Sparky's Turn (Roxanne You're Through)," defending the honor of her fellow Brooklynites UTFO while ridiculing Shanté for being jailbait. It was on NIA Records, which would play a role in providing a weigh station for Juice Crew recording artists before they found their home with Cold Chillin'. NIA was owned by identical twins Albert and Arthur Allen. They called themselves the Ghetto Fighters and recorded background vocals on Jimi Hendrix records, before changing their own first and last names, becoming Aleem.

Monica Lynch: Tunde-Ra and Taharqa Aleem—they were brothers. They were body-builders. They used to come to our office. Aleem brothers had some hits in the early '80s.

Aaron Fuchs: The big difference between Pop Art and NIA was there was no brilliance at its core to Pop Art. The Goodman brothers knew the record business. They just knew how to go about the business of being an independent label. With the Aleems, there was this musical excellence at its core.

Marley had already been helping mix records by a rapper named Captain Rock and also the Aleem single "Release Yourself" for NIA the year previous. To fully capitalize on the Roxanne craze, the Aleems formed a sub-label called Spin Records specifically to release an album containing a re-recorded version of "Roxanne's Revenge," the Sparky single, one more track from each MC, and then a battle track where each artist traded verses dissing each other. Roxanne Shanté vs. Sparky Dee—*Round 1* featured a black and white photo of the two wearing boxing gloves—Hip-Hop as sport. There was no *Round 2,* and it was the only release under the Spin Records imprint.

Shanté released a slew of follow-up singles on her home label Pop Art throughout 1985, all with Marley Marl behind the producer's chair. "Queen of Rox (Shanté Rox On)" employed boastful, simple rhymes about Shanté's story up to this point, name checking Marley Marl, Fly Ty, Pop Art, Dana Goodman, and Mr. Magic in the process. "Runaway" served as somewhat of a public service announcement discouraging young folks from fleeing their homes, with the phone number for the National Center for Runaway & Missing Exploited Children printed on the label of the 12". "Bite This" followed the great "Roxanne's Revenge" technique of dissing established artists, this time taking aim at Run-DMC, Kurtis Blow, and a hot, young MC out of another part of Queens named LL Cool J. Pop Art even created a self-contained series of answer records between Shanté and their marquee Philadelphia rapper Steady B, who was almost exactly the same age and was a nephew by marriage of label co-owner Lawrence Goodman.

I'm Fly Shanté

Grand Dragon KD: We did "Fly Shanté" [by Steady B, b-side of "Just Call Us Def," Pop Art, 1985], and she come back with "I'm Fly Shanté" [by Roxanne Shanté featuring Steady B, Pop Art, 1986]. Her song was a response to "Fly Shanté" that we did.

Fly Ty: We were doing six shows a week at $3,000 a show, in 1985. I would always give new, young promoters a shot because old promoters didn't know nothing about it. That's $18,000 a week, and I'm taking fifteen percent of that. Shanté would take half; the other half would go to Magic and Marley. That's all we saw. We wasn't thinking about the record company.

The Battle For World Supremacy

In 1980, the year before Tommy Boy came into existence, Tom Silverman and three other partners founded the New Music Seminar—an industry networking event. It grew exponentially over the next several years, incorporating DJ and MC competitions that were taken very seriously by its participants. *The Battle For World Supremacy* had an ominous ring to it, but Roxanne Shanté, now at a mature fifteen, felt she could take on anyone. The winner would be given a wrestling-style prize fighter belt. "I didn't come into Hip-Hop to become a great *female rapper*. I came into Hip-Hop to become a great *rapper*," Shanté told Ice-T many years later on his podcast.

Pitted against Fruitkwan, an MC in the newest Tommy Boy signing Stetsasonic, Shanté feigned nervousness before unleashing a fury of insults, targeting his dark skin, yellow teeth and "borrowed" clothes. Feeling himself starting to lose, Fruitkwan grew frustrated and told Shanté to suck his dick. She had him where she wanted him and after making fun of his penis size the crowd erupted in laughter. Shanté won the battle and advanced to the finals where she was to face one of her idols—Busy Bee Starski, a first-generation MC who had been prominently featured in the 1983 Charlie Ahearn Hip-Hop film *Wild Style*.

The rules had changed. Each competitor was told swearing would no longer be tolerated. Just before the battle, Busy Bee convinced Shanté it wouldn't matter if she used profanity. "Go out and do your shit the way you do your shit. Don't worry about the rules. Ain't no rules for you. You Roxanne Shanté. Ain't no rules for you. You go out there and get 'em. We all got everybody else out the way because they were scrubs, and they're all gone. Who's left? Just the two best in the world. Just me and just you. That's right. It's just me, and it's just you," Shanté recollected Busy Bee telling her. She gave her new opponent the Fruitkwan treatment, but he kept his cool. The crowd again cheered for Shanté, but she was either disqualified for swearing or thrown under the bus for other reasons. One of the judges was Kurtis Blow, who asked what score he needed to give her in order for her to lose. The answer was a 2, so that is what he gave her.

"Busy Bee won, but clearly Roxanne Shanté actually won. Kurtis Blow was a judge, and I remember him saying, 'I'mma vote for Busy Bee because he's from the old school!'" recalled MC Chill. "I think that was the first and only time I cried at a battle. I literally cried, because I just knew I was gonna walk away with this World Supremacy," Shanté explained. Years later, she asked Kurtis Blow the real reason he scored her so she would lose, and he said that back in 1985, the world was not ready for a little girl to be the best in Hip-Hop.

By the year's end, Lolita Shanté Gooden had a much larger issue to concern herself with than figuring out why she lost a rap battle—she was going to be a mother. She gave birth to not only baby Kareem, but also to the diss record. The template had been established and was about to reach geographographic proportions.

3
THE BRIDGE

Around the time Roxanne Shanté records were introduced to the streets, so was another product that exploded in popularity.

Craig G: In the '80s, the crack era came. A lot of people started making money. A lot of people went the other way, and got strung out. It got *really* bad in the '80s. As a kid you saw it, it hit close to home, but you didn't really notice it like that, because you were too busy doing your thing as a kid.

Troy Shelton: There was *always* drug dealers around. I'm not going to say drugs and Hip-Hop were synonymous, but there were a lot of records that were financed by non-traceable sources. It wasn't necessarily a label thing. It could be more of an artist thing. The concept of "This is my guy. This is the guy that's gonna be working with me"—he very much may have well been a drug dealer. So if I'm an artist and I'm signed to x label, and I'm starting my own thing with my guy on the outside, he's got cash to do what I need to do because he has an additional source of income.

Many of Hip-Hop's first-generation stars fell into drug addiction, leaving an opening for the next wave.

Aaron Fuchs: I wish I had been present where someone said, "What would you say was the reason there was an old school and a new school?" In the history of rap, you don't think of two eras that are so sharply bifurcated. It's hard to say exactly that it corresponded with the rise of cocaine and its evolution into crack, but if that wasn't a significant part of the cultural picture, and something from which much else emanated, I don't think there's any other factor that influenced the way Hip-Hop evolved as much.

Big Daddy Kane: I think from the '70s to the '80s it became more violent. In the '70s in Brooklyn you had your gangs like the Tomahawks, Jolly Stompers, and Outlaws, and really only the gang leader would have a gun. Everybody else would have brass knuckles or a switchblade. In the '80s, when it became the drug dealer era, everybody had guns, and people getting murdered left and right. The crack era changed a lot of people. In the '70s, heroin and cocaine was a thing, but you didn't really see young cats messing with that. That was was really like the older people that was messed up on the heroin and that was messed up on the coke. In the '80s, you'd see a lot of young people that was messed up on crack—kids I went to school with, people that lived in my building.

Masta Ace: In my neighborhood we had a game room. It was in the next projects over [from me]—Seth Low Houses. That game room was run by a friend of ours' father. There was a candy store, video games, and a DJ set in there. We were allowed to come in there and play music for the people who came into the candy store. We would DJ and rap and play music. People would come in and buy candy, buy soda. Some people would go in the back and come back out. At the time, I didn't know what that was about. I didn't realize until years later that we were DJ'ing and hanging out and partying at a drug spot. I was too young to realize it. Hip-Hop was the front. It became the neighborhood front for a lucrative drug spot. I went away to college right after that time period. The real crack era was my college years. From '84 to '88, I was in college, and that's when crack really went off the rails. I would come home from school, and I would hear stories about nice people from my building that had families and jobs that were now crackheads and lost their jobs and had no teeth. Right before your eyes, you're seeing peoples' lives completely crumble.

Grand Daddy I.U.: It fucked the whole community up! But the young muthafuckas, we was all getting money—the ones that wasn't smoking that dumb ass shit. If you was in your teens and maybe even early twenties, that shit was the best time of your life. That was the most money you were ever going to get. That shit's dead now. In retrospect, it was all fucked up. You was fucking up people and all that, but at the time you so young, you ain't giving a fuck about none of that. You not even thinking about none of that. You just getting money and having fun.

Big Daddy Kane: Gold jewelry is something that everyone that wanted to be fly wore. Even in the '70s, before the crack era, you had the cats on the street that might have been running numbers or just little street thugs. This is when the rope chains wasn't Run-DMC sized, and they were smaller, and they was rocking with the Jesus piece. It's really a church medallion, but we used to call them the "house medallion."

Built in 1939, the Queensbridge Houses were home to almost 7,000 residents. By the 1950s, most white residents had moved out when the city built middle class public housing elsewhere, leaving its mostly African-American residents to navigate the oddly angled greyish brown buildings and elevators that only stopped at odd numbered floors, designed that way to cut building costs. Socio-economic and racial segregation throughout the city persisted into the '70s and '80s, exacerbated by the crack epidemic.

Aaron Fuchs: Queensbridge is just north of the 59th Street Bridge, and I was in Long Island City, which was just north of that. It sort of separated the Italian and black parts of the neighborhood.

MC Shan

Roxanne Shanté may have had records on the radio and lucrative live gigs by 1985, but she was still a fixture of *The Bridge,* as it was called by the locals. She gave those around her hope. Shawn Moltke, four years her senior, felt like he had what it took to be an MC too. Known by his friends as Shan, he had been observing Hip-Hop well before the Roxanne era.

Craig G: Shan lived on 10th Street, which is the next block over [from Shanté]. Everybody in Queensbridge knows everybody.

Troy Shelton: Shan was just cool. He was a prankster, he liked to laugh. He loved to party. He had his little gaudy side, but that was that Queensbridge shit.

Dee Joseph (Vice President of Prism/Cold Chillin'): His hat—the Kangol hat. *Every day,* I never saw him without it. I didn't know if he had hair under there or not, but he always had his hat and his kicks, his sneakers. Shan was a sweetheart.

Grand Daddy I.U.: That's my dude. That's a funny muthafucka too.

Arthur Baker: MC Shan was really, really good.

Kool G Rap: MC Shan, other than a label mate, that was my homie.

Craig G: My brother was in a group called High Fidelity Crew. You had the Sunshine Boys. They were these dudes from different blocks. They were like the main dudes. They would throw parties at the community center on Shan's block. There were big parties there. Sometimes DJs from other areas would come.

Marley Marl Scratch

Queensbridge was a petri dish of raw talent, and it rubbed off on the tall and lanky teenager in intentionally mismatched Pumas. By opening his bedroom window, Shan could hear first-generation MCs like Melle Mel and DJs like Grandmaster Flash rocking the Riis Center mere yards away. One day, during the height of the Roxanne Wars, he crossed paths with Marley while on a Honda MB5 motorbike. Shan told the budding producer he had written a song about him. When Marley invited him to his sister's apartment the next day to show him the song, Shan walked in holding a brown paper bag with lyrics scribbled on it. The result of the session was "Marley Marl Scratch." A re-recorded version of the song credited to Marley Marl featuring MC Shan was released on NIA Records in 1985. Lyrically, Shan turned Marley's name into a backronym, boasting about the DJ's prowess on the wheels of steel. Recorded on a 4-track cassette recorder with a vocal mic missing its ball, "Marley Marl Scratch" came at the tail end of the era where DJs were thought of as the star of any Hip-Hop outfit, with MCs serving as their support.

Jay Quan: Marley was one of the first to structure things where he was scratching the a cappella part of a name. When Dimples D did "Sucker DJ's" she did an a cappella of it. That became Marley's signature. He used it for "Marley Marl Scratch." DJs weren't really doing that on songs yet. "I'm gonna take a piece of what my MC said," or, "My MC said my name, I'm gonna scratch my name." I'm not saying he's the first one to ever do it, but he's the first one to consistently make that a trademark.

Cut Chemist: "Marley Marl Scratch" was an amazing rap from MC Shan about a DJ. You know how's he's breaking down every letter. His cuts were sharp. "Ma ma ma me ma me Marley! Me me me me Marley!" They were really tight, showcasing his DJ skills.

Where Marley was beholden to a specific production style while working with Shanté—the UTFO formula of drum machine sounds approximating the intro of the Billy Squier track "The Big Beat"—he felt unencumbered to experiment with MC Shan. Marley treated Shan's distinctive high-pitched voice as an instrument in the mix on each record. "Marley Marl Scratch" employed another production technique that was discovered, or rather *invented* by accident.

The previous year, while working on mixing "Cosmic Blast" by Captain Rock for NIA Records, Marley attempted to sample a vocal snippet from English experimental band Art of Noise's single "Beat Box" using an E-mu Emulator. "The snare actually recorded first before the sound that I was looking for," he told Red Bull Music Academy in 2014. "I started playing my sampler against the track that was coming through the speakers, and my snare sounded better. So I told the engineer, 'Turn that snare down,' and I played my snare over it. I looked at him and said, 'Wow! Do you know what just happened?' He's like, 'Yeah, you made a mistake and sampled the snare.' I was like, 'No. This means I can take any drum sound on any pre-existing record.' . . . It was a basic, honest mistake that changed everything."

In terms of electronic-based music production, this discovery was tantamount to inventing the wheel or harnessing fire. Marley didn't use the drum sample for "Cosmic

Blast," but he kept what he had learned in his back pocket. Soon thereafter, he bought two Korg SDD-2000 Sampling Digital Delay units that could store a skimpy 4.368 seconds of sampling time each. Ironically this piece of equipment was most closely associated with something worlds apart from Hip-Hop—the signature guitar sound of The Edge from Irish rock band U2, who was filling stadiums internationally by the mid '80s.

In Marley's case, invention was the mother of necessity, and affordable samplers that would become closely associated with Hip-Hop, such as the E-mu Systems SP-12 and the Akai MPC60, were still a few years away from being conceived. By hooking up his Roland TR-808 drum machine to the Korg units, he was able to trigger individual sampled drum hits. This broke Hip-Hop records out of the limits of pre-set sounds inside drum machines into an infinite number of sonic possibilities. "Marley Marl Scratch" was the first record its namesake was actually proud of having made. Marley Marl had arrived as a *producer.*

Dr. Butcher (DJ/producer): During Marley's time, it was coming out of the drum machine era. And Marley using the early samplers that would only have five seconds, he decided that instead of using the drum machine sounds, he would use the break beats. He was the first person to use natural, sampled drums in place of the drum machine drum types.

Kool G Rap: Marley will forever be legendary because he's one of the producers that fore fronted that sampling shit that still exists to this day, and he not only utilized the sampling technique, but fucking killed it. He's always gonna be a legend. His name holds weight by itself.

Feed the World

MC Shan went out on tour with Roxanne Shanté well before "Marley Marl Scratch" had even come out, as he was a known commodity due to the heavy airplay of the cassette of the song on *Rap Attack*. He fast became an idol in Queensbridge, buying candy and throwing it out to kids who surrounded him when he came home. Shan was fully indoctrinated into this new version of the Juice Crew that was beginning to form, whereby Marley handpicked MCs to produce and play on Mr. Magic's radio show, while Fly Ty handled the artist management end. Shan's next single however ended up being a strange misfire—a total aberration from what would become his signature sound. Co-produced by Marley Marl and another DJ named Charley Casanova, "Feed the World" was a case study in why a Hip-Hop act signing directly to a major label in the early days of the genre was seldom a good idea. WBLS had rehired Mr. Magic, and the station's music director May James hooked the rapper up with MCA Records for a single deal. The Music Corporation of America (referred to by many at the time as the "Music Cemetery of America" for their low success rate) had zero background in Hip-Hop. The song itself gave them little to work with—the lyrics were preachy, in a "We Are the World"/"Do They Know It's Christmas?" kind of a way, and the beat was forgettable. Shan was promptly dropped by MCA, and his career was all the better for it. However, this foreshadowed negative experiences with another major he would have in years to come.

Beat Biter

During this time, an NYU student from Lido Beach, Long Island, named Rick Rubin had just joined forces with thriving Hip-Hop artist manager Russell Simmons to help take his record label Def Jam Recordings to the next level. Rubin had self-released his experimental punk band Hose, but his first foray into rap was a T La Rock & Jazzy Jay single he himself produced. "It's Yours" tore up the airwaves in '84, forcing rappers to expand their vocabularies. Rick Rubin and Marley Marl had planted the seeds that grew into the two most influential Hip-Hop record labels in the same backyard—Partytime.

Arthur Baker: I put out the first Def Jam record that Rick did, which was T La Rock & Jazzy Jay. The Partytime label, which actually didn't do all that well—we put out the first Marley Marl record and the first Rick Rubin record. I guess it wasn't bad.

On the other side of Queens from Shan, in the St. Albans neighborhood, another Kangol-clad MC, self-crafted in the image of T La Rock, had scored the first record deal from the Rubin/Simmons era of Def Jam. James Todd Smith, aka LL Cool J ("Ladies Love Cool James"), was sixteen years old.

Dr. Butcher: He grew up in St. Albans, but as a kid, his grandparents lived in East Elmhurst. 100th Street. So me and LL Cool J and another guy named Royal Rich were in a group together, just before LL made his first record, which was probably supposed to be all of us. I was Jazzy Drewski. We were called Extravagant Three.
Starting with his debut single "I Need a Beat," LL Cool J was an instant sensation within Hip-Hop. Boastful, verbose, ambitious, and good looking, he was fast becoming the poster child for what was becoming known as the "new school" of rap—the generation that Run-DMC had ushered in by '83. A few singles later, LL came out with a career-defining anthem—the Rick Rubin-produced "Rock the Bells. "

Jay Quan: There was a show in Connecticut with Shan and LL on the same bill. They were cool with each other. Shan said, "Hey, listen to my new song." The song was "Marley Marl Scratch." The next thing you know, LL comes out with "Rock the Bells." There weren't so many drum patterns, and there were very similar drum patterns back at that time, but "Marley Marl Scratch" is not the same kind of pattern you would hear on a lot of records. It was a kind of distinctive drum pattern. "Rock the Bells" is the same drum pattern, down to the snare and hi hat. There could have been some copying there. That's the accusation.

MC Shan was so sure that there was foul play that he retaliated with something that was fast becoming Juice Crew tradition—a diss record. LL Cool J and his producer Rick Rubin had allegedly violated an unwritten ethic in Hip-Hop—*don't bite;* don't steal someone else's sound or lyrics. "Beat Biter" announced to the world that an impropriety had occurred. The 1986 single was released on Bridge Records, a new imprint of Pop Art Records, which already had a relationship with the Juice Crew via Roxanne Shanté. Bridge Records was for Shan, Marley, and Fly Ty, and distributed by Pop Art.

"We had one show where we were supposed to battle—it was in Syracuse—and I did that 'Beat Biter,'" Shan recollected in a 2012 interview with *Complex*. "Marley was cutting the record up, back, and forth. I went over to the turntable, and I snatched LL's record off and I snapped the record! I still had the microphone in my hand, and when I snapped the record the sound resonated through the speakers, the crowd went crazy and LL never got on stage that night! They tried to turn his limo over, just for that."

B-Side Wins Again

It wasn't "Beat Biter" that had a big impact though. In much the same way UTFO's career was defined by a b-side, so too was MC Shan's when "Beat Biter" b-side "The Bridge" hit the airwaves. Originally recorded by Shan and Marley over a year earlier with the exclusive intention to play as bumper music in between live bands at a festival in Queensbridge Park, the song was a history lesson on Hip-Hop within the housing project. Those who were mentioned in the lyrics included T-Tom, DJ Gas, and Marley's older brother Larry Larr of the High Fidelity Crew, Phase Brothers, Cousin Bruce, Marley himself, Dimples D and the "Sucker DJ's" record, Roxanne Shanté, and the newest member of the Juice Crew—a twelve-year-old rapper named Craig G who only learned he was in it when he heard the lyrics.

Craig G: That ["The Bridge"] is our neighborhood national anthem. That song was such a hit, and it was playing on the radio constantly, and it just made us proud.

Via "The Bridge," Marley yet again introduced a production element to the burgeoning genre—intentional noise. By sampling a tiny instrumental piece of the 1975 record "Scratchin'" by the Magic Disco Machine, adding reverb, and then playing it backwards, he created a sound that was ominous, disorienting, and totally unidentifiable.

Troy Shelton: That's my man. Love him to death. Marley was always super serious about growing as a producer, and he worked at it constantly.

Cut Chemist: Taking that "Scratchin'" horn and wheeling it backwards and making it sound like some fucking synthetic dinosaur—it was psychedelic. He had a sense of psychedelicness to him that [myself] as a thirteen-year-old, those sounds get into your brain a certain way. You're listening to these mix shows and you're hearing these weird sounds, and they're echoing and they're going backwards. It's a trip.

Around this time, a Hip-Hop group was beginning to form out of members of Long Island DJ crew Spectrum City. Signed by Rick Rubin to Def Jam after much cajoling on his part, Public Enemy had its own production team—the Bomb Squad, which included the brothers Hank and Keith Boxley (rechristened "Shocklee"). "I think our favorite producer was that Marley Marl," stated Keith Shocklee on *The Combat Jack Show* in 2014. "That's where that noise come from. That's our influence." Public Enemy's leader Chuck D expounded, "'The Bridge' by MC Shan . . . Marley Marl would have MC Shan rocking the beat, and then the noise would come in the chorus. Our voices were strong enough to rock the fucking noise." Public Enemy and the Bomb Squad would bring Marley's intentional noise formula to a whole new level over the next several years, without ever losing sight of who inspired them.

Impeach the President

Subject matter and noise aside, the other crucial component of "The Bridge" was the sampled drum sounds of what had been an obscure record at the time of its release in 1973 by a high school band backing singer Roy C. Hammond. They were called The Honey Drippers, and their song called for the impeachment of President Richard Nixon.

Dr. Butcher: So [Marley Marl] took "Impeach the President" and sampled that into the drum machine. And he put that on top and layered it with the drum machine sounds. He got credited with doing that.

Aaron Fuchs: I knew Roy C since the '70s. He's a Queens guy. I just crossed paths with him. I was a very popular journalist in the '70s, and I was one of the real first people to write about Hip-Hop. Maybe doing the best job writing about it critically. So people were really coming to me for press. I had become friendly with [Afrika] Bambaataa. I went to see him at T-Connection, and he let me peep his crates. Even though the names of the artists were scratched out, I recognized a lot of the artists from being an R&B collector, and I know my Roy C records. As I was building my catalog, I was able to not be hamstrung by seeing artists' names crossed out. "I know where to get that record. I know who I can buy that record from." I made a number of deals that included some other R&B.

Fuchs estimated that he bought the publishing for "Impeach the President" by The Honey Drippers around 1981. Several years later, he traded a stack of records with Marley in exchange for mixing a single by rapper Spoonie Gee. Marley remembers it being "That's My Style"/"Serve You Right" and Aaron Fuchs remembers it being "Take It Off" (both were released in 1986 on Tuff City). In that stack was "Impeach the President."

Aaron Fuchs: I popularized "Impeach" because when I got in the business there was a series of records called *Ultimate Breaks & Beats*. Basically it was a bootleg series that had records with breaks in them. These were often used by DJs to use for reconstructions. I picked up a box of "Impeach" from a cutout dealer, and it was much easier for me to pay the jocks with breakbeat records. I wouldn't put money in a DJ's hand . . . I'd give them two copies of a funky record. That's how I played the game. I popularized "Impeach" en route to becoming one of the great bedrocks of Hip-Hop construction. What I like about Shan is he always told people that he saw me hand Marley "Impeach."

Marley Marl would sample the drums from "Impeach the President" on at least ten more productions of his own, and it would be sampled by others on well over 700 more records. The sounds of The Honey Drippers' snare and kick drum, even in isolation, grew to be intrinsically associated with Hip-Hop. Using two SDD samplers (one loaded with the kick sound, one loaded with the snare sound) hooked up to his Roland TR-808, and only four tracks to work with, "The Bridge was accomplished as follows:

Track 1: snare (sampled from "Impeach")/hi-hat (from the 808);

Track 2: kick (sampled from "Impeach")/second kick layered on top (from the 808)/"Scratchin'" sample played backwards triggered by 808 kick;

Track 3: sample of Marley Marl's own voice shouting the song title;

Track 4: MC Shan's vocals.

Kool G Rap: As far as what MC Shan is to Hip-Hop, Shan is that dude that made that unforgettable, undying, classic fucking record that still *knocks* to this fucking day. I'm not saying it's the only hot record he ever did. I'm just saying the first thing you think of when you think of MC Shan is "The Bridge." That fucking record to this day knocks so fucking hard. It didn't lose none of its potency. It don't sound dated. Him and Marley Marl is the artists that made that shit, and that's gonna forever hold a certain spot for MC Shan. It was like boom! It's the new era of Hip-Hop that went from drum machines to sampling, and MC Shan is the forefront of a rapper coming out on this new style of production called "sampling" that made one of those classics that the world will never forget. It's etched in stone.

Boogie Down Productions

Marley didn't initially expect anyone outside of Queensbridge to be impacted by a song about his and Shan's housing project. The influence of "The Bridge" spread not only to Long Island via Public Enemy, but also to the South Bronx. Cedric Miller and Scott Sterling lived just about a half mile from 1520 Sedgwick Avenue—the fabled location of DJ Kool Herc's 1973 party that birthed Hip-Hop. The two would become Ced Gee and Scott La Rock, respectively.

Ced Gee (MC and producer for Ultramagnetic MCs, producer for Boogie Down Productions): Me and Scott grew up together. We was childhood friends. He was in the projects, I was in the tenements. He would always compete against his block: two hand touch, basketball, baseball. Herc started playing around the corner. He would come up through Macombs Junior High School. I was on Andrews Avenue, I went to school at [P.S.] 82, but I had to be upstairs when the night fell. My mother and father used to let us sit out on the fire escape of the tenement building. They'd be laying down, watching

TV, and we'd be on the fire escape. One of us would climb down and run around the corner to the school. We'd cover for one another. We took turns. We never got caught. That's the only way I got to see Kool Herc. Herc was an older teenager, where I was like in 7th grade.

Approximately a decade later, after the two friends graduated from college, Ced formed Ultramagnetic MCs with DJ Moe Love and rappers TR Love and Kool Keith. Scott was a social worker at the Franklin Armory Men's Shelter in the Bronx, where he was assigned to a twenty-year-old named Lawrence Parker, who had bounced around Brooklyn, Harlem, and the South Bronx as a youth. Lawrence's mother had been in an abusive relationship with his step-father, and at sixteen he left home for the streets. Being fed by the Hare Krishnas, he became drawn to studying religion and spirituality, and adopted the nickname Krishna, which was shortened to Kris. Kris was in a graffiti crew, and he wrote KRS until he saw the work of others with the same moniker. It was lengthened to KRS-One. Scott and KRS-One were antagonistic towards each other before realizing they shared a mutual interest in Hip-Hop, and a mutual friend—Ced Gee.

Scott moonlighted as a DJ at the Broadway Repertory Theater, and Kris was an aspiring MC, motivated to make it a career by seeing the success of Run-DMC, who were now bona fide superstars, fast on their way to going gold. Scott and Kris' first few groups weren't hitting. There was Scott La Rock & Celebrity Three, which had one single called "Advance" (Street Beat Records, 1986). Then there was 12:41, with the single "$ucce$$ I$ the Word" (Fresh Records, 1985). Third time was a charm when fifteen-year-old D-Nice joined as a beatboxer/auxiliary DJ/MC and future producer. Being from the *boogie down Bronx,* as it was referred to on the street, the group was named Boogie Down Productions.

South Bronx

One day while re-recording their demo track "Poetry" in Power Play Studios just nine blocks from Queensbridge, Kris and Scott noticed Mr. Magic with Marley Marl working. Brimming with admiration and enthusiasm for Magic, and the prospect of being down with the Juice Crew, they tried to meet him. Kris recalled in *Check the*

Technique that Magic said, "Get out of here!" and then later told recording engineer Frankie D that their music was wack after hearing it. Marley remembers being in the studio working on "Bite This" by Roxanne Shanté in the next room, and being told by Magic to walk over to where BDP were working to listen to what they had been recording. Marley's recollection on *The Combat Jack Show* in 2014 was that while playing the recording, "[Magic] stumbles across the room, goes to the big knob on the SSL, turns that shit down . . . it gets silent. 'Yo man, that shit is *bullshit.*' It was Scott, KRS, and five or six other goonies . . . [Magic said] 'You want real Hip-Hop?' He pointed at muthafuckas. 'MC Shan! Marley Marl! Roxanne Shanté! Mr. Magic!' This nigga turned around, walked out and slammed the door . . . now I'm the only one left in the room with these niggas. 'I, I guess he didn't like it.'"

Ced Gee: He [Mr. Magic] wasn't giving them [BDP] a minute of his time. But that was Magic. Magic was getting that payola. You want Magic; you had to come up with some green. That was Magic's thing. They took it personal, but if they had some money they could say, "Magic, can I talk to you?" Pull out a couple hundred dollars, Magic would have been there, listening. Because everybody knew Magic took payola.

Boogie Down Productions were so incensed by what had transpired that they immediately wrote and recorded a new song called "South Bronx." Produced by Scott La Rock with the aid of D-Nice, it was an answer to "The Bridge" that presupposed Shan's record wasn't telling the history of Hip-Hop in Queensbridge, but was rather making the claim that Hip-Hop *as a whole* started in Queensbridge. Following the same vocal cadence as "The Bridge," and using a historical narrative, only this time naming important figures from the Bronx who began making an impact between 1976–1980 (Coke La Rock, Kool Herc, Afrika Bambaataa, Chuck Chillout, Afrika Islam, Grandmaster Flash, Casanova, Nine Lives Crew, Cypress Boys, Rock Steady Crew), "South Bronx" was founded on a faulty premise. No one ever denied where Hip-Hop was born in the first place. It didn't matter though—Boogie Down Productions had their first hit record.

Ced Gee: It was dope. It was raw. It was as raw as you can get.

Jeff Smith (product manager for Warner Bros. Records, 1988–1991): Neighborhood identification and the battling thing was going on. The records really did brim with this raw energy that young people bring to it.

Monica Lynch: The big thing that blew up was the big rap beef between MC Shan and Boogie Down Productions, which was a huge boon for everyone involved.

Cut Chemist: "South Bronx" used the drum beat from "Smokin Cheeba-Cheeba" [by Harlem Underground Band] and did kind of the same thing that Marley did. It's an answer record to Marley too, so maybe there's something to that. And then they went on and did that on the rest of [debut Boogie Down Productions album] *Criminal Minded,* and it was interesting, because I thought they took the Marley template—dirty, isolated drums.

Kool G Rap: I took it personal, but not to the level of I hated KRS-One, but to the level of, "Yo, dat nigga *buggin*'! Dat nigga sleepin' on *Queens?*" I think to the level that all Queens natives took it. Even though he said that, Queens dudes ain't wanna kill him. They didn't have it out for KRS-One like that. Even though I remember a time he performed at the roller skating rink on 74th Street, which was like a hot spot for performers to do shows at back in the days, on Roosevelt Avenue in Corona—Borderline Corona-Jackson Heights. He got chased out of there. I wasn't there, but I had heard about it. United Skates of America.

The Juice Crew's main weapon was used against them. Roxanne Shanté's career started by going after UTFO, but Shan's plan to drag rising star LL Cool J into a beef hadn't panned out. Instead, out of nowhere, BDP utilized the diss record to gain notoriety, and they learned from the best. "South Bronx" was getting played heavily at Latin Quarter in Times Square, which had become the premier New York Hip-Hop venue. Crowds from every corner of the city were losing their minds.

"I did a little answer record called 'South Bronx,'" KRS-One said on *Take It Personal Podcast,* "and [MC Shan] had the audacity to answer me. That is really how my career begins."

Ced Gee: It was an MC thing. It was rap. Shan never ran. He was like, "Okay, we gonna battle." And that's what it was. It was just like a basketball game. You won or you lost, but you came to compete. When you're a boxer, you might lose. You don't go get a gun. You go back in the gym, and you train harder for the rematch.

Kill That Noise

Shan's response was "Kill That Noise," which called out KRS-One and Scott La Rock by name, re-purposed a sample from "South Bronx," and contained a lyric threatening to shoot his rivals with an eight-shot clip .25.

Ced Gee: It was cute. It was cute. Then we went in and we did "The Bridge Is Over" in a half hour.

The Bridge Is Over

Produced by KRS-One and Ced Gee, BDP's "The Bridge Is Over" went for the jugular, making homophobic swipes at Magic, Marley, and Shan, declaring that Shanté's only purpose is for sex, trashing Marley's skills as a DJ, and also poking fun at Shan's sneakers. Musically, it sounded like nothing else at that point. Heavily influenced by dancehall and delivered in Jamaican Patois, KRS-One also played a sinister sounding piano line on the recording.

Big Daddy Kane: In my opinion it all ended with "The Bridge Is Over." I think after "The Bridge Is Over," everyone pretty much selected a winner.

Grand Daddy I.U.: As a fan, I was kind of with Shan first with "The Bridge." I didn't really like "South Bronx." But then goddamn, when Kris came out with "The Bridge Is Over," that shit really *was* over. That was undeniable. "Kill That Noise"—that was aight, but when "The Bridge Is Over" dropped, Shan couldn't say shit else. Like shut the fuck up, try to make something else, try to get off the subject.

Cut Chemist: To me, Shan in his prime kind of ended with "The Bridge." His album *Down By Law* is cool, but I don't think he made anything with as quite an impact as he did as his 12"s. And then you take BDP who has gone on to do nothing but bigger and better things post-"South Bronx."

Big Daddy Kane: I know Shan was seriously upset. With KRS-One I don't really know. With KRS-One, it might have been a strategic move to get into the business by dissing someone that's poppin'.

Shan wanted to return fire. We wasn't going to be played like that. He was a fighter. Marley however didn't want to give BDP more ammunition and thought that anything else at that point would just make the Bronx group even more famous. There would be no response from MC Shan, and this course of non-action would remain a point of contention between the MC and producer for many decades. Lyrical jabbing aside, there was something else about "The Bridge Is Over" that was eating away at Marley. It was the drums. They sounded eerily familiar.

The Mystery of the Missing Drum Reel

Ced Gee: So we got in [the studio], Kris put the cassette on, and said, "Ced, just use stock sounds." I said, "We can't use stock sounds! This is a diss record. We gotta put this thing to bed. Let's use the 'Impeach the President' sample like they did." So I pulled out the "Impeach the President" samples, tuned it up a little, and did the beat. When I did the beat, the cymbal crashes on there I did one time. Scott was like, "Yo, this shit is dope!" He put some more of those in there. Then Kris went in the room and played the piano.

Remembering back on the night of the incident at Power Play Studios, Marley realized he had forgotten to grab his drum reel when he left. He kept his isolated drum sounds stored on a tape reel, which he would then drop into a sampler before making a record. Recording engineer Everett Ramos informed Marley the reel had gone missing the next day. Listening to "The Bridge Is Over" he could hear pops and ticks in the drums that were unique to samples grabbed from his own copy of "Impeach the

President." Boogie Down Productions had made the ultimate diss record against the Juice Crew using sounds that were physically stolen—Marley was sure of it.

Ced Gee: Nobody stole Marley Marl's drum reel. That's the biggest joke maybe in the history of rap. Steal Marley Marl's drum reel? Understand when I said Hip-Hop came to Queens *last*. I had "Impeach the President," I had all those records before Marley even knew what they was. I never took any of Marley's reels. I didn't have a 2-track in my house, so why would I take his stuff? I didn't know that stuff was on 4-track. Nobody took Marley's reels. That's just a joke. Even if somebody took it, it's not Marley's. Those drums were played by The Honey Drippers. You can't claim somebody else's work. That's a joke. All he could say is, "I sampled it first." But to call it yours? Come on. That's sometimes when I question humanity. How people can just go along with silly shit like that. Like Marley got on the drums and played that stuff. It was a drum sample.

"I and Scott La Rock did not technically lift anyone's reel to reel out the studio," KRS-One said on *Take It Personal Podcast* in 2018. "Ced Gee was not using a reel to reel. Ced Gee was using floppy disks. Here's where the controversy comes in. Here's what I think happened: on 'The Bridge Is Over' I used the kick and snare from 'Eric B Is President' [by Eric B. & Rakim], which is a Marley Marl drum sound. Marley produced 'Eric B Is President.' . . . Those *are* his sounds."

Magic vs. Red

Craig G: We liked that song ["The Bridge Is Over"] in Queensbridge. It was a good song! It was also the radio wars, not like physical violence wars. We didn't play it on our show [*Rap Attack*]. You had Red Alert and you had the *Rap Attack*, and it was like a back and forth, which made it very interesting back then.

A driving force in what came to be known as the Bridge Wars was a rivalry that was already in full gear on radio in New York—Mr. Magic on WBLS vs. 98.7 Kiss (WRKS) FM's Kool DJ Red Alert. Born in 1956 like Mr. Magic, Fredrick Crute was a Harlem native, but was most closely associated with the Bronx due to his involvement in Afrika Bambaataa's Zulu Nation collective. He had been a DJ in the Jazzy Five, whom

Magic helped popularize back in 1981. Red Alert had been on Kiss since October of 1983, and was the first to play UTFO's "Roxanne, Roxanne" on commercial radio. Mr. Magic had his Juice Crew in his corner, consisting of Marley, Shanté, and Shan. Red Alert now had Boogie Down Productions in his corner. Fans would record both shows onto cassette tapes that would get dubbed and make their way throughout the country. *Rap Attack*, Red Alert, and the Bridge Wars were being observed on a national level.

Cut Chemist: DJ Eclipse lived in South Carolina. Eclipse was getting tapes from people in New York, I think maybe [from] the Mighty Maestro. Then he would send them to my friend, and my friend would share them with me. That was like '87, '88. We got them pretty quickly. Like an October show we would get in November or December. They'd probably be like third-generation [dubs].

Ced Gee: Red was happy because people had records, and they were good records. Magic wouldn't play them without payola, so then Red started playing them and more people started listening to Red. Magic was saying little side things out his mouth about Red Alert. So that started that rivalry. Red never really had any feeling towards Magic until Magic started saying things about him, like "Duck Alert," "Red a dirt," little things like that. They were competing. Magic dissed us [Ultramagnetic MCs] one time! He was playing "Traveling At the Speed of Thought" when it came out, and you know how when you play a record warped? He didn't even have it going at the correct tempo. He had to drag it. "Boom Bap! Boom Bap!" He had Marley scratch it SSSKKKKKKSSSFFHHFFFAAJCH! And he said, "Take that wack shit off!" We laughed. We laughed hard. That was funny.

Monica Lynch: The chronology is that Frankie Crocker hired Mr. Magic at WBLS, and within a year perhaps, Barry Mayo hired Red at Kiss. My understanding is that Barry Mayo first wanted to get Bambaataa or Afrika Islam I believe. Red Alert wasn't his first choice, but Red Alert was available and had all the bona fides and the credentials, the associations and everything.

Aaron Fuchs: I would say you'd probably describe the word "hateful" a little bit more towards the Magic crew than the Red Alert crew. Red Alert was a DJ who had a couple of hours of DJ time. He wasn't an air personality. Magic was an air personality, so there was fuel for his ego. That definitely affected the character and personality of each posse.

Troy Shelton: Red had a different kind of sensibility. You have KRS-One introducing a new sound with shit going off beat. You got different factions forming. Now there wasn't just twenty records to choose from. Now you had stuff where you could say, "I'm not feeling that. I'm not gonna play that." Or, "I am gonna play that because I am feeling it."

By early 1987, the dust had settled and KRS-One with Boogie Down Productions emerged as the victors. That didn't stop other artists from jumping in and taking sides. On the Queens/Juice Crew side was Noel Rockwell Featuring The Poet with "Beat You Down" (11-A Records) and Butchy-B's "Beatin Down KRS" (Groovy Move Records). On the BDP side was MC Mitchski "The Rappin Comedian" and MB "The Human Radio" with "Brooklyn Blew Up the Bridge" (Ski Records Co.), although no records had made as big of an impact as "The Bridge Is Over."

DJ Scott La Rock

Scott La Rock saw the bigger picture. The Bridge Wars had more in common with professional wrestling than a hostile conflict, and there was money to be made. MC Shan, backed by DJ Cool V, toured the east coast with Boogie Down Productions in the summer of '87.

After returning to the Bronx, Scott received a call from D-Nice. The youngest member of BDP was on the other end of the phone in tears, blood rushing down his face. He had just been pistol whipped by a man in front of the Highbridge Houses near Yankee Stadium. The culprit had accused D-Nice of trying to hit on his girlfriend a year previous. Later that day, Scott La Rock, D-Nice, DJ McBoo, Scotty "Manager Moe" Morris, and their bodyguard Darrell, aka "Robocop," drove to Highbridge to try to squash the turmoil peacefully.

D-Nice explained the order of events on *The Combat Jack Show* in 2014. "While we were standing by the Jeep, Darrell was in front of the Highbridge projects, asking someone if they had seen this group. The kid must have said something smart to him. All we saw was Darrell lift this kid up in the air . . . and just slam him, and that was that. We were still standing out there, like, 'Yo, what happened?' Somebody was in the bushes, somebody ran to the roof, and they just shooting at us. It was a one way street going uptown, projects on the left hand side, we were parked on the right-hand side . . . we had no guns. We were scrambling to get back in this Jeep Wrangler. Darrell was driving, Scott in the passenger seat, McBoo in the left side behind the driver, I'm in the center, Manager Moe [on the right]. They're shooting at us. I see Scott swerving. I look and I can literally see the blood coming out of his head."

Scott La Rock was murdered on August 27, 1987 at the age of twenty-five. One of Hip-Hop culture's first significant casualties, he left behind a young son. KRS-One carried on the name Boogie Down Productions for another half decade, first with D-Nice, then without him, before performing under his own name. Scott and Kris will forever be intrinsically associated with that first diss record that put them on the map.

"I would not have a career if it wasn't for MC Shan," said KRS-One on *Take It Personal Podcast*. "If any book is written, if any movie is done, if any legacy is called, I'm indebted to MC Shan."

4

NOBODY BEATS THE BIZ

What was that sound? Marley Marl heard something coming from the staircase inside his Queensbridge apartment building that sounded like an unrecognizable drum machine interspersed with a vocal sample being pitched up and down through a Fairlight sampler. Whose record was this and who was playing it? He opened the door and laid his eyes upon Marcell Theo Hall, aka Biz Markie, a hulking twenty-year-old who slurred his words when he spoke, and was not attractive by conventional standards. Within five years, he would go onto sell over one million records and be a cultural phenomenon, helping Hip-Hop transcend into the mainstream where it would remain.

Only a handful of people claimed they saw it coming, but did anyone *really* see it coming? Biz hustled for it. Introduced to the burgeoning sub-culture via a live cassette of the rap group L-Brothers in 1978, Biz was now making his presence felt, and he was ever-present.

The Inhuman Orchestra

TJ Swan: When I personally met him he was living in Coram at the time. Suffolk County, Long Island. I know his brother Diamond Shell lived in Brentwood [Long Island], and he would go back and forth. Biz had a lot of relatives. He would stay with a whole bunch of different relatives, because he's constantly going back and forth to the city. Biz could be in Central Islip one minute, and then he could be in Harlem the next, then he could be in Jersey, then he can be back in Brentwood, all in one day. It's like he had superpowers!

Troy Shelton: Biz was like my nephew, and Biz was funny. But he was wickedly, creatively funny. He did a record about black history and people who were important to us. And he did a record about picking boogers. He did one about taking a shit. We had promo items with a toilet, "Toilet Stool Rap." The big thing was Biz was a risk taker. He wasn't the best looking guy. He was always kind of awkward, but the thing Biz had was focus. He wasn't trying to be sexy. He was trying to be funny. The records that he made filled in the space where nobody else was going. If you weren't trying to be political, you weren't trying to be hardcore, or tell a dope boys story, or talk about the girls, you had Biz.

Dee Joseph: Biz is a tremendously talented guy. He knew every record that's ever been made. Trust me; he's got every 45 probably that's been printed. He knows beats like nobody.

Cut Chemist: Biz has an ear. If you want to ask me what his main contribution is, his ear is something fierce.

Monica Lynch: Even to this day, Biz is my favorite MC. I always loved Biz.

Dee Joseph: And of course he had the *biggest* posse. I mean everybody had a posse, but Biz's was the biggest.

Troy Shelton: You had TJ Swan, which added a whole different element to the music. The guy who can't sing, but is singing, but don't sound bad singing what he's singing . . . but he's not really singing.

TJ Swan: I started off as a DJ. I was about twelve years old, and I begged my dad to buy me some Lafayette turntables at RadioShack, and he got them for me. I just loved music because I grew up with it. Both parents were former musicians. I just inherited it. I would DJ, doing all the skating rinks. I eventually got into the rapping part. I tried my hand at rapping. So I entered a contest, came in third place, only rapped for six weeks.

I was fifteen. I got mad because it was supposed to be an amateur contest, and they had two professional rappers that won #1 and #2 spots. I was like, "Yo, I should have been #1. I should have won because you guys are professional and I'm an amateur." It wasn't fair. It just made me ambitious. It made me want it more. So then I started singing over my breakbeats. Back in the days they had this beat called Freedom ["Get Up and Dance" by Freedom, Malaco, 1978], and I would start singing over it. I didn't take it serious. It was just me having fun, until I went out to Riverhead, Long Island, with a friend of mine, Troy Brown. We went to a club one night. These guys was trying to sing in three-part harmony over some beats. I was like, "Oof. That sounds horrible. I could kill these guys." So, the guys said, "Oh really? Get on the mic!" I said, "Cut up 'Freedom' for me," and I started singing over the raw beat. The crowd went nuts. I was like, "Oh my God, I got something here!" Then I started practicing singing over raw Hip-Hop breakbeats. I went back to my hometown C.I. and introduced my new style to my audience, and they went nuts. I started recording all of my performances on mixtapes. Thirty minute tapes I would sell for fifteen dollars, and sixty minute tapes I would sell for thirty dollars. So I was already hustling hard at fifteen, sixteen selling my product. All the DJs wanted me to be a part of they group, but I was like, "When you guys need me to perform for you at the house parties, I do it, but I don't wanna be with no one particular group." Then one day Biz was supposed to do a party in Riverhead. He had another obligation that was lucrative for him, so he took that deal, and he left these guys hanging. One of these guys knew my girlfriend. She said, "Why don't you let Swan do it? Swan beatbox, he sing, he rap, he DJs, he does it all." So they said, "Okay." It was a big success. It got back to Biz, and he was like, "What? Who is he? I wanna battle him! I wanna battle him!" Six, eight months went by, then I finally ran into him. He was like, "I wanna battle you. You beatbox?" I said, "I sing. That's what I do." I didn't interact with him until about a year later. That's when he happened to be rolling through my neighborhood looking for my next door neighbor Andre. I'm coming out the door, and he said, "You know if Andre's home?" I said, "Nah, I really don't know." He said, "Oh, okay. You live here?" I said, "Yeah, sure do." He said, "Okay. Where you going?" I said, "I'm about to go to a block party in Brentwood and perform." "Oh, okay. Uh . . . could I come?" I was like, "Aight, dude. Yeah, you can come." So then we got in the car. I have a 1967 Camaro, and I just gutted out the system, so I didn't have no radio in there yet. I had ordered a new one and took out the old one. He said, "You don't have no radio?" I said, "Nah, man." He said, "Okay." Then all of a sudden, out of nowhere, he started beatboxing. I was like, "Damn, this is dope!" Maybe a good two minutes in while we driving, I started singing to his beat. By the time we got to Brentwood, to the block party, we performed, killed it. We was just incredible from that point on! We never left each other's side. He's a battle type of guy and I'm a battle type of guy, so everybody that would challenge us or try to battle us, we just rip 'em apart. He would kill 'em on the beatboxing; I would kill 'em on the singing. That's the way we build up. All the other crews that was already scared of him by himself, and was already intimidated by me by myself, when we joined forces, they was like, "It's not fair. It's not fair for you guys to join . . . it's not fair!" And we just killed everything in our path.

TJ Swan would paint a mustache on his face with mascara to appear old enough to get into clubs with Biz Markie, four years his senior. Gradually, Biz began forming his own crew before connecting it with the already established Juice Crew. His DJ Vaughan Lee of Elizabeth, NJ, aka Cutmaster Cool V, joined the fray, as did Biz's rapping partner and occasional rhyme writer Big Daddy Kane of Bed-Stuy, Brooklyn.

TJ Swan: Cool V and Biz is cousins, so of course he knew Cool V. On a professional level, me and Biz got together first. Once we got together, then we hooked up with Cool V, and after that was Big Daddy Kane. Me and him [Biz] was actually doing shows before he got with Marley Marl and Roxanne Shanté. We was doing our routine "Something So Different, Something So Dope." He was always going to the city, back and forth, meeting people. So he was grinding for a couple years, he eventually met Roxanne Shanté. That led him to Marley Marl.

Craig G: Biz hung out in The Bridge a lot, and he was always known. Shanté brought him on the road with her. Biz was a funny guy. Marley had everyone waiting for him at his sister's house. You'd always be standing outside waiting for Marley to get there. I would see Biz, and we'd joke around.

Big Daddy Kane: It was Marley that discovered Biz, and they ended up putting him on the road with Shan, because Shan was hot.

Arthur Baker: Magic came to the studio. He brought Biz Markie to my studio, potentially for me to sign him. I did some demos with Biz Markie that was some of the same stuff he ended up having on his first album. At the time I just started not wanting to be around drugs, so I just sort of tipped out on the whole thing of working with Magic. It was a decision I made. I still have the tape of Biz Markie. We were definitely all blown away by Biz. He did some awesome things. At that point I was losing my interest in rap in general, the whole culture, so I passed on it.

Beatboxing was all the rage in the mid '80s. There was the *Original Human Beat Box* Doug E. Fresh making waves with the Get Fresh Crew featuring MC Ricky D, not to be confused with the *Human Beat Box* Buff Love of the Fat Boys. Both brought a unique take on using the mouth as a percussive instrument, but Biz Markie could pitch shift his voice while holding the mic to his neck. He also had the ability to beatbox and rap simultaneously. It sounded robotic, and he christened himself *The Inhuman Orchestra*.

Fly Ty: I found this kid named Biz Markie, making these funny noises.

TJ Swan: Once Biz got together with Roxanne Shanté, she was like, "That's my beatboxer." So she invited him on tour. And he siad, "I already got a partner that I work with, and we got our routine. Is it alright if I bring him on tour?" And she was like, "Yeah, but who's gonna pay him?" He was like, "Well, you're not giving me that much money, so I can't pay him." And she said, "Well *I'm* not paying him." I said, "Look guys, it's alright. Nobody has to pay me. I got money, I'm good. I just want the opportunity." Shanté gave me my first break. I went on a major, domestic tour without any records—just a routine that me and Biz would do in the show.

Gradually throughout the mid 1980s, as the Juice Crew expanded in membership, so did its tour itinerary. Beginning with short stints to northeastern cities like Philadelphia that had a Hip-Hop radio presence, their sphere of influence pushed west and north into Pittsburgh and Toronto, and south into Raleigh-Durham, where record shop owner Mr. Freeze would promote shows. It was in North Carolina where the son of an auto dealer was so enamored of Shanté that he offered the driver's license-less rapper a car, no strings attached. Tours eventually made their way to the west coast and overseas to the UK by '88.

TJ Swan: We [me and Biz] would come on first, do our routine; then him and Shanté would do the hit record that they had together. That had to have been about '85, because we came out the following year. It was everywhere. It was the east, west. It actually went to Chicago, LA. It was a nice tour. Shanté was famous for the "Roxanne, Roxanne" record ["Roxanne's Revenge"], so she had fans all over the place.

Big Daddy Kane: Originally his deal was with Full Force for Select Records. The next thing I know, Biz is on the radio with Mr. Magic, doing the same routine that me and him used to do, but he was doing it with MC Shan. So now he was down with the Juice Crew.

Now under the tutelage of manager Fly Ty, Biz beatboxed while MC Shan rapped a modified version of "Marley Marl Scratch" and Marley Marl himself scratched in Fab 5 Freddy's "Change the Beat" at the Roseland Ballroom in Manhattan. A recording of it was played on *Rap Attack,* which led to an a cappella number—this time recorded at Power Play Studios with Roxanne Shanté. Accomplished in three takes, each time with Shanté rapping off the top of her head over Biz's unique combination of beatboxing and maniacal laughter, "Def Fresh Crew" (Pop Art, 1986) perfectly encapsulated the fun and innocence of Hip-Hop at that moment in time when the culture was just barely in its early teens.

Grand Dragon KD: He [Biz Markie] was quiet. He was cool. He was excited about Shanté putting him on. He said, "Let me do a little bit of what we do in New York." He started beatboxing, and his beatboxing was different from Doug E. Fresh. It was a different sound. With her rapping, it made an impact. That's how he got on, and he went from there.

Aaron Fuchs: Biz was really the last gasp for party MCs as entertainers. Everybody talks about the moment that [Kool] Moe Dee killed Busy Bee [in a 1981 battle]. It represents a transition from rappers that could rock a party to rappers that could rock a record. That tradition was very alive. Biz Markie entertained.

Tom Silverman: The dude is a fucking genius! When you [have a] guy with that kind of genius you got to give it to him and say, "Okay, what can we do? Let's do crazy ideas." Biz was a breakthrough artist in the early part of his career. You know—the human beatbox. Interesting nerd rap—he was the founder. It was never called that, but that's what it was.

Prism Records

After a stint performing as Roxanne Shanté's DJ, it came time for Biz Markie to make his own record. Fly Ty struck a deal with an unlikely partner—a small label founded in 1978 by Lenny Fichtelberg with the help of Dee Joseph. Prism Records followed the transition of disco music in the late '70s into dance music in the early '80s, but had very little connection to Hip-Hop.

Dee Joseph: I'm from LA. I graduated from UCLA, and I was actually doing some writing for a gossip magazine at the time. I had some friends who knew some people who are starting a label—this was back in 1978, '77. Butterfly Records was a dance label. Disco was like the thing at that time. They were just like on the ground floor and starting this label, and I got hired by them and learned everything about a label from retail to marketing to distribution, international licensing. It was a small, independent label, so it was easy to be able to wear a lot of hats and learn everything that I possibly could. We had a couple of hit records—a French record called Je T'Aime [by Saint Tropez], Tuxedo Junction. This label was in LA. I met Len Fichtelberg because I was doing national distribution, marketing, club promotion, and at the time he was at one of the largest one stops in New York City, which was like a middleman. It was called Record Haven.

Fly Ty: Lenny was, how should I put this? Is *philanderer* a good word? *Gigolo?* He looked like Richard Gere, and he knew it. There was no place I could go with Lenny where he was not trying to mess with a girl.

Dee Joseph: Len is from New York, he's a New Yorker, so I was out here and I had met him a couple of times at MIDEM [music industry trade show in Cannes] and we started talking and he said, "You know, I'm going to start this label." At that time Butterfly, which was distributed by MCA by then, were going under. And so he said, "Why don't you come and work for me?" And I was like, "Yeah, as your west coast representative," thinking I'd be on the west coast and he'd be on the east coast. Well, about two weeks into it he called me and he said, "No Dee, I need you here in New York." We started Prism Records together. We were actually on 11th Avenue. We were in the warehouse of Record Haven, which was this one stop distributorship. They distributed everybody—Columbia, Warner Bros., and they would just distribute them to the mom-and-pop retail stores throughout the city. And so we had an office in the warehouse.

Aaron Fuchs: When "disco" became vilified as a word, it took on the name "dance." Dance labels and Hip-Hop labels were different animals. At that time, I was always amazed that Sleeping Bag was able to put out dance records. And then you hear Todd Terry was sampling. He had this wonderful respect for what gains were being made in terms of production style by Hip-Hop. But in general, Prism was a very, God help me, white, gay kind of disco.

Tom Silverman: There are four kinds of dance music right at the time. There was white, gay disco, which is really what Prism did. There was black disco which was like SOLAR Records and was a little bit more funky—"Funky Sensation"—records like that. Taana Gardner "Heartbeat." Those records were black disco records. Those are black straight and gay disco records. Then there was black gay disco records. And there was a black straight disco records. And then there was white gay disco records, and there was white straight disco records, which was more John Travolta/Brooklyn/

Saturday Night Fever kind of disco, and there was overlap. And then there was Latin disco that has more of a salsa beat to it. But it was also enormous crossover.

Monica Lynch: They [Prism] were a scrappy, New York, independent dance label in the post-disco era, when dance music kind of went more underground. Like many of the independent Hip-Hop labels that emerged, the owners and/or the labels themselves started out in the disco and dance era.

Dee Joseph: We started Prism with Lime and Geraldine Hunt. It was straight up disco. We had a little run there. Lime and Geraldine Hunt were from Canada and then we got involved with Chris Barbosa and Mark Liggett and Lottie Golden and Richard Sheer, who were songwriters and producers at that time. Lottie and Richard did Warp 9 and we also had a group called Pure Energy, who was from Jersey and they actually wrote "Holiday" for Madonna. Jellybean [Benitez,] who was like our in-house mixer guy, I befriended because I was doing club promotion and I would spend a lot of time at the Funhouse. He had heard the song "Holiday" and he took it to Madonna. And the rest of it is history for her. Pure Energy had one hit called "Party On," and that was about it. But they're doing fine; collecting royalties on "Holiday" for the rest of their lives I'm sure.

Arthur Baker: They put out "NUNK (New Wave Funk)" [by Warp 9] on Prism. That was sort of an electro record that Jellybean did with friends of mine and I passed on it, because anything that anyone sent me that sounded like "Planet Rock" I wouldn't put out for some weird reason, and I'd even send them to Tommy Boy or I would just say, "No, I don't want to put it out."

Dee Joseph: By that time [mid '80s] Prism was doing okay, but the music started to change again. We did a couple things out at Sugar Hill with Joe Robinson, and we started hearing buzzes about rap and Hip-Hop—this kind of music that was more from the streets. Lenny had a bit of a relationship with Magic over at WBLS, and because we used to promote our records to Frankie Crocker and Magic, we tried to get them to play our music. You could work Magic a little bit. He might throw something in for you. But you know . . . you had to work it. Just being at WBLS a lot, Lenny had developed a rapport. And we had Warp 9. It was dance, but it was more, getting more towards the funkier side of dance. They did rap in it. Not like Biz or Kane, not like the homeboys, but it was our attempt at doing some type of rap. So we did try to get things played, and Magic did play "Light Years." So Magic came to us, because he liked Lenny a lot. He introduced Lenny to Marley. And that's how Cold Chillin' originally started—not Tyrone starting some label without Lenny. Marley was introduced to us first. And then Tyrone, he was the "manager" of all these.

Fly Ty: We met Lenny in France at the MIDEM. They had Alfonso Ribeiro. He was in a play called *The Tap Dance Kid,* and he was in a [Pepsi] commercial with Michael Jackson. How Lenny got him on Prism I will never know. He [Lenny] brought him [Alfonso] to us to play the song. It was a song called "Time Bomb." It was terrible! The song was terrible. We said, "Nah. This is not happening." Disco was dead by that time. Really dead! He [Lenny] was trying his hand at rap, and he thought he hit the jackpot with Alfonso Ribeiro, because he was on TV all the time. He was on a show called *Silver Spoons.* We tried to do a remix. This was not working. I take Biz to Lenny. That's why Biz was on Prism initially.

Prism by and large released 12" singles in label sleeves, devoid of cover art. When photography and art design became a component of their records, George DuBose became the Prism go-to guy. Initially an apprentice for fashion photographers, he broke into the world of sleeve design after photographing the first B-52's New York show at Max's Kansas City, and scoring the cover of their platinum-selling 1979 debut album. DuBose also shot the Ramones for every album cover of theirs from 1983 on, and worked with Soulsonic Force, whose "Planet Rock" was his introduction to Hip-Hop.

George DuBose (Photographer/art designer for Cold Chillin'/Prism Records): He [Alfonso Ribiero] got a record contract with Prism through Island through Warner Bros. They were gonna distribute the album. So I was the art director for Island. I got the job to photograph Alfonso's cover for his Prism/Island Records record. A few weeks later I got a call from Lenny Fichtelberg of Prism, and he asked me if I could shoot another artist for him. Since my agreement with Island Records was I was allowed to freelance, I set up an appointment to meet Biz Markie.

Make the Music With Your Mouth, Biz

Big Daddy Kane: Biz wanted to do this song "Make the Music," and he wanted me to write the rhymes for it. I was so used to me rhyming and him beatboxing, I was like, "Yo, don't you mean you want *me* to say the rhyme about *you* making the music with your mouth, and then *you* make the music with your mouth?" And Biz's exact words was, "Okay, Kane." And I didn't see Biz no more!

TJ Swan: When me and Biz came along with the "Make the Music," they only had a small budget left. So they took a chance, they gave us $1,000 a piece to sign the contract. Actually, they didn't even want to sign me. "We don't want no singer. We want rappers." Singing was so prevalent with the R&B movement and that dominated the music game forever. So this Hip-Hop came along—that was the new movement. They was not interested in a singer at this point. But Biz stood his ground. He said, "If you don't sign Swan, you don't sign me. We a team and that's *it*." They had no choice. We went on and did "Make the Music." The record was so dope, because nobody ever heard that type of format before. You had groups that would do five-part harmony, four-part harmony—[Grandmaster] Flash and them, Cold Crush, Kurtis Blow—all those guys did them type of things. But you never, ever heard a vocalist sing a record like I did with the hook, the melody, the breakdown, the adlibs. And it worked. When you come out with something so unique and so different, you know it's gonna work, because me and Biz was doing it for years. All we did was take what we did and put it on wax. There was no doubt in our mind that we had a hit record. The record took off really fast.

George DuBose: Biz came to me—I remember he was wearing black shorts and a black and white striped shirt. He looked like a sports referee. We made some pictures, and he brought two of his pals with him. In the beginning, a lot of these Hip-Hoppers were a little stage shy. They would have a DJ, who they didn't really need, or they would have hangers on come along with them. I took the pictures to Prism Records, and they liked them. I said, "Who is going to do your graphics?" They said they had no idea, so I said, "I could do that too." I'll never forget—Biz had a hat from the shooting that had these letters "BIZ MARKIE" on it. The letters were in this font called Fraktur. This was a font you could buy the letters in many shops in Times Square, and you could have them ironed on your T-shirt, on your jacket, on your Levi jacket, or on a baseball cap. I found a shop in Times Square, and I bought the letters to make "BIZ MARKIE" and I bought the letters to make "MAKE THE MUSIC WITH YOUR MOUTH, BIZ." So that's how I designed Biz's first single, using this Gothic-looking font. I learned this later, but that font was also being used at the same time by some of the street gangs up in the Bronx. It was just an iron-on, and there weren't too many choices. This font went on to become I think the most used font in Hip-Hop and many of the early Hip-Hop artists had tattoos using it. I had a photo exhibit in Berlin, and one of the viewers who was a German woman came up to me, and she said, "This is Nazi font." I said, "Nazi font?" I didn't know it was a Nazi font. It was just a Gothic font, but it turns out in Berlin that's what they used for all their street signs for hundreds of years or whatever.

TJ Swan: Just think about the genius of "Make the Music." That's straight up rock radio. You wouldn't think that a Hip-Hop kid was getting ideas from people like Peter Frampton, Elton John, Kiss, the Rolling Stones, Frankie Valli and the Four Seasons. But that's the kind of diverse music we all grew up on in Long Island and the Tri-State area. We didn't just listen to black radio. We listened to everything.

With Biz rhyming the verses and TJ Swan singing the choruses to the tune of "Na Na Hey Hey Kiss Him Goodbye" by Steam, Marley Marl still needed to lay down a beat. He recorded one, but quickly scrapped it. The Juice Crew's newest creative force needed a record that hit hard—something that could be immediately recognized coming out of cars from blocks away. Marley constructed an entirely new beat using the kick and snare from "Impeach the President" that had proven to be so effective on MC Shan's "The Bridge" and Eric B. & Rakim's "Eric B Is President." With his TR-808, he added an on-beat hi hat and an off-beat hi hat, with an off-beat bass drum hit that only occurred once per measure. Doug E. Fresh & The Get Fresh Crew's "The Show" had been a huge record the previous year, and featured a shaker sound effect. Marley didn't have access to this sound, so he sampled his own voice saying, "Shhh!" into a cheap microphone, and added it to the beat. After adding a loop of the piano from Isaac Hayes' "Ike's Mood I" sped up to 45 rpm, he noticed Queensbridge residents dancing outside his window to the song. Biz, Marley, and Swan had a hit before they were even finished making the record.

TJ Swan: We was lucky because we had Mr. Magic. He was on BLS, along with Marley. We would get those spins. But then it crossed over to Kiss FM. Red Alert and them was playing it. Then it started getting daytime spins. Then it started getting the countdowns. You know how great that feels? Your debut single, and you on the Top 8 at 8, and you hit #1, taking out R&B singers? *Professional* R&B singers? And you just a young, Hip-Hop, rapper, beatbox guy, and you come in there and take those spots. It was amazing. The lights was about to get cut off at Prism. They put their last dime into the "Make the Music" project. If it wasn't for "Make the Music" blowing up, there would have definitely been no Cold Chillin' Records. That was the blueprint. That was the premise of the success. That was what gave everybody light. You had other artists. You had Shanté on Pop Art, you had Shan on MCA. But when it comes down to Prism Records, which was about to fold, "Make the Music" saved the day. Then we came out with "Nobody Beats the Biz." And we just kept hittin' 'em.

To the Break of Dawn

Also released by Prism, Biz Markie's next single followed some of the same formulas of his debut record: photography and design by George DuBose, TJ Swan singing the hooks, Marley Marl behind the board, and a handful of strategically placed samples. This time around, Big Daddy Kane, a consummate lyricist, wrote the rhyme. DJ Premier, one of the most successful and prolific producers in the Hip-Hop world, would always trace his own style back to this one song, particularly the rhythm of the scratching in the intro, which featured Shanté's voice from "Def Fresh Crew."

Monica Lynch: Biz was such a genius at grabbing those huge, huge pop riffs. Here's a guy that takes the jingle for The Wiz electronics chain in New York, which is huge. "Nobody Beats the Biz"—that's a fucking radio commercial! That's what it is. That ["Nobody Beats the Wiz"] was the jingle for The Wiz stores. I think that Biz always had a very keen and big and warm and fuzzy ear for those big records.

Cut Chemist: In the mid-'80s, in '85 and '86 things were so hard, and kind of cold. You had to be tough. Biz, with the Marley production, which was tough in its own right, comes with a lot of warmth and laughter, and not taking himself seriously a little bit, and taking himself seriously enough, because he had skills. It was a brilliant combination of the two. And he was a dope MC. His voice was amazing, and the way it's EQd over those drums. Remember "Nobody Beats the Biz"—["Hihache" by] Lafayette Afro Rock Band. Nobody was fucking using a Lafayette Afro Rock Band beat. Marley was. With "Fly Like An Eagle" [by the Steve Miller Band]? I wish I could go back to the first time I heard that record again. And then you have TJ Swan, and it gives a singing element, but it's not R&B. It's still kind of psychedelic. We were thinking, "What the hell is this?" Biz threw curveballs at you. It was like, "I'm trying to make something different," and it *was* different. And he kept doing that. Him as a music selector, because he's a collector, brought a lot to the game.

TJ Swan: He [Biz Markie] was a beat guy. He was an idea guy. He always had these great ideas. He said, "Swan, when I find that beat, it's over." He called me, he said, "Swan, get to the studio. I found the beat." So we went to Marley's studio, and I was like, "Oh my God, this is beast. We got another hit." It was the Steve Miller Band "Fly Like An Eagle." He asked every DJ he knew. I think he finally got the beat from Grandmaster Flash. Once he got that beat, oh, my gosh, it *was* over. He wanted to let everybody know he was not a one hit wonder.

The Birth of Cold Chillin'

On the heels of Biz Markie's initial success, Len Fichtelberg made a deal to create a Prism sub-label by which Marley Marl would produce every record for his and Mr. Magic's stable of Hip-Hop artists, who were by this point all managed by Fly Ty. Marley would be a salaried employee at $65,000 a year, not an owner like many thought. The Juice Crew could finally be under one roof. Graphic designer Eric Haze, who had created logos for Tommy Boy Records and the Beastie Boys, would draft an emblem in instantly identifiable bubbly cursive letters for the new label after the first handful of releases. Towards the end of 1986, Cold Chillin' was born.

Dee Joseph: Eventually we realized that we needed to have a separate entity and we kinda moved Prism to the back burner because it was really our dance label, and we wanted to have a new identity and we wanted to have something that was more appealing to the kind of audience that rap appealed to.

Fly Ty: I wanted a name comparable to Def Jam and Uptown. I couldn't have a bad name. They [Russell Simmons and Andre Harrell] were my best friends, but we were competitors—extremely competitive. We came up with all kinds of names. Tar Records. Killer Records. Street Records. One day I bump into Shan. I say, "What you doing?" He said, "I'm chillin'. I'm cold chillin'." I said, "That's it! 'Cold Chillin'!"

Dee Joseph: Lenny came up with Cold Chillin'. He had a boat. His boat was named Cold Chillin'. I think one night we were sitting around stoned and just throwing out names.

Grand Dragon KD: Shan was never signed to Pop Art. He wasn't bound by any contract. I think it was kind of similar to what Shanté did. She wasn't locked in. She was really free to go where she wanted to go, and that's how she wound up on Cold Chillin'. In response to that, Pop Art developed the Hilltop Hustlers. They came with [Philly MCs] Cool C, Steady B, and Three Times Dope was added. This was a subsidiary of Pop Art Records. It was Hilltop Hustlers Presents, under Pop Art. That's when Cool C came out with "Juice Crew Dis," dissing the whole Juice Crew. Cool C, his voice sounded really similar to MC Shan. That was a bit of bitterness released.

Dee Joseph: Marley was our producer. They did not give him a piece of the label. He had a production deal, a fairly lucrative production deal for that time, so we thought.

Fly Ty: Starlite Gentry was the best publicist. We used to call our listeners "Super Listeners" on the radio. She could get through every time. "Hi, it's Starlite from Flatbush." She's an older woman. The reason she liked our show on the weekends is she would have a *Rap Attack* party at her house on Friday and Saturday night. That way she kept her six kids in the house. No one could understand how much this woman loved Hip-Hop. It wasn't age-appropriate, but she loved it.

Dee Joseph: Starlite—she was like the fan club for the Juice Crew. I don't know exactly what she did so much, but they gave her a job to work on fan promotion or something like that.

Fly Ty: Then you had Earl Sellers. He was the best national promotion guy you could find, because Earl had been in the business for years. He was an older guy too, but he knew what buttons to touch. Then there was Keith Jackson in marketing. A guy named Rick Barry is the first [basketball player] to go from the NBA to the ABA. Keith Jackson was that to me. He came from RCA to Cold Chillin' because he liked what we were doing over here. Dee Joseph was unbelievable. Dee was co-president. I always say without her, we would have done closed. I don't want to use the word "administrative," but knowing what goes where. That was Dee. Alonzo Brown ended up actually working at Warner Bros. in publicity. Alonzo was in a rap group called Dr. Jeckyll & Mr. Hyde with Andre Harrell. Alonzo was the first person I ever hired. Alonzo went on to Motown, and produced the Judge Mathis show. Ernie Singleton was the head of Urban at Warner Bros. before Ray Harris. I hired his nephew. Then there was my bookkeeper Esther. She was a little Jewish lady. She was sixty-five years old when I hired her. She would take the bus home. On the bus would be a lot of high school kids. She would hear them talking about rap. She'd say, "Uh uh! Kool G Rap is better than him! And Big Daddy Kane!" They would look at her like, "Whoa!"

Down By Law

Biz Markie would temporarily stay on Prism, as the two label designations were fairly arbitrary during the first year. New singles by MC Shan ("Jane, Stop This Crazy Thing"/"Cocaine"), Roxanne Shanté ("Have a Nice Day") and a duo calling themselves DJ Polo & Kool G Rap ("It's a Demo") all bore the Cold Chillin' imprint in 1986–87. The first album for the new label was MC Shan's debut full-length *Down By Law*, containing both "The Bridge" and his Bridge War answer record "Kill That Noise." The cover was a still life photo shot by George DuBose showing the Queens rapper's trademark mismatched Pumas, Kangol, and track suit. Showing off Shan's more sensitive side was the lead-off single, co-written by Marley Marl's mentor Andre Booth, and featuring Biz Markie's right-hand man TJ Swan.

TJ Swan: Shan was like, "I got this song I want Swan to sing on." I went to the studio at Marley's house. They had the beat already; he already wrote his rhyme. So I'm listening to the record and I was like, "Okay, where's the lyrics?" He was like, "What? Man, write your own lyrics!" Shan was a real G dude! I was spoiled, because Biz would have everything set up for me. All I had to do was sing. Shan was a different beast. When you listen to "Left Me Lonely," I did it in five takes. It was all adlibbed—all top of the head. Me and Shan would go out on double dates. We had success. "Left Me Lonely" was so big, we was on tour with superstar R&B artists, Colonel Abrams—whoever was out at the time, the hottest R&B acts—we was opening up for them at different universities and colleges. We had a good run with "Left Me Lonely."

Andre Booth: I would just play them tracks. They would say, "Okay, I like that," and we would just build off of that. He [MC Shan] said he wanted a tune like LL Cool J "I Need Love." I said okay, and we laid it down. At that time everybody was party rapping, and when LL came with "I Need Love" with the sensitivity, he was like, "Wow, I need one of them on my album."

Marley remembers instructing Booth to come up with a melody like producer Larry Smith had for Whodini's hit "One Love." For the remainder of the decade it became standard practice for Hip-Hop acts to include one or two songs per album "for the ladies."

Pickin' Boogers

While Shan rapped about heartbreak, Biz and his wingman Big Daddy Kane were crafting an album with Marley that covered slightly different topics. When Biz asked Kane to write lyrics for a song called "Pickin' Boogers," he thought his friend had lost his damn mind, but nonetheless he obliged. When Cold Chillin' held a label showcase at Harlem's hallowed Apollo Theater in 1988, Biz took the stage by falling out of a giant, novelty-sized nose and performed the song to a captivated audience.

Jay Quan: Biz Markie kept it more authentic to what rap was originally like. On "Pickin' Boogers" he rapped over an old break by Graham Central Station—"The Jam." Biz said he came to the studio with all his records, but he didn't know how to work the equipment yet. Even if it's a silly record, it can still be very lyrical. I can tell all day that's Kane on "Pickin' Boogers" without even looking at the credits.

"'Pickin' Boogers' is me. That came from my heart," Biz told UK Hip-Hop mogul Tim Westwood on his television program *N-Sign Radio* in 1988. "All those incidents really happened." He went on to speak convincingly about a song literally about throwing snot on people in public places.

TJ Swan: Biz is like, "Yo, we got another record we gonna do for the album." Me and him always talking about the Albee Square Mall. That was our hangout spot. He just wrote about what we knew. So he wrote "Albee Square Mall" and I sung the hook. Once again, he came up with the great ideas, and I just rolled with it.

The Vapors

For everyone who ever doubted the man's ability to become a star, Biz was going to shove it back in their faces. For much of his early material, Biz came up with an overall theme for a song, and instructed Kane to write a rhyme to it using a specific rhythmic pattern expressed to him in gibberish. "Zippa zippa zay, zippa zippa zippa zay!" The idea for this new recording was that each verse would tell a true story about a different member of their posse being disrespected, and subsequently treated like royalty after finding success. Kane gathered up real life stories about Cool V not being able to get a job at a record shop, Biz being rejected by other MCs and DJs in his formative years, TJ Swan being dissed by girls because of his job at the United Parcel Service, and Kane himself being being looked down upon as a hoodlum before making records.

Kool G Rap: "The Vapors" beat was originally made for me. That was one of the things Polo did. There wasn't too many ideas Polo came up with that I wanted to do. Polo and Marley did "The Vapors" beat, and when they presented it to me I wasn't crazy about it because it wasn't my style, not that it wasn't a hot beat. It just wasn't for me. It wasn't for G Rap. And I don't think G Rap could have did what Biz did with it. Now that I look back at what Biz did with the record, it wouldn't have been the same record if I would have did it.

TJ Swan: The thing with Biz is we hung out together, we was partners, we really partied, had a good time, dated. So he knew everything about my life that came out of that. In that time period, there's girls that you can date, and there's girls that won't date you because you're not an athlete, or you're not a drug dealer—because those are the money guys. I'm just a regular guy trying to kick it to a fly girl, and got rejected. When we went on tour I became TJ Swan, I'm driving in my brand new $80,000 Jaguar, and I got the silk suits on, the jewels all the way down to my bellybutton. So now I got the hit records. All of a sudden it was a totally different beast. Now the same girl that was frontin' is on it. He said she caught "the vapors." So the story is pretty accurate. I worked for UPS when I was in college. Fran was a fictional character. While me and Biz was grinding, we would work all day, all night, then I would leave him about 2:00

or 3:00 in the morning, then I would go to work around 8:00. I would gas up the UPS trucks.

George DuBose: I can't remember the original concept for Biz Markie's first album, but I remember at the end of the day we were shooting Biz, I needed additional pictures for publicity. So I hung up a piece of Mylar film—it's a silver, plastic foil—and I let it sort of wrinkle. I shot Biz's reflection in this Mylar. It was kind of distorted. It looked like you were looking at the picture while on LSD. Tyrone Williams saw those pictures and he said, "Yeah, just use that for the cover." It was something completely different from what we had planned. Biz is all warped and melting. Biz wasn't a very handsome guy to begin with, so this didn't do him any damage, and certainly made an interesting cover.

Def Jam had inked a deal with CBS's Columbia Records in 1985, followed by Andre Harrell's MCA-distributed Uptown in '86, and 1987 was the year for Russell Simmons and Harrell's former roommate Fly Ty and his new partner Len Fichtelberg to hitch on to a major. With Run-DMC (Profile), Fat Boys (Tin Pan Apple/PolyGram) and a hardcore-punk-band-turned-rap-group called the Beastie Boys (Def Jam) all going platinum, Hip-Hop had big business potential, and big business wanted in. Biz Markie's debut album *Goin' Off* would also be the first new material resulting from a partnership between two labels—one indie and one major. The corporation Cold Chillin' was jumping in bed with also needed to be prepared for something street . . . something raw.

5
THE WRATH OF KANE

A white, Realistic brand microphone sat inside a book bag, newly purchased from RadioShack. Its owner, the fifteen-year-old son of a truck driver and nurse living in Bedford-Stuyvesant, Brooklyn, saved up for weeks before he had the twenty-five dollars to afford it. He was on a mission.

Big Daddy Kane: The two rappers in Divine Sounds was Disco Ritchie and Shelton D. They had "What People Do For Money" [Specific Records, 1984]. They were street legends. Brooklyn heroes. They made it—they had a big record and video. But Mike Music the DJ would still come out and do park jams on Van Buren or Lafayette or Lexington. He did one on Van Buren, and I was going, "I'm gonna ask Ritchie for a battle! I'm gonna ask Ritchie for a battle!" I asked him, and Ritche was like, "Let's do it! Little man wanna battle!" He rhymed, and after he said his rhyme I'm like, "Okay, aight." And I reach for the mic so I could go, and he knocked my hand out the way. I'm a little kid. Ritchie is a grown man, about 6 foot 4! And he just knocked my hand out the way like, "Nah, shorty, you gotta get your own mic! You can't battle me with *my* mic." And I'm like, "Okay."

Disco Ritchie didn't know what he was in for. Antonio Hardy was still developing the perfect combination of skills, bravado, and determination to conquer and stomp other rappers with ease. He didn't spring from the earth fully formed, and he didn't descend from the heavens. The MC who would soon declare himself the Big Daddy Kane was years in the making.

Get Into It

Big Daddy Kane: I started off DJing first. I originally started writing rhymes around '79 for my cousin Nicole who was calling herself Nicky B. That's all it really was until another one of my cousins named Murdoch started rapping in '81 or '82. I looked up to him. In '82 I started writing for myself because I wanted to be down with him. I was using [the MC name] Tony T. Then when I got to high school, I switched to MC Kane. The name Kane I got from the David Carradine show *Kung Fu*. I never knew how it was spelled on the show, so I just used a K. I believe on the show it's C-A-I-N-E. We be outside playing on Thursday night when *Kung Fu* get ready to come on, or *Kung Fu Theater* on Channel 5 get ready to come on. "You gotta get someone else to play. I'm gone. I'm going to watch karate." They'd say, "Young Grasshopper," or, "We just lost Bruce Lee," or, "We just lost Kane." So out of those nicknames that they teased me with, I thought Kane was kind of fly, so I used it as my rap name. Boxing did play a very, very important part in my battle style. I was a big Muhammad Ali fan, so I was always that person that would study my opponent and use his weakness against him. For example, if he was the type of battle rapper that used a bunch of big words—because that was popular when LL [Cool J] and T La Rock first came out—I would crack jokes on him and just clown him to keep people laughing so they can't really focus on what he's saying. Or if it was the type of person who *tries* to be a funny rapper, I would use big words, but I would use them in a way where he don't know what I'm saying, to make him seem like he's not intelligent. Or if it was the type of thing where I'm battling a rapper and he got a crew with him, where they're just screaming for everything he say, and trying to make it seem like I'm corny, then I would incorporate his crew into my rhymes. I'd say something real fly about his man's hat, but say it in a way where I'm dissing him.

With Muhammad Ali's fighting instincts and his own father's sense of style, MC Kane had one more primary influence: Grandmaster Caz of the Cold Crush Brothers. The first-generation Bronx rapper had a way with words that put him in an elite set of MCs that included Melle Mel and Kool Moe Dee. When Kane first heard Caz, he threw away his rhyme book and started over.

Aaron Fuchs: We were so enamored of Caz's lyrical skills. I told him he had a way with words that would have impressed his English teacher. This is an "A" paper with your English teacher.

Big Daddy Kane: I was a major fan of Melle Mel and Kool Moe Dee. In fact, connecting the end of one line to the next one—I learned that from Moe Dee. But Caz just had that dude at the pool hall that would be sinking shots, talking shit the whole time while he's taking your money. [He had that] pimp/player/slick talking/"I'm the man" swagger.

On that glorious day in 1984, Kane marched half a block from his home to Lafayette Avenue between Lewis and Stuyvesant, twenty-five dollar microphone in hand, ready for battle. Disco Ritchie may have had a song on the radio, but he didn't have a prayer in the street. Kane crushed him. And then he crushed Mike Ski of the Dismasters. EZ-L-Double E of the Mighty Mic Masters? Crushed. The legendary Kool Moe Dee? Near miss.

Big Daddy Kane: In 9th grade, I went to school in Manhattan, at Park West. One time, one of my boys said, "There go Kool Moe Dee. I dare you to battle him! I bet you won't battle him." And I asked Kool Moe Dee for a battle. Moe Dee's like, "Nah, you don't want it, shorty. You don't want it, shorty." I'm like, "Yeah yeah, I want it." And he's like, "Nah, you don't want it," and he just kept walking.

Just Rhymin' With Biz

Street by street, borough by borough, a king was being self-made. Nothing was handed to Kane. He fairly earned the respect of his peers by *never* losing to any of his opponents. The most storied battle of Kane's career happened in Downtown Brooklyn around 1984.

Big Daddy Kane: I had a friend in Central Islip, Long Island, who used to always tell me about this guy named Biz Markie Dee, and one day he said he was in the Albee Square Mall. I was like, "Yeah? Right now? Well take me to him. And after I bust his ass, you go to your Biz Markie Dee man and tell him about MC Kane." So he took me to meet Biz, and we battled. When I asked to battle, he let me go first and I spit some real lyrical stuff at him. He tried to come back with something lyrical. And I spit some *more* lyrical stuff, but this time really *going* at him. So he saw that wasn't his way to go, so Biz switched up and tried to do a funny rhyme about a girl. So I switched up and said a funny rhyme about *four* different girls, but it was like eight lines about each girl. Each one would end up with me saying, "Learn to pick the right bitch." He started crying laughing. After we battled, Biz was like, "Yo, you dope. You need to get down with me. I *promise* you we gonna make a record one day."

Kane and Biz, who would go on to sell over one million records each by the start of the following decade, were now a team. Kane was unmatched as a lyricist, and Biz understood the psychology of an audience like no one else—he could rock a party. He also understood how to craft rhymes into actual *songs,* which he taught Kane how to do. They both made each other better. Soon after meeting Biz, MC Kane made up a rhyme where he referred to himself as "Big Daddy Kane."

Big Daddy Kane: Biz thought it was funny and said, "Yo, you should use that." Around '84, I started calling myself Big Daddy Kane.

Kane's posse was growing. He had already befriended Calvin LeBrun, who became his DJ for the next decade, while going through a few name changes of his own.

Mister Cee [Calvin LeBrun]: I'm from Lafayette Gardens projects in Bed-Stuy, Brooklyn. I'm older than Kane by two years. We went to the same high school—Sarah J. Hale High School in Brooklyn. I was part of a rap crew called the Magnum Force Crew. It was two DJs in the crew—myself and another DJ named AJ Fresh. Then there was four rappers at the time before Kane got in.

Big Daddy Kane: I got down with them [Magnum Force Crew], but then later on they decided to do other things, and me and Mister Cee was just really rocking together.

Mister Cee: Master Cee was my first name that I came up with, because at that time everybody was "Grandmaster" this. My aunt was selling office supplies to build up money for her senior dues when she was getting ready to graduate high school. I ordered some personalized pens and pads to get made. When the order came back, it came back "Mister Cee" instead of "Master Cee." The only person who had a "Mister" at that time was Mr. T from *The A-Team*. Even though the pens and pads came back as a mistake, I just fucked with the name. When people got to know me, they knew me as Mister Cee. "Master Cee" never really materialized in public. It was always Mister Cee.

Big Daddy Kane: Cee started DJing these parties with this guy Eric D. We wasn't really around each other that much, so that's when I started running with Biz. As I was running with Biz, Biz would take me to Latin Quarter, and that's where I met Scoob [Lover]. Scoob was with a whole dance crew called the I.O.U. Dancers. Finally when I got my deal, I came back and asked Scoob, "Yo, you wanna get down as one of my dancers?" I saw a James Brown thing where he did the splits and Bobby Byrd pulled him up by the hair, and I'm like, "I need dancers." I asked him if he want to get down, and I asked him which one of the I.O.U. dudes he wanna put down. He said his man Laze. It was me, Scoob, and Laze at first until Laze left. Then Scoob put Scrap [Lover] down.

Mister Cee: Kane was more closer to Scoob and Scrap than he was to me, even though I was there before Scoob and Scrap. Our relationship was really business-related and always has been business-related, even from the time of coming in my projects and getting to know my crew, because me and Kane have nothing in common. At that time Kane likes to drink forty ounces and all that. I don't drink. Kane liked to hang out. His particular clique of people wasn't my particular clique of people that I hung out with. All these years I've known him, since high school, we never hung out. We have the best relationship, but we're not the best of friends. When it's time for show time, I'm there for show time. When it's time to record, I'm there to record. We're not gonna have a beer afterwards.

Aaron Fuchs: I saw him [Big Daddy Kane] from day one. Biz Markie brought him out at Union Square, and he was the most foul-mouthed rapper you'd ever hear. And there was a stunning evolution towards marketability with his spectacular way with words. You wouldn't imagine that his origins were so hold-your-nose nasty. I think it's a case where cleaning somebody up was for the good.

Kane, Biz, and TJ Swan rocked X-rated a cappella routines such as "Protection" and "XXX-Mas Freestyle," where Kane rapped about Santa Claus putting off delivering toys to children on Christmas Eve so he could solicit prostitutes in Times Square. A far cry from the greatness that was to come, it established the wit and humor that would be driving force in their respective recording careers.

Big Daddy Kane: I met Marley in '86. I would come to Biz sessions, and I was in Power Play the night Biz did "Def Fresh Crew" with Shanté. That was the first time I met Marley. Biz had took me to Marley's crib a few times when he was working on stuff, and I thought from that, me and Marley was cool 'cause I done been in his house. The day he was supposed to record "Nobody Beats the Biz," we spent the night at my grandmother's crib, and he went and brought the drum break for it, but then said he had to go to the City to get the Steve Miller Band part. I told him, "I'm going to school. I'm not cutting school." So I went to school, and he went to the City. After school, I went to Marley's crib to bring him the rhymes. Marley told me Biz wasn't there. He had a chain on the door and wouldn't let me in. I'm like, "I'm supposed to meet him." He's like, "Biz ain't here. I don't know what to tell you." So I was like, "Aight, homie, whenever he do come these are the rhymes for his session today. Just give it to him." He was like, "Yo, you be writing Biz's rhymes?" I'm like, "Well, I wrote that." He said, "How does it go?" I said a little bit of the "Nobody Beats the Biz" joint, then he opened the door. He was like, "You rhyme too?" I'm like, "Yeah." He said, "Come on in. Let me hear something." I came inside and rhymed for him, and we cut "I'll Take You There" that day.

Have a Nice Day

Big Daddy Kane: I was rolling with Biz, doing little cameo appearances with him originally. Then one day at a Juice Crew rehearsal, me and Shanté's DJ battled on the turntables. That's when Shanté found out I could DJ and what I could do. She asked me to be her DJ instead. That's when I started traveling with Shanté. She asked me, and I was like, "Well I be doing the joints with Biz." She said, "What Biz pay you?" I said, fifty dollars, she's like, "I'll give you $250." I was like, "Well let me go talk to Biz." We went on the Def Jam tour with Whodini, LL, and Eric B. & Rakim. Touring was great because Shanté showed a lot of love. She always took care of you. She'd go into a fancy restaurant, and she'd be like, "Come on with me." She'd got to the mall to Foot Locker to buy new sneakers, she'd be like, "You want some sneakers?" Me and Eric B's brother Ant [Live] was already cool, so me and Eric bonded, and we was cool. Jalil from Whodini was schooling me on the industry, telling me the do's and don'ts.

Kane was brought into the fold with Fly Ty as manager, and signed with Prism in 1987. Ty told the MC that in order to be full-fledged member of the Juice Crew he would have to end the Bridge Wars once and for all with the ultimate diss record against Boogie Down Productions. Kane refused, but a compromise was reached when he agreed to write lyrics for Roxanne Shanté with the Bronx group squarely in her crosshairs. It was to be Shanté's debut single for Cold Chillin' and her last significant record.

Big Daddy Kane: Me and KRS was cool. Me and Red Alert was cool. Red Alert didn't play Shan or Shanté records, but he played me and Biz's records. KRS-One and Ms. Melodie [of BDP's crew] helped me move out of my parents' crib into my first apartment. I didn't have a problem with BDP. I didn't have a problem with Red Alert. There was beef between Shan and them with those cats. I did write the rhymes dissing KRS and Scott La Rock for Shanté. I wanted to put it in her style, but they said, "No, do it in your style." I'm like, "I go kinda fast for Shawnee. She might not be able to keep up." [Fly Ty] was like, "Nah, we'll make sure she keep up. Just do it in your style." Surprisingly she kept up. That was "Have a Nice Day." After I wrote it, I told KRS. He was like, "You said something about my nose?" We just laughed. Then finally when he did hear it, he called me and was cracking up laughing. That was his graffiti name, but he said, "KRS *does* sound like a wack radio station! I never even thought about it that way. This is hilarious!" We was cool.

Somethin' Funky

Kane's first single of his own was "Get Into It," engineered by Marley Marl.
Big Daddy Kane: That was my idea, because when I heard that "Kool Is Back" beat [by Funk, Inc., 1971], I was just like, "Imagine if someone had an off-beat rhyme style following that beat." *Boom Gat! Boom Boom Boom Gat!* Gat dada gat a gat gata . . . you know. Rhyming just like that—doing the off-beat stuff. I was like, "Yo, that'd be crazy."

Mister Cee: The funny thing is that when we originally signed the contract with Prism, the group name was supposed to be called DJ Mister Cee & Big Daddy Kane. Like Jazzy Jeff & The Fresh Prince, like Eric B. & Rakim. Back in the '80s it was all about the DJ and the rapper name being named together as a group. So when we signed, we signed as a group. Fly Ty had a conversation with Kane about the suggestion of dropping my name—having it be called Big Daddy Kane. Fly Ty just felt like the name Big Daddy Kane was such an odd name, but it just kind of stood out. He told Kane we should drop the Mister Cee name out. Then Kane had the conversation with me and asked if I'd be cool with it. We were signed as a group, so I was getting the royalties and advances as if we were signed as a group. It didn't matter to me because I was still getting paid. As long as everything in the contract was fulfilled as far as what I was supposed to be getting, it didn't matter that my name got dropped at the last minute.

After "Somethin' Funky" (the b-side of "Get Into It") was laid down, Kane, Biz, and a female rap duo Marley had been producing named Frick And Frack all took turns rhyming over the beat, in what is known as a cipher. Before the record was pressed, Marley was playing both versions on *Rap Attack*, and getting more requests for the version with multiple MCs. It was added to the b-side of the single as "Just Rhymin' With Biz" with Frick And Frack's verses cut from the final version, giving the song a sudden ending. It was a local hit and proved to be influential to the next generation of Hip-Hop producers, being sampled on over 300 other recordings.

"When Biz Markie brought out Big Daddy Kane for the first time ever, Big Daddy Kane had a Jamaican hat on," recalled Bronx rapper Fat Joe on a 2016 episode of *The Cipher,* recalling the two performing "Just Rhymin' With Biz" at a New York club. "I literally watched human beings try to run up the wall. He ripped it so much that the crowd went so crazy that they were trying to run up the wall. I was seeing them try to defy gravity. They couldn't even control themselves. Niggas was *losing their minds*."

Big Daddy Kane: LL apparently heard "Just Rhymin' With Biz," and he was like, "Yo, you that dude?" Me and him was cool, so it was a lot of love.

However, on the recording Biz's verse preceded Kane's, leading many rap fans to believe they were listening to a Biz Markie record. Kane needed to come with something that would make an impact to help his own career. Meanwhile, at Cold Chillin'/Prism HQ, Len Fichtelberg and Fly Ty were hatching a plan to take their label to the next level. They were in talks with Warner Bros. Records, who had tried to get in bed with Def Jam two years previous, after releasing the soundtrack for *Krush Groove*—a film loosely based on Rick Rubin and Russell Simmons' label, oddly enough made before Rick and Russell had even released their first rap album.

Bugs Bunny Money

Mo Ostin (former CEO of Warner Bros. Records): We went to Def Jam to make a deal with them. So I met Rick at that time. He wanted to do the movie, so I talked the film company into making *Krush Groove*. We actually entered into a contractual negotiation [for the Def Jam label], but at that time the industry was being killed by independent promotion—costly, corrupt, payola—all the kinds of things that can get you in real trouble. So we took a position where we would not work with independent promoters. Def Jam, in their contract with us, wanted us to guarantee that we would work with the independent promotion people, and I wouldn't do it. Independent promoters were the guys who were involved in the payola, and there was a big scandal associated with them. CBS was willing to do it. They dealt with them pretty regularly.

Clive [Davis] was very much into it. He would deny it in RIAA meetings, but the fact was that he recognized that they had value, as did Atlantic. Atlantic was part of the Warner group, but Atlantic had made some kind of independent arrangement with them that somehow passed muster with the corporation.

Fly Ty: Russell talked to Benny [Medina] and said, "Ty's my man. You don't miss on this one too." MC Shan was very hot. Roxanne Shanté had a big name. Russell sent Lyor [Cohen] to meet with Benny and bring Benny to my house.

Jeff Smith: I had been friends with Benny Medina. We were kind of high school friends; mostly we had a lot of mutual friends. Around that time was also when the Raiders were here [in Los Angeles]. His mutual friend and I had tickets to the Raiders, and we used to go to games together. We became kind of friendly over that, and hung out. I was out of a job, he knew my dad [former Warner Bros. Records president Joe Smith], and I knew him when he was working at Motown. Kerry was one of our mutual friends, Barry Gordy's son. Benny got plucked by Mo to go run a substantial or more substantial black music division. Benny was pretty steeped in Motown kind of soul music—singers, bands, and all this other stuff—but he recognized that he was missing something.

Mo Ostin: Benny Medina is very knowledgeable. He was weaned at Motown, and then he had his Warner Bros. experience. He attributes a lot of what he learned from those two sources. He grew up in Beverly Hills. He was taken in by a family called Elliott. The father of the family was Jack Elliott, who was a very important TV composer. He was at a home for children who were without parents. He's a fountain of information. We had him work with Prince, and he was great with him. Prince liked him a lot, and he'd go to Paisley Park pretty regularly. He brought in Kerry Gordy, who was Barry's son, who he knew from his Motown days.

Dee Joseph: I was in New York and Warner Bros. approached us about a deal. Tyrone and Lenny were partners, and they took several trips to LA and met with Mo. I'm positive it was Benny and *he* brought the deal to Warner Bros., and Lenny and Tyrone met with Mo and eventually they were able to close the deal.

Fly Ty: MC Shan combined with Roxanne Shanté caused Benny Medina to start looking at us. Benny was telling me how badly Warner Bros. wants us, but I didn't want to go with a major. I wanted to be independent. I said, "Thanks, but no thanks." Our allure was more than just the records. Our allure was we had radio. So automatically what we make is going on the radio, which you had to get to promote a record. Then a guy named Mo Ostin calls me, and I don't know who he is. "Hi, I'm the chairman of Warner Bros. Why don't you just come out and talk." "There's nothing to talk about, Mo. I'm telling you." "Just come on out. We can discuss it. It will be on our dime. If nothing else, you get a vacation in California." Sounded good to me. Then I went out there. They gave us a deal that they never gave anybody else again. David Altschul was the head of business affairs. He said, "We're gonna give you twenty-five points." Or thirty points. Something like that. I was like, "Points? Does 'point' mean percentage?" He said, "Yeah. We're gonna give you thirty percent." I said, "But I get 100 percent now. Why would I take thirty?" We left. And they called back with a deal we couldn't refuse. It was a joint venture, and they gave us money for each album. It was a lot of money. More than anybody had ever seen. I cost everything against me. I didn't cost against the artist. For example if they gave me let's say $10 million . . . let's use that number. The first ten, that came in from all the artists. I ended up having twenty-two acts on Warner Bros. If the first three recouped that $10 million, then the next nineteen was all gravy. The next nineteen albums was all free money, because we already recouped on the first three albums. I was very young. I wasn't quite twenty-nine yet. We needed Lenny Fichtelberg in that, at that time we didn't have much money. Lenny didn't have much either, but he had office space, and he knew the game. He knew the record business. And he knew wholesale/retail.

Warner Bros. Records set up a five year distribution deal with Cold Chillin', now co-owned by Len Fichtelberg and Fly Ty, where both labels would work in tandem to promote the artists. This differed from Warner's deal with Hip-Hop label Tommy Boy, made two years previous.

Monica Lynch: The deal between Warner and Tommy Boy is that Warner Bros. owned half of the label and Tommy Boy maintained the other half, and there was an arrangement wherein there was mutual discussion about, "Hey, if we've got a big Force MDs album, it would be best served going through Warner Bros. and get the benefit of a full-fledged black radio staff and distribution that could help us get into large accounts more easily." The leverage a large label has. But at the same time, I would say the vast majority of our releases still went through independent distribution, where we could move more quickly, get things out, not have to live or die by getting in the queue for whatever was happening at Warner Bros., which of course was at any given time *a lot*.

Fly Ty: Warner didn't distribute singles for us—only albums. So we did our own singles. That way we could put out a record any time we wanted to. We didn't have to wait for the Warner schedule, which was most peoples' dilemma. You had to wait for their schedule. To us, it didn't matter. We put out records all the time.

Big Daddy Kane: Warner Bros. didn't want me at the time. When they [Cold Chillin'] did the deal, all Warner Bros. wanted was Biz, Shan, and Shanté. I know that when Cold Chillin' got the deal with Warner Bros., we were all ecstatic. We were happy, but then Tyrone explained, "Yo, they're only taking such and such, and I got an option for another artist, but this all they want right now." Okay well, that's what it is.

Under this new system, Prism Records became used as an independent, farm team imprint for newer artists to prove themselves via 12" singles. Cold Chillin' was now the major leagues, connected directly to Warner Bros. Records and plugged into their black music department, headed by Benny Medina. Do well on Prism and you get bumped up to Cold Chillin'. Kane, along with Kool G Rap & DJ Polo, was relegated to the farm team. Then came "Raw."

R-A-W

To Marley Marl, there is Hip-Hop before "Raw," and there is Hip-Hop after "Raw." It represents an evolutionary leap for the genre—a sea change in both production and rap style. In addition to kung fu flicks, Kane was a connoisseur of '70s Blaxploitation. He brought Marley the *Black Caesar* soundtrack in order to sample the squealing sax from James Brown protégé Lyn Collins' "Mama Feelgood." Intentional noise. Marley wanted to pound out a beat á la "The Bridge," but Kane had other plans. He went to Downstairs Records on 6th Avenue in Manhattan and picked up "Hot Pants" by Bobby Byrd. Marley was instructed to loop the drum intro, played by John "Jabo" Starks, in such a way that it was off-beat, with Byrd's "I'm coming!" vocal up front. Mister Cee scratched in James Brown's voice from "Get on the Good Foot"—the Godfather of Soul and his band comprised 100 percent of the sample choices. Up-tempo, aggressive, and jarring, "Raw" didn't include any sounds originally recorded after 1972, but it sounded like the future. Kane's fast-paced, braggadocious lyrical assault was laced with metaphors and also punchlines, a trademark of the deep-voiced Man With the Given Gift of Gab.

Big Daddy Kane: I'm thinking we done with "Raw." Marley's the one that came and was like, "Yo, check this out." He added a tambourine. "You hear it? In the original there's no tam there. You don't hear it?" He added it there, so Marley really defined the whole art of sampling.

Jeff Smith: I remember one of the first things Benny Medina did was he played me Big Daddy Kane's song "Raw." I was just knocked out. I guess I was a pop-rap kinda guy. I liked Grandmaster Flash—that kind of thing. The stuff that became pop hits too. But this was something different. The energy was just pulsing out of it. It was awesome. I have to say, wow that was really *raw,* and it was the name of the song! I think he [Benny] made a connection, like I *knew* something. He [Kane] was just great. I really was kind of floored by it. It was something really new. The sounds on it—the high pitched *weee weee weee!* That was something that nobody was doing yet, and it was very dissonant and quite different from the rap music that I was familiar with.

Big Daddy Kane: When we put out "Raw," I got the call from Tyrone saying, "Yo, guess what? They told me to stop pressing up 12"s. They want to put it on this movie they doing called *Colors,* and they wanna reissue it with a Warner Bros. logo. So we gotta do this deal."

Jeff Smith: I was involved kind of in everything that happened with Cold Chillin', and because it was a new thing to Warner Bros. They had no Hip-Hop. They had Ice-T through Sire Records, who was really making a name for himself, and was starting to work towards a gold album. While we were there, the soundtrack for the movie *Colors* came out, and was kind of a watershed moment for Warner Bros. to have a big event like this.

Released in April 1988, the Dennis Hopper-directed *Colors,* starring Robert Duvall and Sean Penn as two Los Angeles police officers, was a grossly inaccurate depiction of the rising street gang problem in Los Angeles. Released on Warner Bros. Records, the soundtrack provided a vehicle not only for new Cold Chillin' signings MC Shan, Roxanne Shanté, Kool G Rap, and Big Daddy Kane, but also for Ice-T. The LA rapper who painted vivid pictures of street life, pulling from experiences in his criminal past, managed to get himself signed to Warner-distributed Sire because oddly, he reminded label head Seymour Stein of calypso music. Ice-T was now labelmates with Madonna. In practical terms however, he was in the same boat as Big Daddy Kane, as both were being handled by Warners' black music department. More than ten years apart in age, the two hit it off.

Ife Kiara (Artist Relations for Warner Bros. Records, 1987–1996): My first and foremost artist was Big Daddy Kane. Ty Williams brought him into the office when he was first coming out, and rap was so very new. He introduced us in the hallway, and Kane just looked so mean.

Dee Joseph: Mr. Moody. Kane was very dark and moody. Man of little words, except when he needed to have words.

Ife Kiara: Ice-T is so funny and he's very open, and I think that pulled Kane out of his shell, and he relaxed his guard a little bit, and we were able to get along better then.

With Biz Markie's debut album already on the streets in early '88 and making huge waves on both coasts, Kane was next up at bat. By chance, he found himself working with Mark Howard James, aka The 45 King, for one song. Based in Northern New Jersey, The 45 King and his Flavor Unit were the mirror image of Marley Marl and the Juice Crew—a collective of MCs with a producer/DJ at the center.

Big Daddy Kane: We was at 45 King's house with Biz. He was playing beats for Biz. He played this beat: *bzzt cack boo doom ba doom cack*. Biz didn't like it, and I was like, "I'll take it." I was like, "Yo, is there any way you can speed it up?" So he turned it up a little bit, and I'm like, "No, no, no. I mean *much* faster." He said, "It's funny you say that, because it actually goes faster." Then he played a different version. I was like, "Yeah, I want that." But he said it was something he did for a Public Enemy remix. If they don't accept it then I can have it. I guess they didn't accept it, so I ended up getting it.

Mister Cee: Cool V did the scratches for "Set It Off."

The a cappella intro of "Set It Off" was modeled after James Brown's "Get Up (I Feel Like Being a) Sex Machine" and became Kane's own personal favorite song to perform. "Set It Off," "Raw," and "I'll Take You There" b-side "Wrath of Kane" pushed tempos in both the music and the rapping itself to a point no one had taken them previous. This new, faster style wasn't dissimilar to punk music's evolution into hardcore, and Kane was at the center of it. However, his album's centerpiece would be slower and prove more influential in shaping the sound of Hip-Hop into the next generation. The seeds were planted by Mister Cee's neighbor—a fellow DJ named Osten Harvey Jr. who went by the name of Easy Mo Bee.

Ain't No Half-Steppin'

Easy Mo Bee: I can remember that when Big Daddy Kane had Mister Cee as his DJ, he started to come around on the block on LG because of Mister Cee. Because he was coming, a whole bunch of other people were coming over there too. So one day, Biz Markie was on the block. Somehow he ended up in my room, in my apartment. Me and my homeboy next door Norman G, aka Witchdoctor from the Bluez Brothers was in my room. I'm playing mad 45s. Then I pulled out "Blind Alley" by the Emotions. Biz in that Biz Markie voice, he knew me real well by my family nickname and he said, "Boobie, what's that?" So I showed him the record, and he left.

Big Daddy Kane: I was at Cool V's crib. That's when Biz used to stay with Cool V. We were going through a record bag that Biz had there. Me and Cool V heard that ["Blind Alley" by the Emotions] and he sampled it in the mixer, when they had those mixers with the sampler. I'm rhyming to it and I'm like, "Yo, this is crazy." I started writing a little something to it and Biz called. He was yelling and screaming, talking about, "I finally found it! I finally found it!" I believe what he found was the Lee Dorsey drums that he used on "Just a Friend." He was so excited that I was like, "You so happy about that, then you probably don't need this Emotions record here." He was like, "You can have that shit!" I was like, "My man!" I told V, "Well you heard him!" I took the 45 and the cassette tape of the way Cool V sampled it up in the mixer. I'm sitting at home trying to figure out what to put to it. I heard the Heatwave joint—the "Ain't No Half Steppin.'" I was like, "Yeah, this would be dope for the hook." And then I'm a big fan of noise. I tried several different things. I was just going through *Ultimate Breaks & Beats* to try different stuff that had noise on it, at that tempo, because it was a little more mid-tempo. When I heard the ESG joint ["UFO," 1981], I was like, "Oh shit. Yeah, this will work." I put that on. The actual day in the studio, I had some 45s that I had bought. One was a Monk Higgins joint. I had bought it actually because it was something that Biz used. I didn't buy it to use. But when I played the flipside ["Big Water Bed" by Monk Higgins and The Specialties, 1972] I heard the horn *Baanum*. I'm like, "Oh yo yo yo, Marley—we need to throw this shit in there too." Me and Marley had a big argument that day because he told me, "Yo, you cluttering the record. It's too much shit. You need to take all this stuff out. Just use 'Blind Alley' and just let me cut up 'Ain't No Half Steppin' on the hook." I was like, "Man, fuck that."

Mister Cee: I wasn't there in the very beginning process of Marley and Kane putting the record together or Kane telling Marley, "Hey, sample this record," or, "Do this," or whatever. But then when it came time to do the scratches, I come in and I do the scratches after Kane and Marley kind of put everything together with the music and the vocals. That was kind of the routine.

Easy Mo Bee: Maybe a month afterward, we listening to the radio, me and Norman G. "A world world world premiere premiere premiere! World world world premiere premiere premiere!" Mr. Magic. And then it dropped. "Mmm mmm mmm." And I hear the sample. Me and Norm looked at each other like, "*Oooooohhhhh,* no you see that? Yo, they jacked us!" What's key is that Biz said, "Boobie, what's that?" Those are the key words: "*What's that?*" So he had never heard that before. And I know that there was a lot of sharing in samples. I was flattered at the time. I ain't gonna lie. I wasn't mad or upset or anything. I was flattered. And if anything, with no product out on the market, it made me feel good. That right there proved to me that my ideas were good and that I was on the right track as far as picking samples and stuff like that. I felt like, "Yo, I'm doing the right thing, because if Kane is rocking on something that was my idea, I *must* know what I'm doing."

Big Daddy Kane: I think it was perfect timing because sampling was just finding itself—that whole art of sampling, and especially what Marley had created with it. I think Kurtis Blow might have been the first person to sample a song, but Marley really defined it. Now it was the park jam. What Marley is doing is the park jam, where the breakbeat is playing repeatedly. But then Hank Shocklee and them [Bomb Squad/ Public Enemy] was finding different ways to add extra stuff and make it more busier and change it up from the norm. It was all a building process, and I think it came at the right time.

By standing his ground, Kane crafted a record that pushed Marley to be a better producer. In the lyrical style of "Raw," "Ain't No Half-Steppin'" was boastful, employing metaphoric language referencing TV commercials and programs—Ginsu knives, the Roy Rogers restaurant chain jingle and the Letterman character from the PBS children's show *The Electric Company*. He also drew attention to his hi-top fade hairstyle he referred to as his "Cameo," a nod to R&B group Cameo's frontman Larry Blackmon, who sported the same 'do. The man behind it was Eugene Shelton.

Eugene Shelton (Publicist for Warner Bros. Records, 1988–1996): Ice-T was the very first rap artist I ever worked. Then it went to Cold Chillin' with Big Daddy Kane, Biz, Roxanne Shanté, MC Shan, and all the rest. But I did not have the relationship or work as much with any of them as I did with Kane, because that was a mutually beneficial relationship. I just saw something in him. I could see how I could sell Kane, because he had that image.

Big Daddy Kane: Gene just loved me to death. They sent him out with Ice-T, they sent him out with Biz, and he said he never want to work with a rapper again in his life. But he went out with me and enjoyed it. He was like, "You don't understand. I got you in magazines you never been in, but I did things that I never done in my life. I've never had the experience of walking through the hood while people interviewing you, and dealing with *Rap Masters* and *Word Up!* [Magazine]. I'm from an older generation, but I feel like I'm solidified and respected in Hip-Hop now. I have relationships with [*Word Up!* contributor] Kate Ferguson, [*Right On! Magazine* editorial director] Cynthia Horner, and all these people from Hip-Hop publications because of you." That's the type of relationship me and Gene had. Gene was actually the one who told me to take my rasta joint off. "You should show your features. You wear your hair like that. You have Egyptian features, youngblood." Gene is the one who convinced me to do that in a photo session—to show my flat top.

George DuBose: I met him [Kane] when he was nineteen. We talked about his concept for his first album cover. Kane had been writing some songs for Biz that are on Biz's first album. So I knew Kane was gonna blow up. Biz was doing pretty well. Kane's idea was to be carried in a chair, or what they call a litter, with two black guys in front, two big black guys in back, and then four dancing girls in the front of this parade, and four dancing girls in the back, all throwing rose pedals. I said, "Kane, where am I supposed to shoot this Cecil B. DeMille production? Central Park? Besides, Kane, you're a handsome guy. By the time I get all you twelve people, thirteen people on the bottom of a 12" package, you're gonna be small. On a cassette, you're going to be tiny." I took Kane's concept of being a Black Caesar, and that was his nickname I guess—Black Caesar—and confined that to him sitting on a throne with three slave girls feeding him purple grapes and yellow apples. I tried to color scheme the whole cover as purple and gold. We wound up with a shot that suited his original concept, but was more refined and marketing-esque.

Jeff Smith: He [Kane] was something. He was really something to behold. It was clear that he worked harder. He wrote better rhymes. He was working at it all the time. He's different. He showed a little bit more. The whole thing was about the fame, the Dapper Dan suit, the gold chain. It was all part of one thing. It was all put together. Kane was busting out. *Long Live the Kane* I think finally creeped over into like 501,000 sales, and we very quickly got it certified by the RIAA before the returns started coming back, and they issued him a gold record.

Released in June of 1988, Big Daddy Kane's debut *Long Live The Kane* was certified gold fourteen months later. Cold Chillin' had its first plaque. Still a teenager, the MC was riding high, but the competition from within the Juice Crew was heating up.

6

MEN AT WORK

Approximately five miles directly east of Queensbridge lies the neighborhood of Corona, Queens. Before there were homes, there was the Fashion Race Course, where the first professional baseball game ever was hosted in 1858. Since the late nineteenth century, Corona's ethnic makeup changed in waves: Jews, Italians, and after WWII, African Americans followed by Dominicans. Long before proclaiming himself the *Kool Genius of Rap,* Nathaniel Wilson was shaped by the Corona of the late 1960s and 1970s.

Kool G Rap: My mother divorced my father when I was about five. I end up growing up with a stepfather who was there the day my mother left the physical realm. My stepfather had a couple of different jobs. He wasn't highly educated or nothing like that, so he did custodial type of work for a community center out in Queensbridge where he resided for a certain time in his life. He also worked in a supermarket. My mother married very young to my father, so she didn't have any substantial education. Her and my father got married at the age of seventeen—the just-making-it-legal age. Corona had different parts. Some parts of Corona were very working class, and then you had other parts that was public assistance. It was a culture change. I was born in '68. My experience of it changing is in the mid '70s—it was more closer then. Black people stuck more together. Of course there was fights and still homicide and all that in environments where it induces that. In other neighborhoods, two working parent homes, there was more closeness. More unity. That would change in the years to come, coming up out of the '80s.

Streets of New York

Dr. Butcher: You had to be careful not to go to certain places and certain blocks you want to avoid. It was good for the most part. I saw a lot of things, but I personally never had issues. You definitely weren't in the slums. Brooklyn and other places—I know what slums look like.

Masta Ace: When I grew up, I didn't even know Queens had projects. To me Queens was like Beverly Hills. There was actually people from my neighborhood [of Brownsville, Brooklyn] who finally moved out of the projects, and they all moved to Queens.

Dr. Butcher: Our entire area was middle class/working class. Louis Armstrong lived there. My sister used to go to his house after school with his wife. Langston Hughes. You would just see them taking the train and doing things. Bugging out. Malcolm X lived there. The Muslims blew his house up. The house they blew up was on 98th Street in Corona.

Masta Ace: Queens had all the nice houses, the tree-lined blocks. You could leave your car out and nobody mess with it. That's how I viewed Queens. I didn't know about the PJs.

Kool G Rap: Crack was one of the things. Because, even with dope in the '70s, you still had more unity. In the early '70s where I grew up at, there wasn't so much a dope epidemic in my face on a particular block and area that I lived in. But not far off, a few blocks away, was where all the action was at, which was certain parts of Northern Blvd. from maybe 112th all the way up to like 96th Street. All up that strip you would see the presence of drugs, the presence of violence, the presence of dope fiends, which would later on turn into crack fiends in the '80s. I spent a chunk of my childhood away from that. Then when I got about eleven years old, we relocated from the area where it wasn't like that, to dead smack in the area where it was like that.

Northern Blvd. between 96th and 112th left such a profound impression on Nathaniel's psyche, that he brought what he witnessed on that strip into the rap world through his vivid, cinematic lyrics, recited with his trademark lisp. But his ascent in Hip-Hop didn't happen overnight.

Kool G Rap: When I started seriously writing rhymes I was about thirteen. I would begin to really develop my writing skills at the age of fourteen—my just-getting-into-high-school years. [My influences were] Grandmaster Caz from Cold Crush 4, Kool Moe Dee, Spoonie Gee, Melle Mel from the Furious Five, and a cat by the name of Silver Fox from the Fantasy Three, which I got to know a little later. Spoonie Gee and Melle Mel—those dudes had records that was knocking through the neighborhoods. When I lived in LeFrak City, one of my peoples that I got close with out there, his name was Joe Grant. Joe Grant's father had a club in Harlem—he had a little after-hours spot. We used to go up there as kids on the weekend. Joe Grant would go up there and be the house DJ on the weekends. Cats like Silver Fox used to come through there, Doug E. Fresh, I met LL [Cool J] there through Silver Fox before LL ever made any record.

Polo's Beats

Another Corona native named Thomas Pough was a high school classmate of Marley Marl. By the early '80s he had developed a local following as DJ Polo, but his main income source came from pimping.

Kool G Rap: I had heard of Polo since I was eleven. He's probably about five years older than me.

Masta Ace: Polo was just the coolest guy ever. Just an overall nice guy. Someone you could have a basic conversation with, laugh, crack a joke, whatever.

TJ Swan: Polo was the first baller in the Juice Crew. He had the Benz. He was dope as a DJ.

Dr. Butcher: He always used to drive around in nice cars with pretty girls. I always admired him. He took a liking to me as a little kid and would bring me to his house to see his turntables, and pictures of him with all these naked women because he DJ'd at a strip club. As a little kid, I loved seeing that stuff. "Whoa, this dude is the coolest dude!"

Dr. Butcher: He had a lot of pretty girls, what can I say?

Craig G: I knew Polo before I met G Rap, because Polo had a different MC before G Rap. His name was Frost.

DJ Polo hooked up with Frost (aka Frosty), and recorded one single as The Terminators on the short-lived Prism-distributed label Snowflake in 1986. "Forever Dis"/"Polo" failed to make much of an impact.

Dr. Butcher: [Frosty was] another guy from our neighborhood. He was an older rapper. They called him Frita Frost. So initially, The Terminators were supposed to be Polo and my cousin Shmoo. I don't know what happened. He just wasn't focused, and Polo went and got Frost to do the song. Actually he wanted me to be his partner. Me and G Rap were the best rappers in the neighborhood, so a lot of people would either go to him or come to me.

Kool G Rap: Frost didn't really want to do promotional shows to help get the crew out there. If it wasn't about paper, he wasn't really with it. Me and Polo knew *of* each other, but never formally met. I used to see him moving through the hood sometimes; he probably seen me, but Eric B. formally introduced us. Polo had told me he had heard of me throughout the neighborhood. I was about sixteen.

Dr. Butcher: Polo, being that he knew me since I was a kid, was like, "Yo, I want you to do this for me." I wasn't really focused on making records at that point. I was like, "Yo, I have another dude that's probably the best dude out here. This guy named G Rap!" He was like, "Yo, that's funny, because I just left Eric B and he told me the same thing." He said, "I bet you that's the same guy Eric is talking about." I said, "It *is* the same guy Eric is talking about. Yeah, he's incredible. Go get him." So they linked up. If you listen to G Rap and Frosty, there's no comparison.

From East Elmhurst, Queens, a bordering neighborhood of Corona, Eric Barrier was another DJ who had recently discovered a profoundly talented MC. Hailing from Wyndanch, Long Island, William Griffin went by Kid Wizard, but soon changed his name to Rakim Allah. Marley Marl, who remembered Eric from when he was an ice-cream man who would frequent Queensbridge, engineered the duo's single "Eric B Is President"/"My Melody," released on the Zakia label in 1986 under the name Eric B Featuring Rakim. MC Shan mixed the record and played keyboard on "My Melody." The group, whose name was later modified to Eric B. & Rakim, sounded so different than anything that had come before it; Marley and Shan would stand in the kitchen and laugh between Rakim's vocal takes. Why wasn't he shouting the lyrics like everyone else?

Craig G: I was there and I wasn't impressed with Rakim at first, because he had a different way of recording. It was a lot of punch-ins, so I didn't get it back then. When I heard the song on the radio, I was like, "Holy crap! This is one of the best songs I ever heard in my life." But during the recording process, I didn't have a lot of faith in it.

Eric B. & Rakim swept the Hip-Hop world by storm, becoming platinum-selling recording artists on Island Records' 4th & Broadway imprint and later on Uni/MCA while signed to Rush Management, falling outside the Fly Ty-managed Juice Crew system. On the contrary, the new duo of DJ Polo & Kool G Rap fell squarely within it.

It's a Demo

Kool G Rap: After Eric B introduced us, it wasn't that long before Polo would take me to Marley's house. I think he was excited to take me to Marley's house because he was really pumped up about my skills as an MC. Polo was seeing something happening that might have not happened with the group of him and Frost. We went to Marley's house immediately. I cut my first record "It's a Demo" [Cold Chillin', 1986] first time going to meet Marley. It was intended to be a demo because back then I was doing demo tapes trying to get discovered. I recorded with Hurby Azor that managed Salt-N-Pepa and Kid 'n Play. I did recordings with Disco Twins. I was in this demo tape making phase, so I thought this was gonna be the same exact thing going to Marley's house. And that's why my first song ever is titled "It's a Demo." Marley just started playing the recording [on *Rap Attack*], and the shit got hot. Then they pressed it up because it was a demand for it.

Dr. Butcher: That was a tape loop. He [Marley] just recorded the loop and put some 808s underneath, and a hi hat. That's what most people would do. Just run a hi hat, an 808, and run the loop.

Masta Ace: It was my second session at Marley's crib, and Polo walked in with his new rapper, and that was Kool G Rap. He came in there wearing a Hawaiian short set, which was in style at the time, and they actually recorded "It's a Demo" that day. G Rap was mad skinny and super lyrical. "It's a Demo," at the time they recorded it, I didn't really get it. It was in the *early* days of sampling. People weren't really sampling like that yet. It was more still drum programming. "It's a Demo" sounded a little foreign to me. I didn't like it at first. A year later I heard it in a club and I was like, "Oh, this is dope!"

Kool G Rap: At first the name of the group was DJ Polo & Kool G Rap. I wanted it to switch because I was pretty much doing the majority of things, except for "It's a Demo." It was Polo's idea I believe to use the [James Brown] "Funky Drummer" beat. That was the first and last time that I rapped over a beat that Polo had anything to do with.

Dr. Butcher: Polo comes from the era where DJs played records, and they were known for sound systems—who had the loudest sound system. A lot of those guys were called DJs. They couldn't really scratch or get crazy on turntables, but they were known as

DJs because they had expensive sound systems. Because everyone knew he was from that era of DJs, he could still walk with that name and consider himself a DJ. But things had progressed.

Trilogy of Terror

By 1987, it was clear that Rakim, Kool G Rap, and new arrival Big Daddy Kane were leading the pack in terms of pure MC skills, pushing the art of rhyming into a new era of lyrical exceptionalism.

Troy Shelton: G Rap is probably one of the most underrated MCs ever. Those guys worked *hard*. It's kind of like that competition thing. G Rap always rapped harder because he wanted everybody to know how dope he was. He was always underrated. I'm like, "This guy can eat a lot of peoples' faces off!" G Rap was one of the best lyricists to ever spit.

Ced Gee: When we used to go on the road with them—Kane, us [Ultramagnetic MCs], and G Rap, we had a routine where when we was going up to the shows, we were battling. We would just rhyme all the way up. Like we was going to Philly—we would just rhyme for two hours. All the other groups wouldn't get in the cipher, because it was just the real MCs. Me, G Rap, Kane, Kool Keith. We would rhyme all the way to wherever we were going, and then on the way back we would snap. Just joke. We'd have crazy fun. We was juiced up by then. Everybody would get their five cents in. We would just say crazy stuff.

Big Daddy Kane: When me and G Rap met, we were rhyming the way we rhyme. I know with me and G, we both used to use a lot of words that rhyme in one line. I know I got that from [Grandmaster] Caz. With G, I don't know where he got it from. But I got that from Caz in '82. Rakim to me sounded more like a 1981 [Kool] Moe Dee—just an advanced version of Moe Dee. Rakim didn't really rhyme that fast. Rakim was more slow, making his rhymes in syllables. That's what Moe Dee used to do. I think that we all are equally great. For someone to say, "Kane is my favorite rapper," or someone to say, "Kane is my second favorite under Rakim," or, "Kane is my second favorite under G Rap," I wouldn't be mad. I think that we all rank equally. I think that we're all incredible lyricists. The people wanted to know who's better [between me and Rakim]. "We need these two to battle." They tried everything they could to get us to battle, but it never happened. We were even offered money in 1990. I think [the televised special] *Rap Mania* was '89, so the following year they tried to turn *Rap Mania* into the battles. And they tried to make it where I battle Rakim, LL battles Moe Dee, Shanté and Sparky D, and Furious battle Cold Crush. This was a pay-per-view event, but they couldn't get dude [Rakim] to sign on. It never happened. I reached out to Eric, because me and Eric was cool. Eric's exact words to me was, "Ah nah, we gon' bust ya ass, Kane. Don't worry about it. It's a done deal. We gon' bust ya ass." I thought it was gonna happen. But they told me Ra didn't sign on, so it never happened.

Masta Ace: Up to that point, the basic pattern was the last word in the second line would rhyme with the last word in the first line. Rakim was rhyming multiple words, three or four words, in the same line. To me that was mind blowing. "Eric B. Is President"—the very first one. It was being played on the radio in my neighborhood, right next to my building. We were sitting on the bench, and we were all talking about that song because it had just played on the radio the night before. We kept rewinding it and listening to it. Less than a year later I heard Kane. He was on a song "Just Rhymin' With Biz." To me, Kane took what Rakim did and he upped the ante a little bit, because he added to that style the concept of punchlines. Lines that made you go, "Oooohh!"

Kool G Rap: I might have had two battles in my life in the street or in a club. I never really had many battles, especially after making records.

Big Daddy Kane: There certain things people gotta understand about battle rap. Rakim is a *phenomenal* MC. He's great at what he do, but battle rapping is something different. I think that's something people didn't really understand. I would have rather battled KRS-One, because KRS is a battle rapper. You got to know how to think. Sometimes you're looking at something, like you looking at the *power* of George Foreman, the *power* of Sonny Liston, and not understand the *skill* of Muhammad Ali.

Kool G Rap: If you ask me and you ask a lot of people that grew up on Hip-Hop in that era, they gonna say the Big Four—Big Daddy Kane, Rakim, G Rap, KRS-One. People got that because somebody did an image a long time ago where they had me, Rakim, Kane, and KRS-One looking like we was etched in the Mount Rushmore monument. When you say any of those artists is part of the Big Four, what you're saying is they're monumental.

"I'm Fly

Unbeknownst to Kool G Rap, he was helping plant the seeds of a new rap sub-genre along with Schoolly D in Philadelphia and Ice-T in Los Angeles. The latter dubbed it "reality rap," but it gradually came to be known as "gangsta rap."

Kool G Rap: I still had that street edge when I did records like "It's a Demo," but it might not come out on the very first record I would ever do. This is why you would hear it more on the album, where there is a variety of material. On the b-side of "It's a Demo" is a record "I'm Fly." It's still talking that street shit, mentioning money, still talking about guns. The main focal point of the song is I'm fly, but you hear street elements in that song.

Glamorous: He [Kool G Rap] was always deep to me. Heavy. He scared me sometimes, but I loved him. He just looked gangsta. I'm from the suburbs.

Dee Joseph: G Rap was intense. He had an intensity about him. He was quieter, and Polo was like his comedic sidekick. He was very funny. G Rap was very serious about his shit and, and Polo was more lighthearted.

Kool G Rap: I had heard an Ice-T song after I already did "It's a Demo," "I'm Fly," possibly even "Road To the Riches." I didn't know who Ice-T was until Polo played him for me. Polo said, "Yo, check out this brother from Cali, cuz!" I liked the song. But I didn't hear it before I made songs like "Rikers Island," "Road To the Riches."

Jay Quan: He [Kool G Rap] was doing that before there was any Biggie, before there was any N.W.A. He would make a record like "Rikers Island" on one hand, which is a cautionary tale, and on the other hand make a record like "I'm Fly" with tons of gangster imagery in there. It would get more and more gangster with every album. His legacy is gangsta rap, subject matter-wise. Stylistically, his legacy is multi-syllabic phrasing, and splitting up his sentence structures. Not rhyming every last word with the last word, but coming back.

Masta Ace: G Rap is another funny guy. People get caught up in his gangsta image and his stuff he be rapping about, but they don't know that he's a serious joke cracker. He's hilarious. People don't expect him to be that way. He is a funny dude. He says some funny stuff. I got a lot of love and respect for him. He's definitely one of the best to write a rhyme and to spit a rhyme.

Jeff Smith: I remember going to see them [Cold Chillin' artists] I think it was in like Peru, Indiana. There was a guy named Darryl, who was like Tyrone's cousin or something like that, and they would just prank on him all the time, but the most infantile pranks you can imagine. They would put a bucket of water on a door that was ajar, and they'd ask him to come in. It would fall on his head.

Poison

"Rikers Island" was released as a single by Cold Chillin' in 1987, and Kool G Rap & DJ Polo, names now permanently reversed, put out "Poison" the following year. With the Cold Chillin'/Warner Bros. deal in effect, the single was released on the Prism label, so as to fall outside the major label machine, just as Kane's early singles had. A few years later, G Rap's voice from "Poison" was immortalized after being sampled by New Edition offshoot Bell Biv Devoe on their debut single of the same name. It peaked at number three on the *Billboard Hot 100* in June of 1990, and their *Poison* album went quadruple platinum.

Kool G Rap: They [Bell Biv Devoe] didn't clear it with me because you had a thing with the sampling at that time. You couldn't use more than four beats, which equate to one bar. That didn't exceed that level, so I don't think technically by law they would have had to clear it. But since it was used so many numerous times throughout the record, they would invite me to the video shoot and all that, just in case there might be any sort of discrepancy. I guess they figure that gesture would smooth it out. But I can't say that's the only reason they invited me to the video. I was cool with them. I didn't feel disrespected or jacked, or nothing like that. To me, it was honorable that a group like them, that sprung off from fucking New Edition, who was like one of the biggest groups—they were very reminiscent of the Jackson 5—so who the fuck didn't love New Edition? And BBD was the fucking same thing. I had an awesome amount of love and respect for them. I loved they records. I looked at is as, "Yo, I'm honored!"

Rhymes I Express

Dr. Butcher: The way he [Kool G Rap] puts his words together, his thought process, the metaphors, the stories . . . He's a smart guy. He does a lot of reading. He comes from a family where if you go to G's house, his older brother just had a room full of books. So he was well-read. If you sit down and talk to him, he could talk about a million different subjects. LL Cool J is the same way. They were not ignorant rappers. They were definitely more in tune with society, political things that were going on, and spiritual things going on. So we all just enjoyed talking. He put a lot of thought into his stuff. It wasn't just about walking in the studio and spitting off the top of the head. G would sit there and really go into a trance with his writing. Once he starts writing, he blocks everybody out. That's just a natural gift. You don't see that in many people.

Kool G Rap: Shortly after I did "It's a Demo" and "I'm Fly" and some of my first singles, I was already working on a full-fledged album, so I had material. The people just ain't hear it yet. But these shits was being recorded. "Road To the Riches," "Men

At Work"—I came into Marley's studio bringing the records myself and telling him, "I wanna rap over this drum loop, I want you to put this guitar loop over that drum loop," and then Marley would add his little things too, whether it was cutting in a roll from a drum or horns. But I always had a general idea of what I wanted to do. There was records Polo did scratches on. When I was working with Marley, if there was any cuts and stuff like that, for the most part of it, Marley would do it. Not with the intention of "Yo, I just want to do everything." It was with the intention of everybody's excited because we producing some dope sounding shit, and he comes up with an idea like, "Yo, I'ma put a scratch here!" I remember a couple of times we told Polo, "You gonna do some scratches?" And Polo would do some scratches.

Death Wish

Road To the Riches, the debut album by Kool G Rap & DJ Polo, featured the almost incomprehensible feat of verbal dexterity that was "Men At Work," where G Rap launched into a seventy-eight bar verse. It was released on Cold Chillin'/Warner Bros. in early 1989, several months after its original intended release date.

Kool G Rap: It took a while to come out. I went in the hospital, and that kind of put me on the back burner of the release roster of who would come out next. I was young; I was getting high and shit like that. Sniffing coke. Me doing that wasn't the cause, but it made the condition I developed worse. I used to get nosebleeds ever since I was young. Maybe around twelve or thirteen years old, if the air was too humid, my nose would start bleeding. I already had a condition of sinusitis. I was in Jersey with a girl I was messing with at the time. She took me to a hospital that was out there. People at the hospital would eventually call my mother. My mother panicked and called my man Fly Ty, who was one of the people that would bring me into Juice Crew. He was like a father figure to some of the people in Juice Crew. He was older. We was all kids. Him and Magic was in the same age group. She called him, and he said he had just finished reading an article where New York Hospital had specialized in whatever surgery they were saying that I needed, which was a craniotomy. He ended up speaking to the doctors at the hospital I was in. I was in South Amboy Hospital in Jersey. He said he wanted me transferred over to New York Hospital. They told him, "He might die by the time he gets from over here to New York Hospital unless he's taken by helicopter." But they didn't know who they was talking to. They didn't know who the hell Fly Ty was at the time, and probably didn't know he had the ability to pay for a helicopter. So they told him that a little sarcastically. He asked them how much it cost and he said, "Yo, I want him flown in a helicopter."

Dee Joseph: I don't know if Tyrone did it, but the emergency vehicles did it! Again, Tyrone in his private helicopter. I think it was the medivac helicopter.

Kool G Rap: That's how I ended up in New York Hospital—flown in a helicopter. Fly Ty arranged it. I was one of his hot artists on his roster. He wasn't trying to lose a hot artist! And at the same time he wasn't trying to lose a friend either, because we developed a relationship. And that money was nothing compared to what G Rap would generate, and he knew that. A craniotomy is pretty much where they cut your skull open.

Dee Joseph: I just remember poor G had brain surgery.

Kool G Rap: In my case, they had to clear an infection off the side of my brain. They told my mother that I don't even have a 50/50 chance to live. They have to put me under with the anesthesia in the condition I'm in. My mother was panicking. I was really in so much pain, I wasn't conscious of living or dying. The cool thing about people that die from failure of the body—you would think that you would fear dying, but you just not feeling good to the point where all that don't really register to you. I told my mother on my deathbed, "My head hurts so much; I don't care if they cut my whole fucking head off." She was trying to explain to me what they gotta do. She was upset. I'm like, "Ma, I don't care if they have to cut my whole fucking head off." And I wasn't the type of person to curse. I was so fucked up at this point. I would never curse with my moms. I had ultimate respect for my mother, but this is the condition I'm in, that I would talk like that to my mother, because that's how much I meant it. I was out of the hospital in a month. I remember wanting to be out the hospital so fucking bad, and wanting the doctors to say, "Okay, he's good to leave," that I actually did a fucking split. That's how bad I wanted to get the fuck out of there. I hate hospitals to this day. So I did a fucking split, came back up, did it perfect, and they was like, "Alright, you can go home."

Dee Joseph: The poor guy had a bad scar after the surgery. He was able to bounce back, you know, thank God he was young enough.

Kool G Rap wasn't the only Juice Crew MC who was using. "'Jane, Stop This Crazy Thing,' 'Cocaine,' all of that—I was being the biggest hypocrite in the world," MC Shan told VladTV in 2016, looking back on his first single released on Cold Chillin'. "Because after I did that song, guess what? [sniff sniff] You get what I'm saying? But I would never enforce that on the children listening to my music. I would do a song like 'Cocaine' where you thought I was talking about a girl through the whole song, and all of a sudden . . . it's cocaine. 'Jane, Stop This Crazy Thing'—I was talking about what the crack epidemic was doing to the projects." Shan was swept up in that very epidemic, but G Rap was determined to bounce back and land on his feet post-surgery.

Kool G Rap: I remember wanting to prove to myself that ain't nothing change. So I was gonna write the most ridiculous shit that I could possibly write, with as many punchlines and complex flow patterns as possible. I wanted to prove to myself, "If anything, I'm *better.*"

7
THE SYMPHONY

1988 was the year the wave crested and then crashed into the homes of Middle America. Rock ‘n’ roll had 1956, the British Invasion had 1964, punk and disco strangely shared 1977, but ’88 belonged to Hip-Hop. In the middle of it all was Marley Marl, wearing a pilot’s uniform, decked out in Big Daddy Kane and Kool G Rap’s gold chains and sitting inside the cockpit of a private plane on Long Island.

George DuBose: It was at Farmingdale Airport [Republic Airport in Farmingdale, Long Island]. We chartered a Lear Jet, because Marley wanted to be in the cockpit of a Lear Jet.

Dee Joseph: I had to arrange it, but I did not go out to the field where they did that. That was George’s thing.

George DuBose: We got him into the cockpit, and he says, “Where’s all the dials?” I call the leasing company at the airport, and I say, “My artist is complaining there’s not enough dials.” He said, “You should have rented a Gulfstream. It has many more dials.” I was shooting that picture from outside the plane. I was standing on a ladder, shooting through the window. It was quite a photo shoot.

In Control

Cold Chillin’/Warner Bros. was releasing a compilation album consisting of previously unreleased recordings produced by Marley Marl. Featuring rappers Craig G,

Queensbridge native MC Percy (aka Tragedy), MC Shan, Roxanne Shanté, a duet between Biz Markie and premier Uptown Records rapper Heavy D, and an unknown Brooklynite named Master Ace (modified to "Masta Ace" after 1991), *In Control, Volume 1* was being marketed as an album *by* Marley Marl—producer as artist. It was the first of its kind for the genre.

Aaron Fuchs: It was a great moment for Marley. When you're running a record company, if you've got a dollar, you can tell your distributors you have two pieces of product: you have a dollar and you have four quarters. A great idea and something deserving, because there was a style he developed. All the acclaim he got was warranted.

Jeff Smith: Marley Marl was kind of a Phil Spector-y kind of a character. He had all these acts. Of course they were all on one label, and he seemed to have a very deft touch with all of them. He gave everybody their own musical identity. I think a lot of them had their own ideas, but a lot of them didn't. These were not schooled musicians. He knew how to lay it down, how to get the sounds right, and the voices. He was tremendous.

George DuBose: The same day, somehow all the other Cold Chillin' artists, with the exception of Roxanne Shanté and DJ Polo, showed up for this iconic Juice Crew All Stars photo on the back cover.

Dee Joseph: Shanté was never on time to *anything ever*. And if she didn't show up, how could we put her in it? And there were times when Shanté didn't show up. We'd book something, and she's supposed to be there for an interview. I'd make an appointment for her, and then she wouldn't show up. Shanté didn't show up for this.

George DuBose: I don't know why she didn't show up. She missed the bus? I don't know what to say. I don't know the politics that day. I don't know why DJ Polo didn't show up either. He was part of Kool G Rap & DJ Polo.

Droppin' Science

At fifteen, Craig G, né Curry ("'G' just sounded better than 'C'"), was the youngest member of the Juice Crew, but he was already somewhat of a veteran, having released a pair of Marley-produced singles on Pop Art in 1985.

Craig G: My mother was a nursery school teacher in Queensbridge. She retired there. My mother and stepfather were really religious. They were church people. He worked at an elevator company. Marley lived in my building on the sixth floor, so I used to hear him playing music. I lived on the second floor. At probably eight or nine years old I was just freestyling on the block and battling dudes on other blocks. It wasn't serious. My grandmother lived in Harlem, right across the street from Harlem World [Cultural and Entertainment Complex]. My brother would come home to Queens with tapes—the routines from the Force MCs and the Cold Crush and Fantastic Five. A lot of those guys were dope, but when it comes to lyricist lyricists, I believe when I heard "It's Yours" by T La Rock was when I was like, "Wow! Okay." He was spitting all these big words and intricate styles. That's exactly what did it to me. Marley just came to my house one day. He knew I rap, and they had an idea for a rap version of "Shout" [by Tears For Fears]. I just went to the studio and did it. The funny thing about it was I wasn't even writing rhymes yet. I went to the studio and rapped for five minutes, and Shan had to help me put it in song mode. I didn't know anything about making a song. I just rapped. No one took it seriously in '85. I got $150 for "Shout" rap. "Transformer" was the second song I did with them. It was a popular cartoon. That's what they tried to capitalize on, because I was a kid.

Troy Shelton: Craig was serious about his craft. He was always trying to perfect his style. The thing I remember most about him is that he gave a damn. He gave a damn about what he was doing, what he was trying to do, and where he was going to go. He was one who did not want to accept mediocrity.

Craig G: I started answering the phones at the *Rap Attack* for maybe a couple of years. Marley had moved away from The Bridge, but not far. I went to his house one day. I used to go after school because my school wasn't far from there, and he played me the "Droppin' Science" beat. He was like, "Yo, you spit something dope to this or I'm giving the beat to Biz." So I took it home, and I made "Droppin' Science" over that beat. And it was so dope. I loved it. A week later, Marley played me the version with the Lou Donaldson beat, and I hated it at first. That's the more famous version. On the single it has the Lou Donaldson sample ["Who's Making Love"], and on the album [*In Control, Volume 1*] it has the James Brown sample ["Make It Funky"].

Masta Ace: I hadn't even heard the album in its entirety, so I didn't know who was on there and who wasn't on there.

Craig G: It was hot as hell that day. I was already hanging out with Ace a lot, and he had just graduated from college. He had this Hyundai Excel that we all drove out there [to the airport], and we did the shoot.

Masta Ace: I was just happy I was there. Steady Pace was my DJ. He was lucky to be there.

George DuBose: I show that [back album cover] picture to European Hip-Hop experts and *nobody* can name them all. When I put out *The Big Book of Hip Hop Photography,* I ran a contest on Facebook where anyone who can name everybody gets a free copy of my book. No one could name DJ Steady Pace. Not one.

Masta Ace: They think he's TJ Swan. I hear that a lot, because TJ Swan isn't in the photo either.

The Posse

Big Daddy Kane: When I did "Raw," me and Kool G Rap did a little freestyle off the beat afterwards. Marley started playing the freestyle on the air. People started calling up BLS saying, "Yo, we want that 'Raw' remix with G Rap on it." That's what they was calling it. A lot of people was loving it.

Ced Gee: Kane and G Rap, when they used to do their little freestyle thing that Marley use to have, they made you re-write. It was certain MCs that after you heard them you said, "Damn, I gotta step up." They ain't playing.

Big Daddy Kane: So Marley said, "Yo, I need you and G to do the same thing, but to a new beat for *my* album." We said, "Okay, cool." That was the plan. Then I guess when Craig G found out about the concept, he said he wanted to be on it. When Marley asked about Craig being on it, Craig had just did this song called "Duck Alert" dissing Red Alert. I thought it was dope so I was like, "Yeah, why not? Throw him on there."

Craig G: That was a term of disrespect too. Like, "He's a duck!" The way "Duck Alert" happened, I used to freestyle every weekend on WBLS on the air. And one day Marley was just cutting up the Antoinette song ["I Got An Attitude"]. I was just freestyling to it, and we both looked at each other like, "Yo, we gotta go record this." So I just made up a song for it. Even back then, Red Alert was just one of the coolest dudes I know. But I was just sticking up for my crew. Even with "South Bronx" and all that, it was never personal back then. Battling was part of the thing. We [also] felt like a lot of [Salt 'N' Pepa producer Hurby Luv Bug's] beats were similar to what Marley was doing. And that was a conversation between us. I'm an Aries so I just put it in the song. But when you think back on it, *everyone* was using those sounds.

Masta Ace: After that photo shoot [at the airport], Marley was going to his apartment in Astoria to record one last song for the album. I heard him talking to Kane and to G Rap and to Craig about coming to record this one last song. There wasn't enough room in Marley's car to take everybody. I was driving. Me and Craig had become really cool from that first day that I met him on the bench in Queensbridge. I was like, "Yo, I'll drive you over there." That was the first day I met Kane. I never met him before. He was an influence. He was somebody that I looked up to from a lyrical standpoint. I just wanted to be around him. I was down to take Craig, just so I could hang out and watch and listen and see dudes do their thing. That was why I went.

Fly Ty: Shan and Marley is another situation. Shan and Marley are close in age. Shan and Marley are like brothers. He was mad at Marley at the time.

Masta Ace: Shan was supposed to be on it as well.

Craig G: Shan was like the main dude back then. Maybe he had a show too, or maybe he didn't have time, or just didn't feel like doing it.

Big Daddy Kane: When I first started rolling [with the Juice Crew], me and MC Shan didn't really get along at all. For a lot of the shows, he would drive himself if I was in the limo. He never really called me by my name. He used to just refer to me as "the new nigga."

Masta Ace: When we arrived at Marley's crib, somebody, might have been Kane, said, "What happened with Shan?" Marley's like, "Shan ain't trying to be in no song with a bunch of new jacks." That's what Marley told us. Nobody thought nothing more of it. Shan later came out and said that wasn't true. He never said that. That was something Marley just told us I guess. He said that Marley was notorious for trying to get people to come to his house to "make tapes," but what he was really trying to do was get free services—get you to rap on something that he was gonna then go and put out and sell and make money off of, and you were never gonna see any money from it. That was what he [Shan] said his reasoning was for not going. Shan was already established. He was already crown prince of Cold Chillin'. Maybe he didn't feel like he needed the extra exposure, but everybody else was just trying to get some shine. Whatever it was, they was just down to do it, and I was just happy to be there. Everybody's writing their rhymes. The beat is playing over and over again. When it came time to spit, there was this debate over who was gonna rhyme first. Nobody wanted to go first. G Rap was like, "Go ahead, Craig!" Craig was like, "Go ahead, Kane!" Everybody was passing the buck. There was this back and forth going on.

Craig G: To be honest with you, Ace wasn't even supposed to be on the song; we were taking our time to write, and Marley was getting impatient. He was like, "Yo Ace, what you got for me?"

Masta Ace: So he [Marley] looks over at me and he says, "Ace, you got anything for this? Why don't you go over in the booth and spit a little something just to warm the booth up. These guys are acting scared." Something along those lines. I was like, "Aight. Yeah, I got a rhyme." So I went in the booth, and we started the recording process.

Craig G: Kane had came up with the hook. And Kane was already huge, so he had to leave. He had a show.

Big Daddy Kane: Marley was like, "Yo, this is my new artist Master Ace. I want to put him on the song too." Ace was a real humble, quiet dude, and he had these funny looking glasses on. Me and G Rap was calling him "Glasses," saying, "Yo, I ain't doing this joint with Glasses. We not messing with Glasses, man. Let's go the pizza shop and say we going to get some pizza, and let's get the hell up outta here."

Craig G: Ace did his verse, and it was dope.

Big Daddy Kane: I guess it took too long and Ace ended up doing his verse. I told G, "Yo, Glasses kinda nice, man!" Then Craig did his verse. Then G Rap was like, "I don't know. Glasses' verse might even be better than Craig's!" Then we was cool and we embraced Ace.

Masta Ace: They played everything back and then they're [Big Daddy Kane and Kool G Rap] hearing my rhyme for the first time. It wasn't until that point when they heard my rhyme that they were like, "This kid is aight here!" I think they looked at me as a little bit of an outlier and didn't really know who I was. "Who's new dude? What's with the big glasses?" I was different, and I was new. I didn't know what was going through dudes' heads back then. I had confidence in myself, but I had no idea how they were looking at me. But I get to hear these stories now. They wound up liking my verse.

Big Daddy Kane: G Rap, I don't know why but all his rhymes he used to write *super* long. One verse might be about three pages.

Kool G Rap: Marley told me, "Yo, I need you to lay something on this." So I laid something on it, but the rhyme that I kicked was the very first verse of [Kool G Rap & DJ Polo song] "Men At Work," and it was attached to the verse [that ended up on] "The Symphony." When I spit all that shit, the tape had ran off the reel. I had to split that shit.

Craig G: G Rap actually rapped till the spool came off the tape.

Masta Ace: I don't know how many bars it was, but it was too long. Marley says, "You gotta chop that down. Shorten it."

Big Daddy Kane: It still was just so *fire*.

Kool G Rap: That was a freestyle rhyme that I had wrote. Especially in those days, I would always write something in case somebody ever tried to battle you, or you would get called out, you need that one ferocious shit that just lay everything to rest. That's what it was.

Big Daddy Kane: I think it came out great. Everybody did they thing. Nobody was wack.

Just as Kane threw away his rhyme book and started over after hearing Grandmaster Caz in the early '80s, so had Craig G after hearing Kane several years later. Now they were on a record together. Rap had taken the next evolutionary step towards complexity and lyricism. Opening and closing with Marley speaking in an affected voice in the style of Walter "Junie" Morrison on Ohio Players' "Funky Worm" record, "The Symphony" was composed by looping the recognizable piano intro from Otis Redding's "Hard To Handle" over a largely unrecognizable beat.

Cut Chemist: In the loop era, he started to use really obscure shit that these bootlegs didn't have, like "Do It Your Way," the [Rory-O &] Chuck Colbert 45 for "The Symphony" beat. No one had that.

"That was one of the loops that I got from WLBS library," Marley Marl told NPR in 2013. "I was privileged enough to have access to one of the greatest libraries in music history. I had [radio personality] Hal Jackson's records. He used to keep all his records at the WBLS library, and that was one of them. The drums under it ["The Symphony"] was one of them.

Aaron Fuchs: Marley didn't know who the Ohio Players were. I gave him the early Ohio Players records on Westbound with Junie doing those high voices, and then bang—Marley adopted this grandma character for the radio show.

Juice Crew All Stars

"The Symphony" was a *posse cut*—Hip-Hop parlance for a song featuring verses by four or more MCs who normally stand alone as separate artists. These records hearkened back to the park jam days of the culture's infancy, when several people would take turns rhyming on the mic over a breakbeat to keep the party going. During the first several years after rap had graduated to the recording studio, posse cuts were fairly uncommon. There was "Zulu Nation Throwdown" by Afrika Bambaataa Featuring Cosmic Force & Zulu Nation (Paul Winley Records, 1980), "Here Comes That Beat!" by Pumpkin and the Profile All-Stars (Profile, 1984), "Krush Groovin'" from the *Krush*

Groove soundtrack (Warner Bros., 1985), and "Uptown Is Kickin' It" by the Uptown Crew (Uptown/MCA, 1986). Even Cold Chillin' released a Marley-engineered single in 1987 credited to the Juice Crew All Stars. The b-side, simply titled "Juice Crew All Stars," featured Craig G, Glamorous, Kool G Rap, MC Percy, MC Shan, and Roxanne Shanté. The a-side "Evolution" was a lesson in black history—MC Shan rapped as Martin Luther King, a Bronx MC named Debbie D played Harriet Tubman, Kool G Rap was Malcolm X, Glamorous was Maya Angelou, and TJ Swan sang the chorus.

Craig G: When we recorded the "Juice Crew All Stars" song, we all recorded our verses separately. We weren't all in the same room when we did it. I was fifteen maybe. I went to the studio, I did my verse, and I had to go home, and I heard the finished record a couple of days later.

TJ Swan: We did "Evolution." The whole Juice Crew did that. That was incredible. We were celebrating Martin Luther King's birthday and all the historical figures. That record's classic to this day.

Glamorous: I portrayed Maya Angelou [on "Evolution"]. That was Fly Ty's idea all the way. He put that together. I went to the library in Amityville [Long Island] to do my part. I sat there and wrote my whole verse, then hopped on the train by the library to Marley's house.

Yo! MTV . . . Raps?

With the Warner Bros. machine behind it, "The Symphony" hit bigger than "Evolution," and soon became the gold standard for posse cuts. The sound coming off the record wasn't the only thing that gave it legendary status. Just before the release of *In Control, Volume 1,* a television program opened the rap floodgates, pushing Hip-Hop into the consciousness of anyone with a basic cable subscription in the United States. On August 6, 1988, *Yo! MTV Raps* premiered on a network with a proven track record of being resistant to black music. There was now a long overdue national stage for Hip-Hop music videos, which had previously been relegated to Ralph McDaniels and Lionel Martin's New York-based *Video Music Box* on WNYC-TV. The videos for Shanté's "Roxanne's Revenge" and "Queen of Rox," MC Shan's "Left Me Lonely," and "Marley Marl Scratch" had local eyeballs, but suffered widespread exposure by virtue of existing long before *Yo! MTV Raps*. The timing for "The Symphony" video couldn't have been better. The filming of it however, was not without its own complications.

Kool G Rap: We went up there to record that for days. It was upstate New York I believe.

Masta Ace: The Adirondacks.

Jeff Smith: They went up to shoot the video. John Beug [senior VP of video, Warner Bros. Records] spent a lot of money on some of these videos. They found an abandoned town that they were going to use as a set, and it was going to be a Wild West thing. All the guys were going to be cowboys. There was going to be a saloon. They're all taking the bus up from Brooklyn.

Masta Ace: It was two buses, and we were like three hours late leaving. G Rap was like three hours late getting to the bus.

Jeff Smith: Kane at this point is like an elder statesman of the rappers. He's got his dancers there, and G Rap's there, and they've got their dancers, so this is like a bus full of twenty-year-old Hip-Hop artists and dancers and goofballs. They get into a food fight on the bus. They start throwing sandwiches at each other.

Kool G Rap: Something happened on the bus. Kane got into a confrontation with somebody that I was with at the time.

Big Daddy Kane: [laughter] An incident happened, and I had to leave the video shoot.

Jeff Smith: Kane pulls out a gun and shoots at one of G Rap's dancers, who's gonna be in the video, and the bullet misses him, and ricochets around, and winds up hitting I don't know who.

Kool G Rap: Kane shot at him. I don't think he was trying to shoot *at* him. I think he was just trying to shake him up, but the bullet end up hitting somebody that was sitting on the bus, because it bounced off the window.

Jeff Smith: This stops the food fight in a hurry, and Kane realizes what he's done has now caused a bigger problem than the one that he was setting out to fix.

Kool G Rap: Kane end up going home—or went somewhere—I don't know exactly where he went. I have no idea about the guy who got hit. I don't even remember who got hit. I just remember somebody got hit in the arm. I don't recall who that was.

Fly Ty: I used to have two phones in the house—one for the regular people, one for the artists. If my artist phone rung at 2:00 A.M., my wife would say, "Please honey, don't answer it." That's not a good call. Somebody's arrested somewhere, somebody shot somebody, somebody got caught with some guns, somebody got caught with something. I would have to get up and go there.

Liz Rosenberg (Senior Executive Vice President of Publicity for Warner Bros. Records/Madonna's publicist): I was working with someone named Pat Smith who was representing him [Kane]. Her office was next door to mine. She came running into my office and was freaking out about the incident. My boyfriend at the time was an assistant DA. His name was William Forde. He actually became a big producer on *Law & Order*. I called him because I didn't know anyone else who might have understood the case to help figure it out. There was a lot of back and forth going on about what to do about it.

Jeff Smith: Everybody's in a terrible mood. I got a call, I think it was Gene Shelton calling to tell me, "There was a shooting on the bus for the video." And I said, "Don't tell anybody . . . or do we tell *Page Six?*" It was a little bit of, "Which way do you go with this news?"

Fly Ty: Lyor [Cohen of Rush Management/Def Jam] did the opposite of what I did. I instructed them to never give their artist name. "Give them your real name—your birth name, and call me;" where Lyor said, "Tell them your artist name." He used that to promote them. He uses "you got shot six times" to promote your record. Or if you shot somebody, "Oh, he's a real thug!"

Jeff Smith: I remember the punchline, if there is such a thing as a punchline to a shooting on a bus, was that ultimately the settlement was that the guy who got shot wanted Big Daddy Kane's leather Gucci suit from Dapper Dan and a chain and like $5,000. The tracksuit was actually the ticket out of this story to keep the guy quiet!

Liz Rosenberg: In the midst of considering all different options, they resolved the issue by the gifting of the gold chain and the suit, the outfit. And there were no charges. It was very dramatic for three days. At that time I was very good at trying to maintain bad news about anybody in as small a way as possible, and keeping it private. That was a big goal of mine with Madonna and lots of people I worked with. If bad things happened, we didn't want the press to know about it. We didn't want to make it a bigger story. Of course in the rap world, that may have been considered very cool. I don't know.

Masta Ace: But we made it up there [to the set]. It was *freezing* cold. You wouldn't be able to tell by the video. It looked like a nice, hot western. But it was super cold—probably 15, 20 degrees Fahrenheit up there that day. We had to pretend that we weren't cold. They had these tubular heaters that they use at NFL games sometimes on the sidelines. They would fire that thing up and have that going. When you weren't shooting your part, everybody would just run and huddle around this heater to try to get some warmth. Then it was right back to it. My first manager was this lady called Monica Meachem. She was actually dating Andre Harrell's partner Alonzo, from Dr. Jeckyll & Mr. Hyde. She's actually in "The Symphony" video. On Kane's part [shot separately on a soundstage], there's a lady who sits on his lap. That was my manager.

Almost immediately after "The Symphony" hit, it became standard practice to include a posse cut on Hip-Hop albums. The following year saw a significant uptick in these collaborative exercises, as De La Soul ("Buddy (Native Tongue Decision)"), The D.O.C. ("The Grand Finale"), and Jungle Brothers ("Doin' Our Own Dang") gave their posses shine. "Self Destruction" was an epic posse cut attributed to The Stop The Violence Movement, consisting of over a dozen New York area MCs. "The Symphony" also represented a high point for the Juice Crew and Cold Chillin' as an identifiable, creative force within rap. However, by the end of '88 cracks were forming within their camp.

8
THE GOLDEN ERA

Fly Ty: Biz was like this—he does the opposite of what you tell him. Shan, if you yell at him he's gonna do better. He gonna want to show you, "I could do it." Kane is gonna get withdrawn. He ain't gonna do nothing. You yell at Kane, he just gonna close up. Yell at Shanté before the show, she gonna get vicious. She gonna go out there and tear the show up. Everybody had a different personality. I couldn't treat them all the same. G Rap—you had to baby him. You had to rub him on the head. "It's gonna be okay." Now at the same time, I'm like dad, Magic is Uncle Magic, Marley is the younger uncle who they could kind be like a friend at the time. But Marley reserved the right to pull uncle status on you. He could be your friend until you got out of line, then he gonna be Uncle Marley.

"The only juice I'm down with is pineapple, orange, grape, know what I'm sayin'?" Big Daddy Kane proclaimed live on the air at WBLS in 1989. "Ain't no beef between none of them there. I just ain't with that movement no more. It's time to get paid and leave that whole phony family alone, because it ain't working."

The Juice Is Loose

Not even a year after "The Symphony" had established the Juice Crew as the greatest posse in Hip-Hop, it was all coming apart. In February, Mr. Magic's contract was not renewed by WBLS, and *Rap Attack* was no more. Marley Marl was handed the slot, and the short-lived *In Control* radio show was born. Marley's first order of business was distancing himself from his former partner, referring to him as "Mr. Tragic."

"The Juice Crew was formed around Mr. Magic, but a lot of people said he caused trouble. He'd diss people, and because of him a lot of people held grudges against the

Juice Crew," said Marley Marl in a 1991 interview with *The Source*. "That's how that whole thing with KRS-One started: Magic dissed Kris on the air. At a certain point, everybody in the Juice Crew said, 'Yo! We don't need to be carryin' [Magic's] burden no more.' We dispersed."

Kool G Rap: There was no formal breakup like, "Yo, we gonna dismantle this shit!" It was a gradual thing. It just took its natural course. It happened over years. It's not like it happened, "Yo, in 1990, everybody came to the table and said, 'Yo, we parting ways!'" It ain't no shit like that.

Craig G: Everybody was just doing their own thing. Nobody said, "Okay, we broke up," because we were never really a group. We were just a collective of artists.

Big Daddy Kane: We was on this Public Enemy tour, the *Bring The Noise* tour, and I was going on right before Public Enemy. Somewhere in the middle of the tour, the show switched. I just found out that Erick Sermon [of EPMD] is the one who wanted to switch the order. They started putting on EPMD after me. I had an issue about it and complained about it. Chuck D told me who made the decision—this guy named Lyor Cohen. So we went to see Lyor Cohen, and we had him surrounded in this restaurant, getting ready to pound him out. He explained that he did this because EPMD was "Rushian." That's the term they used to use for they artists—they called them "Rushians." He said, "EPMD are Rushians. This is what I do for my artists. If you was with Rush, I would do the same thing for you. I understand what you gotta do, so do what you gotta do." I told my boys to just chill, and I said, "I don't know. I think I want to be down with Rush, man!" He explained other things to me like, "Are you making merchandise money? Do you have somebody taking pictures on your backdrop? You're making more money than EPMD, but they're making almost the same as you doing their merchandise every night." That's when I really wanted to be down with them. Then I found out your record label is not supposed to be your manager as well. That's a conflict of interest. I was nineteen when I first signed, so I didn't know what I was doing until I find out all this here stuff. That's when I got down with Rush.

Eugene Shelton: When Kane was being managed by Lyor Cohen, I remember him directing Kane's career. It showed a great deal of opportunity and promise.

Big Daddy Kane: We worked out some sort of agreement, and we restructured my record deal with Cold Chillin'. I got a bigger advance and more points. They [Cold Chillin'] were the label and Rush became management. We just kept the ship rolling. That was '89.

Mister Cee: Once we started being managed by Rush Management, no disrespect to Fly Ty, Kane wasn't listening to Ty no more. We was managed by Russell Simmons and Lyor Cohen, so we was listening to them and Warner Bros. Fly Ty didn't have our ear no more. He didn't have our attention no more. All he was doing was putting the records out.

Jeff Smith: It wasn't that hard to see. Look at what happens over at Def Jam. They've got all these platinum acts. [The Rush-managed group] Run-DMC is all over the charts and on MTV, and this kind of thing. Kane got with Lyor Cohen, who of course had Def Jam, but more significantly, and more importantly to this story, was also Russell's partner in Rush Management. He stole Kane from Tyrone. He [Kane] was still on Cold Chillin'. Lyor always said the "g" where the apostrophe is. "Cold Chilling." Without fail. Sometimes you hear somebody do something like that, and you go, "Okay, I like your way better."

Fly Ty: Somebody said that was double dipping. Okay, I started the label—should I not sign my artists? I should just sign other artists? Is that what you're telling me? No. I sign *my* people. That's what I did. I never took record money from them. I took show money, but never record money. Being on Cold Chillin', just being with me meant you didn't have to pay management out your money. I never recouped from them because I recouped collaterally on everything. So everything that a Cold Chillin' artist got was a *signing* bonus.

While Kane had disassociated with the Juice Crew as a concept and moved to Rush (who was also engaged in "double dipping" with some of its own Def Jam artists such as LL Cool J and Public Enemy), the remaining Cold Chillin' roster of Biz, Shanté, Shan, and Kool G Rap & DJ Polo continued to be managed by Fly Ty. Kane also began severing ties with Marley Marl. The nature of the falling out revolved around their conflicting viewpoints regarding the age-old question: *what is the job of a record producer?*

Big Daddy Kane: [On *Long Live the Kane*] Marley produced "I'll Take You There" and "The Day You're Mine." Pretty much everything else was produced by me. "Set It Off" of course by 45 King. Marley was really the engineer. [I was] showing him what part to sample, or how to connect. "Take that part and use that as the first bar, and take that one and use it as the second bar, so that off-beat snare fall here instead of there." Stuff like that. It was more than just, "Take this record and throw it on." I think a lot of people make that mistake. They say they produced something because they gave someone a record. But if someone take that record and put it together for you, that's a producer. [Marley got production credit] because I was a nineteen-year-old idiot.

Craig G: Marley probably had a falling out with everybody, but I kind of stayed out of that. From what I understand, a lot of people brought him sample ideas, and he was getting the credit for it. But personally I don't think it was all him. I believe that's how the label had it set up. Marley was the producer. In a business sense, if you bring ideas to it, you should be co-producer and you should get co-producer money.

Andre Booth: The way Ty had it set up, I was there when they had the meeting, Ty told Marlon that he would be the sole producer. He don't care if Quincy Jones came in, he said, "You still going to be producer." He gave him everything to produce that walks through that door. If you came in with your band, and you already producers, and you already know what to do, y'all wasn't getting in unless he produce y'all.

Aaron Fuchs: Cold Chillin' was a label where there was a lot of weight hooked up to one horse.

Masta Ace: We were all talking to each other. Kane was talking to G Rap. Biz was talking to Kane. Everybody was basically comparing notes and saying, "Yo, that's my sample! I brought that record there. I told him to sample that. I told him to loop that. I told him what I wanted to do to that." The credit comes out and it just says, "Produced by Marley Marl," straight up, nobody's getting credit. Had he handled it differently, he would have been able to do a lot more albums on these artists. But everybody was like, "Yo, this guy's taking all the credit. He's not passing any credit off to nobody else, so we gonna show that we can do records without him." And that's what everybody was determined to do.

Big Daddy Kane: Shan started working with other producers. Also Shan stopped letting Marley DJ for him, and he got another DJ. It was all falling apart at that point.

MC Shan's sophomore LP *Born To Be Wild,* produced by Marley Marl and released by Cold Chillin'/Warner Bros. in 1988, was sonically superior to its predecessor *Down By Law.* However, during that one year interim, Hip-Hop's climate became hyper-competitive, and Shan got eclipsed by an array of artists as diverse as N.W.A, Public Enemy, DJ Jazzy Jeff & The Fresh Prince, and even by his labelmates Kane and Biz. It didn't help Cold Chillin', which had paid Marley $200,000 in 1988 as a staff producer (up from $65,000 the year before), that almost all its acts began separating themselves from him, or vice versa.

It's a Big Daddy Thing

By '89, Kane was working on assembling his second album with himself as rightfully credited producer for the lion's share of the songs. He also handpicked a few outside producers to help fill Marley Marl's shoes. One of them was Stetsasonic's Prince Paul, who was having enormous success that year, having produced Tommy Boy trio De La Soul's debut *3 Feet High and Rising.* The Long Island DJ/producer contributed "Ain't No Stoppin' Us Now" and the title track for *It's a Big Daddy Thing.*

Big Daddy Kane: I thought Prince Paul was dope on the De La stuff. He has a weird sound. He has a gritty Hip-Hop sound. The music has such a pop appeal, but it's *gritty* as hell. So I'm like, "I really want to work with Paul." I was excited about working with him.

Mister Cee: "The House That Cee Built" on the second album I did. But then you have a record like "It's a Big Daddy Thing" that Prince Paul produced and did the scratches on.

Big Daddy Kane: Then Mister Cee comes and he says, "You need to listen to some of these beats from Boob from my building." I'm like, "What Boob? Little skinny necktie Boob?" He like, "He make beats and he gots *fire!*" That's when he brings Easy Mo Bee in. I was like, "Oh wow!"

Easy Mo Bee: I produced "Another Victory" and "Calling Mr. Welfare" featuring Kool DJ Red Alert.

The widespread police practice of racial profiling was discussed by Kane in "Another Victory."

Big Daddy Kane: When I had my Volvo, I didn't even have a license. But back then, you get pulled over without a license, you get a ticket. You don't go to jail. But due to the fact that I didn't have one, I'm being very cautious—obeying all traffic laws, but still getting pulled over. I'm not doing nothing. I got a seat belt on; that was like the wackest thing in the world in the '80s. How you gonna be hood with a seat belt? You supposed to be laid back, chillin' with the music blasting. I'm sitting up with a seat belt on, with my music on normal. Plus I'm listening to Marvin Gaye, Otis Redding. I ain't even blasting Hip-Hop, and still getting [pulled] over. You can only call this one way. There's *gotta* be something racial. I never seen my pops get pulled over. I think it was more or less about black youth in fancy vehicles. My pops was driving a two tone Seville, all white Coupe de Ville with white fur interior. He was driving that pimp shit. He was a grown man.

Easy Mo Bee: "Another Victory," the beat for it actually started as a pause tape, where you would use the pause mechanism. It was basically just another form of tape editing. They were doing the same thing in the studios with the legendary DJ remixers and re-editors like Tee Scott, Walter Gibbons, you can't forget Tom Moulton. You listen to "Love Thang" by First Choice and "Ten Per Cent" by Double Exposure, both on Salsoul Records, they would edit the tape to extend the song. Basically at home, what the Hip-Hop DJs was doing with the pause button, we were doing the same thing. It's just that we weren't splicing tape. We were doing the connections and making the edits with the pause button. I had it looped on pause on a cassette. That concept, that idea is what Kane heard and he loved. I just promised him, I didn't have equipment at the time, I was *begging* him to get on. I didn't want the opportunity to pass me up. I was like, "Yo, if you just take me into the studio, we can loop the record." He saw the vision, and we went in. It is him, Big Daddy Kane, who I have eternal love for, and I kind of feel like I owe a big part of my career to him, because he's the one who put me on. He's the first one to take a chance on me, and give me my first commercial entry into the business. That was the first record that ever appeared commercially on an album, on a major label [that I produced]. Kane gave me $3,000 for those two tracks. That's $1,500 a track. So with that $3,000, *immediately* upon being paid that, I *ran* down to 48th Street to Sam Ash, which is no longer there now. The developers tore down the buildings. I bought an SP-1200 [sampler].

Big Daddy Kane: Me and Marley was having a beef about the thing I did with Antoinette called "Raw Attitude." It was a radio promo, but he gave the beat to Shan for Shan's album ["They Used To Do It Out In the Park" on *Born To Be Wild*]. I was pissed about that, like, "Yo, that's my beat. How you going to give it to Shan? You owe me a beat." He was like, "What you want? Pick out a beat you want." What was so funny is one day at a session he played the "Young, Gifted And Black" beat for me and told me it was for Shan. I was like, "Shan don't need this. *I* need that!" And I hid the disk in Marley's house. So when he told me I could have whatever I want, I went straight to it and said, "Yo, I want this." When Marley popped it in he was like, "Yo,

I've been looking for this!" That's how Marley ended up doing "Young, Gifted And Black."

Marley Marl's last contribution to a Big Daddy Kane album, the title of which referenced Lorraine Hansberry's 1957 play *To Be Young, Gifted and Black,* utilized the intro to Albert King's "I'll Play the Blues For You." Marley would many years later explain how he saw Kane as a true artist, in direct contrast to MCs who just rap over beats.

Gods & Earths

"Young, Gifted & Black" included a piece of a speech by Minister Louis Farrakhan of the Nation of Islam, a controversial figure who Kane admired. The MC however identified as a member of the Five-Percent Nation—an offshoot of the NOI founded in New York by Clarence 13X in 1964. Five-Percenters teach that black people are the original people, and that black men are "Gods" while black women are "Earths." Additionally, an elite ten percent know the truth of existence and strive to keep eighty-five percent of the world living in ignorance, while the remaining five percent know the truth and are determined to enlighten the world. Both Kane and Rakim subscribed to its ideology, peppering their lyrics with terminology from the teachings.

Big Daddy Kane: I think my moms was Christian and my pops Baptist, but we never said grace or anything. When I was in 7th grade in junior high, a lot of Five Percenters I was hanging around, they would be building and saying a lot of stuff that I was impressed by. I started studying the lessons myself, and I eventually became a Five-Percenter. As time went by, I converted to Islam. There are so many chapters and divisions. I just find it much easier to say Islam. I feel it definitely influenced my rhyming because not only did I just want to brag about how dope I was—I also wanted to educate and try to instill knowledge in others.

Kool G Rap: Everybody knew about the Five-Percent Nation. Me feeling it in my personal life was in the early '80s—'82, '83 I start to feel a presence from the Five-Percent Nation. A lot of cats I was around converted to become Five-Percenters. That would continue for a long time in my life, with me knowing dudes named John or Tommy, and now they "Born Justice" or "Understanding." Rakim came out around those times where it was beyond the explosion. He was already in the aftermath of the explosion. It was pretty much substantiated that the Five-Percent Nation exists, and especially in the hood. Dudes always associated Five-Percenters with knowledge.

Smooth Operator

Religious teachings were a tough sell to commercial radio and MTV, but Kane had another asset that worked perfectly for those formats: sex appeal. The two biggest hits to come out of *It's a Big Daddy Thing* both revolved around his skills with the ladies: the self-produced "Smooth Operator," and "I Get the Job Done," produced by Teddy Riley. Riley was the primary architect of an uptempo genre called New Jack Swing, which sat on the fence between R&B and Hip-Hop, working equally well for singers and rappers.

Mister Cee: Back then we was working at this studio in Queens called Libra Digital Studios. He would bring the samples in and tell our engineers at the time Tony A. and Tony P. what to sample. They had a Synclavier sampling keyboard. It looks just like an organ. We never even worked with this thing ever again. I think that thing could sample two minutes long, which was unheard of at that time. Kane was ahead of his time, as far as the music that he was making—the whole mix of Hip-Hop and R&B. Kane and Heavy D—I have to put them in the same kind of category. They was among the few that bridged the gap between Hip-Hop and R&B, as far as using old '80s and '70s R&B records and making it into a Hip-Hop record, with "Smooth Operator," with us using "All Night Long" [by] Mary Jane Girls.

Big Daddy Kane: The Teddy Riley thing was Benny Medina's idea. I was completely against it, because as much as I like [Riley's group] Guy and Bobby Brown, I didn't like his Hip-Hop productions. I didn't like "Go See the Doctor" [by Kool Moe Dee]. I didn't like "How Ya Like Me Now" [by Kool Moe Dee]. I didn't like "We Got Our Own

Thang" or any of the Heavy D stuff. I wasn't crazy about those beats. But this was one of those Benny calls like, "This *got* to happen. This priority over anything."

Aaron Fuchs: He [Teddy Riley] did a couple Spoonie records for me. You knew you were watching brilliance at work. And he also was working out of his mother's living room at that time in Harlem. His brilliance wasn't lost on me or anybody else. I turned to his mother and I called him a genius, and she practically yawned in my face, she heard it so often. Really, she had to stifle a yawn. But I said that to her and it absolutely didn't impress her. It's like she had known that forever.

Big Daddy Kane: Me and Teddy ended up talking and I was like, "Yo, I don't want no Moe Dee or Heavy D stuff. I want what you give Guy. Give me what you give Guy." He started laughing and was like, "Not a problem!" I feel like that's what he did.

Masta Ace: The women at Warner were smitten with him [Kane].

Liz Rosenberg: He was *gorgeous*. He was such a beautiful man. I think I must have been telling Madonna incessantly he was so handsome.

Ife Kiara: Kane was the young, dark chocolate stud, and from eight to eighty they were just all over him. I had to check who's underage. We wind up in a club doing promotion, and as we're walking out he just grabs a girl and puts her in the limo with him. We had to fly to somewhere the next day. I come downstairs, and here *she* comes. He just snatched her, and she just went and left her girlfriends and everything. He didn't even introduce himself. They hadn't even met.

George DuBose: Kane's concept was that he wanted to be photographed in a Jacuzzi on the back of a stretched limousine. *Is* there such a thing? He said yeah, he saw it in New York City. So I called a couple limousine companies and I got one of them, and I said, "Do you have a stretched limo with a Jacuzzi on the back?" And he says, "Yeah." When they sent the goddamn car to this location, it wasn't a Jacuzzi. It was just a rumble seat.

I called the company complaining that, "You promised me a limousine with a Jacuzzi." It was really kind of a cluster fuck, because the guy said, "Go ahead and put a plastic sheet in there and fill it full of water." I said, "That's not the point." The lid of the seat comes up and blocks the whole view. The rumble seat wasn't working for me. Kane was cool about it. We went on and did the shooting. If you look at the photos in the booklet, this house was owned by Justin Lipman. He was a garment manufacturer on 7th Avenue in Manhattan. I was friends with his daughter. She was the stylist on the shooting actually. The house is called Five Chimneys. It's in Westbury, Long Island. It's a pretty big mansion with a swimming pool. After we did the limousine shots, we went down by the pool and did some shots, and Kane, horsing around, threw the makeup artist into the pool. She had a belt on with all her makeup in the belt. And she couldn't swim. It was kind of a disaster there at the end. Often the rappers would have, I don't want to say delusions of grandeur, but *illusions* of grandeur. They wanted to be photographed in a place where they didn't live, but where they *wanted* to live. They wanted to be in a car that they didn't own, but they wanted to own. Kane always seemed to like luxurious houses.

Released in September 1989 by Cold Chillin' and the revived Warner Bros. imprint Reprise, *It's a Big Daddy Thing* was certified gold two months later—one seventh the amount of time it took *Long Live the Kane* to reach the 500,000 mark. Kane was ruling Hip-Hop. He was *the* man. It was difficult to imagine anyone else outshining him, especially from within the label.

The Biz Never Sleeps

Dee Joseph: Biz wanted to produce himself. He decided he was producing, and that Marley really didn't help him do anything. So he convinced Lenny that he could do this and he wanted to be in charge of his direction and where he was going. That was like fighting words to Marley.

Big Daddy Kane: Biz just built his own studio and was like, "I'm not coming to Marley's crib." We always worked at Marley's crib. So Biz built his own studio and was like, "I'm doing my stuff at home."

Dee Joseph: Biz had just come off a really successful record with "Make the Music" and *Goin' Off*. It was a constant balancing act because you didn't want to piss the artist off, but then you had the producer who was bringing the talent to you. I think at this time Marley started to venture out a little bit on his own, producing other stuff.

Just a Friend

Biz Markie's strategy was to produce his sophomore album with his DJ Cutmaster Cool V, using a handful of engineers, including Ivan "DJ Doc" Rodriguez and Paul C. McKasty, aka Paul C. Finally, Marley Marl would mix it. One record was an interpolation of Freddie Scott's 1968 single "(You) Got What I Need," using the piano from that record with the breakbeat from "Get Out of My Life, Woman" by Lee Dorsey underneath it. In the pre-internet age, it had literally taken years from the point Biz first heard the Dorsey record to the point at which he could identify and purchase it. Now he held what he believed was the key to making his own smash hit, but the samples just didn't match up tempo-wise. To resolve the issue, engineer Shane Faber at Calliope Studios in Manhattan replayed the Freddie Scott piano part so that it lined up with the drums. Biz sang the choruses, changing the song title to "You Must Be On Speed," quickly changing his mind and making it a tune about heartbreak.

Fly Ty: Remember that song "Just a Friend"? I *hated* that record. It was with Biz rapping all the way through. It was the first album I let Biz produce on his own. I took the tape and gave it to Marley. I said, "Marley, this is *garbage*. What am I gonna do with this?" Marley listened to it and he said, "I know what to do." At the end of the record Biz was singing, and Marley made that the hook. That's the only part anybody knows anyway! So Marley produced the record. Biz: "I produced that!" No you didn't. Now Biz, so you understand how he was, he said, "We don't need that as the hook!" [If] you don't have that as the hook, that's not the biggest record you ever made. To show you how ornery Biz was, on the next album he did a song called "What Comes Around Goes Around." He does the same thing—no hook. In the beginning and the end—if you make that the hook, it's a better record.

TJ Swan: I wasn't on the second Biz album because I was actually working on my solo album at the time. I worked with him on that album, the "Just a Friend" project. I just encouraged him: "Do it like this," "Do it like that." The way "Just a Friend" went down is he came to me and said, "Yo, I got this dope record. I want you to sing." I was like, "Yo B, I'm tired of the TJ Swan/Biz movie. Let's try something different. Let's have some fun. Why don't you do it?" "What? Nah, nah, nah, nah!" Finally between me, Cool V, the rest of us, we convinced him. He did it. Marley came, worked on the production early on, got everything arranged. Then Biz took the project to mix it out.

George DuBose: The back cover [of *The Biz Never Sleeps* album] was the original concept for the front cover. Here we are again with Biz, making music with his mouth. We had done something with these gold, plastic Christmas ornaments. We had done something before, I forget what. Biz wanted to be eating a bowl of these instruments. The cereal was called *Diabolical Crunch*. First we had to make the cereal box, which meant I had to do a photo shoot for the cover of the cereal box to make the cereal box, and then do another photo shoot for the actual front cover. As it turned out, the front cover is way more powerful than the back cover concept. Although the back cover is fun to look at, and there's lot of little interesting things to see—like the cereal box weighs 10,000 lbs.—you can see that on the album cover. But as it turned out, the cover of the box was the most interesting photo from the whole project, and we used that for the front cover of the album. Thirteen cups of coffee—that's my lucky number. I was born on the 13th so it's not unlucky for me.

TJ Swan: When the project didn't jump off, when "Just a Friend" didn't get hot, he looked at me, "This all your fault." I was like, "Listen, once you do the video, let everybody know it's not serious, like you just having fun, you just jumping around, everything will be alright." Because Don Cornelius wouldn't let us on *Soul Train* with it, Arsenio Hall wouldn't allow us on his show with it. Because it was at that time when Milli Vanilli and all that stuff was going on with lip syncing and all that crazy stuff; so they just found it as a mockery.

Dee Joseph: The video—we shot it out at Post College out in Long Island, and Biz put my dog in it. She's got a gold record too. Krystal. When he's sitting on the park bench the dog was sitting under the bench. It was a lot of fun. We could film an entire movie with all the people that he had, and he wanted them all in the video.

TJ Swan: Once the video came out and they saw it was comical, it was funny, and the director said, "I want you to play the 'Just a Friend' guy—you're the guy that Biz catches in the dorm room with his girl," I was like, "Cool cool cool."

George DuBose: I think Hip-Hop was still not really accepted by white, teenage America so much. A lot of kids were into it because it was radical, but the majority of the white kids were maybe a little bit afraid of Public Enemy and the "shoot the white people" and the kind of violent, gangsta rap. We did this cover for The Diabolical Biz Markie. The video company took the [mad scientist] white wig, and turned him into Mozart playing a clavichord for "Just a Friend." That's the MTV video. That video made Biz's record go gold, because it was such a funny video. It was non-threatening to white folk. They could identify with the clavichord. There's a stupid ballad by a real ugly guy who's kind of funny.

TJ Swan: Next thing you know, it was getting a lot of love, it was doing very well, but then it still wasn't doing what we wanted it to do, and I was still getting the backlash. "You should have sung the record. It's your fault." I was like, "Listen, give it a chance. It's doing well." Then the record got played one night live through Z-100 at a club. Once that record was played, the next day it started selling like hotcakes. That was amazing. To this day, Biz will tease me, "See Swan, I told you to sing the record!" "It wouldn't have been the same, bro!"

Jeff Smith: When that song "Just a Friend" came out, that was one of the *strangest* hit records of all time. It has to be. He's a *terrible* singer. That's what made it such a successful thing. People could relate to it. "I'm a terrible singer too!" It was like a novelty record, a joke kind of. Somebody started playing it somewhere, the phones lit up, and it's like they made us put it out.

Stu Cohen [National Promotion Director, Warner Bros. Records]: Big Daddy had 'Black Hits,' but none that were crossable to pop. "Just A Friend" crossed Pop, because a Pop station in Washington, D.C. heard it on Black radio, played it, and got an enormous response. WAVA, I think. So I instinctively jumped all over it. You never know where your next hit is coming from, so you have to be alert.

Monica Lynch: I was very concerned when "Just a Friend" was out, and I strongly believed that Warner wasn't really as fully invested in making it a hit single as they could have been or should have been. And I remember being out in Burbank. Periodically I would go out there and hang out around the Warner buildings and see if I could get Tom Draper drummed up to promote Force MDs. But I remember meeting with Mo [Ostin] specifically to tell them that I thought they were missing the boat on "Just a Friend," and that it was the biggest hit since sliced bread, and they should really make it a priority. That's major label-speak. "But, is it a priority?" Was [Senior VP of Promotion] Russ Thyret gonna crack the whip and say, "This is like the next Madonna single, or Prince, or Fleetwood Mac," or whoever it is?

Jeff Smith: It was by far the biggest hit that Cold Chillin' ever had. As a single by ten-to-one, and as an album by at least two-to-one. It was huge.

The man who had appeared outside Marley's Queenbridge apartment beatboxing five years earlier, had a gold album and a platinum single to his name. Marley never considered himself the producer of "Just a Friend," but he believed he *fixed* the record by strategically dropping the beat out of the mix in certain parts of the song, including the intro, and finding Biz's best (or least worst) vocal performance of the hook to use in every chorus section. The tradeoff for Marley's work on "Just a Friend" was that Biz would allow him to take back an instrumental track originally intended for Biz to rap over. Marley used the track as a remix for LL Cool J's "Jinglin' Baby," which would help resurrect the Def Jam icon's floundering career.

Against all odds and expectations, Biz Markie was a bona fide pop star.

Dee Joseph: It's amazing, even to this day, I think it was a Michelob commercial, or Heineken, and they're playing "Just a Friend." And it's like there was something else recently and another commercial, like Target or something, like I'm like, "Oh my God." So many years later it's still being played. That's our platinum. Listen—there are labels that never had a platinum record.

THE NINETIES

9
TAKE A LOOK AROUND

A live bullet sat on the desk of Len Fichtelberg, his initials etched into the side. Just moments earlier, the scene at Cold Chillin' HQ was one of chaos.

Masta Ace: My album was done, they gave me a contract. The contract said I was gonna get $12,500 as advance. I had personally known that G Rap and Kane both got $25,000 advances, and I felt like they were trying to disrespect me and sell me short, because I was totally expecting to get what everybody else got. I called up Lenny and I was like, "Yo, why does this contract say $12,500 when everybody else got $25,000?" He basically was like, "You get what we give you. You lucky you getting that." He talking super tough on the phone. I made a couple of phone calls.

Can't Stop the Bum Rush

Dee Joseph: Lenny and I shared an office and when Ace showed up with his posse—they never traveled alone—they told me to get out of the office. They closed the door and they wouldn't let me in, and I knew that they were hot. They thought that they were owed more royalties or something. That was always the argument—over money.

Masta Ace: I called up my man Harry who used to do security for me. I called up my man Martell [Ellis], who later [was in] the group Blahzay Blahzay. I called up Jeru [the Damaja]. It was me, Harry Fobbs rest in peace, Jeru, Martell, my man Shah from Howard projects, who was my road manager. He was a gun carrying, official street dude. I brought him along for the ride. And Steady Pace. We went up to Cold Chillin' and barged into Lenny's office with this group of dudes. Kane had already done something similar maybe six months or so previous over another incident. I heard that story and I heard he got his way, so I followed suit. I brought goons up there, and we barged into Lenny's office.

Dee Joseph: Lenny told me that Ace put a bullet down on his desk with his name scratched in it. All I could hear from the outside of the door was some really loud yelling. It made me a little nervous, but I didn't call the police.

Masta Ace: He was sitting at his desk looking like was about to piss on his self.

Dee Joseph: Lenny was chicken shit. He could get scared.

Masta Ace: I told him my advance better be $25,000 when I get the new paperwork or it's gonna be a problem. When we left, my boy left a bullet on his desk with "L.F." [Len Fichtelberg's initials] engraved on the side of it. We walked out of the office and the next paperwork said, "$25,000." There was a different way to handle that. The way to handle that wasn't to be an asshole to me. It was to say, "Come on up. Let's talk about it. Let's have a conversation." He didn't respect me. Where I'm from, the only way to get respect is by force. I can't talk you into respecting me. I have to physically threaten you for you to understand that you can't talk to me any old kind of way and think it's gonna fly like that. If I let that go, who knows how my career would have went?
Fichtelberg may have misjudged Ace because of his quiet demeanor. The only college-educated member of the Juice Crew was just as street smart as he was book smart, and he had learned to navigate between both worlds. Like so many of his peers in Hip-Hop, the man born Duval Clear was raised in public housing without a father present. In his case, it was the Howard Houses in Brownsville, Brooklyn.

Howard Park

Masta Ace: Those apartments are based on income and assets. The entire system is designed to keep families broken up. Women can't receive public assistance if the father of the children lives in the home with the kids. In fact *no* male can live there. "If you want this free money and reduction in rent, you can't have a male role model in the home for the children." Terrible. My mom and my grandmother—those were my two parents. My grandmother worked out in Bensonhurst. My moms was really trying her best to get a fresh start somewhere else. She wanted to get me out of the projects. That was her ultimate goal. When I was in 4th grade, she got a job in Boston. I moved to Boston and I did 4th and 5th grade in Boston. The job didn't work out. We moved back to New York, back to projects. I'm going into 6th grade, she moves to Atlanta. She had another job offer down there. She tried to make that work. While she was away in Atlanta trying to build this new life, my grandmother was my parent back in Brooklyn. I lived by her rules. I did everything I was supposed to do. But at the end of 8th grade, I was supposed to be moving to Atlanta, something happened with that job she [mom] was counting on, and she had to move back to Brooklyn yet again. That's why I wound up going to high school in Brooklyn in Sheepshead Bay. I was actually a latchkey kid starting out in 7th grade. I had two uncles that lived in the apartment too, but they both worked. I went to the University of Rhode Island. I came in freshman year and I majored in chemistry. After my first semester, I switched to marketing. I remember my mom having a lot of marketing books around the house. That's what I got my degree in. I had a minor in advertising. My goal when I graduated was to get a job at an advertising agency. I wanted to write commercials and write print ads, and join an ad firm. [Going to college] helped me in a lot of ways. It helped me to think more logically. The things I learned in some of my marketing classes, I was able to apply to my own career. Just being exposed to different types of people was a big thing. So many of my friends coming up never really lived around or had opportunity to interact with white people. They were like a foreign thing to them. But going to high school in Sheepshead Bay and leaving there and going to Rhode Island, I was the minority in these schools, as opposed to in my neighborhood where everybody was black. It made me a little bit more of a well-rounded individual.

While in college between 1984 and 1988, Ace paid close attention to the fast evolving New York Hip-Hop scene that he had been fanatical about since first hearing "Rapper's Delight" in '79. He became aware of the rise of the Juice Crew like any fan during that era, and he also started rapping himself. There was no grand scheme on his part to get into the collective. Like the stories of so many others, it all happened by chance.

United Skates of America

Masta Ace: I think one of the earliest [influences on me] was Slick Rick. He had this joint called "La-Di-Da-Di," which wasn't a song at the time—it was just a routine he did at a party. As time went on and lyricism became even more intense, it would be LL, Rakim, and Kane. That was the main four early on. I was home for Christmas break, '85. We had just finished dinner and my boy Scooter Rockwell called me up. He said he was going to this rap contest out in Queens. United Skates of America was the name of the skating rink. I entered this contest. On the first night, I did this little rhyme called "Silver Suckers." At that time in Hip-Hop, silver was played out. You couldn't wear silver no more. You had to be wearing gold or nothing. I had wrote this rhyme about cats that were still wearing silver. It just so happened that there was a guy in the audience that had on a whole bunch of silver chains. It appeared to the crowd that I was talking about this specific guy, but it was really a rhyme I had pre-written and pre-memorized for the contest. It worked in my favor because everybody thought that I was talking about him. Everybody screaming, yelling, and laughing. That rhyme led into this other rhyme called "A Ho Is a Ho," which is about meeting a girl and thinking she was a nice girl, then finding out she's was a ho. I threw some surprise endings in there and caught the crowd off guard with the punchlines. The lines were set up perfectly to have the person right on the edge of their seat. "Where's this story going?" and then *boom*—you hit them with a line, and everybody go crazy. The drum machine was programmed so that every key line that I wanted people to hear, the drum machine would drop out. Then it would come back in. I had to sit there and count the bars and make sure that the beat lined up perfectly with my rhyme so that the music would stop on the perfect lines I needed it to stop on. It wasn't like I had a week to plan for this. If you can imagine me in the waiting area, with the headphones on, programming this Dr. Rhythm drum machine to match up with my rhyme, I had to do all that right there at the skating rink. That day it was a total of twenty-one people that entered, and they picked the top five. I was one of the top five. They had another round the following week. That was right before I went back to college. It was the New Year's weekend. I won first prize. That was the beginning for me. First prize was six hours of studio time with producer Marley Marl.

Keep Your Eye On the Prize

Masta Ace: It took me six months to get to that six hours of studio time. They gave me a phone number. All I would ever get was his sister on the phone. She would be like, "He's not home." I was persistent. I'm back in college now. I'm thinking that maybe this guy's not gonna give me what I want. I wound up calling the skating rink. I was crying foul. I was like, "I still haven't got my six hours. You need to call this guy." The manager was like, "I'll call him. I'll see what's up." I didn't get any answers. That winter I call again, and his sister by now knows my name, she knows my voice. "Hi, Ace. Nah, he's not here." Then one day, she's just like, "You seem like a nice guy. Here's his *real* number." It wasn't that it wasn't his number; it's just that he didn't live there. I called him. "Who's this?" I got an attitude. "Yo, this Master Ace and I had won this studio time back in January. I'm owed my time. I need my time." He was like, "Aight." It's spring '86. Six months later. Finally I go out to Queensbridge projects. He told me to meet him at 2:00 P.M. Me and my boy Steady Pace sat there from 2:00 P.M. probably till 6:00 P.M. when he finally pulled up. I met Craig G that same day. He saw me sitting on the bench. He said, "Who y'all waiting for? Marley?" "Yeah." "He always have rappers out here waiting." He sat down on the bench and we started talking about everything under the sun. That's how I got to know him.

Craig G: Me and Ace were really close.

Masta Ace: I did my first session that day. He had me in the back bedroom. MC Shan was doing drum programming for me. I talked to MC Shan recently about this whole thing and he don't remember that specific session, but he's like, "Marley knew I didn't know what I was doing, so if he put you back there with me, it's probably because he didn't know what you had. He always did that. He would just throw the cats back there that he was trying to get rid of, that weren't a priority. He knew I didn't know how to work none of that equipment." It was his way of burning time, and do what he had to do—give this kid six hours. But what happened was he wound up hearing something I rapped over. I guess Shan made some kind of beat. I rapped over it; he [Marley] liked it. Then he started actually working with me. At the end of my six hours, he asked me to keep coming back. I kept coming back and recording demos. The first song was a joint called "Power Move." It never came out. Marley and Shan had a song on the *Uptown Is Kickin' It* compilation album—"He Cuts So Fresh." The original verses was me. I was an unknown. Marley had to submit a song for the compilation. [Uptown Records founder] Andre Harrell was like, "Who's this dude? Get Shan to do it." Shan wound up doing the song. There was another joint called "Howard Park," which was actually about my neighborhood and the park where we used to play music at. He played that on the radio once or twice in '87 and never played it again. Then he asked me to be on Marley Marl *In Control* [*Volume 1*] the following year, '88. Those ["Keep Your Eye On the Prize" and "Simon Says" from I*n Control, Volume 1*] were records from my mom's record collection that I brought up to Marley's crib. I liked the loops. I wanted to rap over them. He did all the drum programming and everything, but I walked in with the loops that I wanted to rap over. That was before "The Symphony."

Ced Gee: Ace is dope. I think he's highly underrated. He was dope—his lines, his delivery.

Brooklyn Battles

When Ace burst onto the scene via "The Symphony" in '88, he assumed he was walking into the ideal situation career-wise. He had just joined the most powerful Hip-Hop collective, on a label backed by a major with hit records blowing up the airwaves and TV. What no one on the outside could see was the dysfunction brewing behind the scenes. It was an uphill battle for him from day one.

Masta Ace: I was the college kid, so I was a little bit more savvy I guess, a little smarter, and I knew it was a conflict of interests for the manager to be the label, because who's gonna fight for you when the label don't do the right thing? Here I come walking in with [my manager] Monica [Meachem]. She had a tough time. She didn't get a lot of respect. They would try to ignore her, not take her call—just real petty stuff to make her life miserable. I specifically remember when I came in with Monica for the first time and said I wasn't gonna sign the [Fly Ty-owned] Superstar Management contract, Fly Ty saying, "If you not down with Superstar, you not Juice Crew." He was saying little stuff so I could hear him. "He ain't Juice Crew! He not down with Superstar." I think that was his way of trying to take digs at me, I don't know if he thought it was somehow gonna make me sign or do something.

Fly Ty: Mr. Magic did not like Master Ace. He was just on a *Marley* record. He was never on a *Juice Crew* record. He was on a *Marley* record.

Masta Ace: I didn't like Magic. Other people kissed up to him because of his name. I had a couple of experiences with him that soured me from very early on. The first experience was Marley inviting me up to the station to rap on *Rap Attack*. The way BLS was set up, when you got up to that floor, there was a receptionist there and there were seats. On this particular day, I think Marley was late. He hadn't gotten up there yet. Magic came out and was basically like, "Who are y'all?" And I said, "I'm Master Ace. Marley told me to come up and rhyme on the air." He was like, "Y'all gotta wait outside." He was real dismissive. We [me and Steady Pace] had to get on the elevator and go down to the lobby and stand *in front* of the building. The whole time we were waiting, I was just boiling inside. That built up the first sense of animosity towards him. Then, I guess "The Symphony" had come out, so I was somewhat of a known commodity, with no album. There was an event happening at a college in Coatesville, Pennsylvania. Magic was hosting and he brought DJ Chilly Q with him as the actual DJ, because Magic didn't really spin records. He [Mr. Magic] was the one being paid to be there. I was asked, not by him, but by a third party. We go there, we do the show; everything is cool. We get back in the limo. We're on our way back on the New Jersey Turnpike. Apparently he [Magic] had promised Chilly Q some amount of money for the gig and what he gave him wasn't what he had promised him. So they started arguing. Chilly Q's like, "I'm tired of this. I'm tired of you trying to play me," almost in the fashion of a little kid tired of his older brother bullying him. He starts wailing on Magic, punching him. Me and Steady Pace is looking like, "I can't believe this is happening right now." He's tussling with Chilly Q in the back of the limo, we're sitting there with our mouths open, Magic screams to the limo driver, "Pull over! Pull over!" Limo driver pulls over, Magic gets out of the limo, closes the door, and tells the driver, "Go! Just go!" The driver goes, and we left Magic on the New Jersey Turnpike. He chose to find another way home. He didn't want to be in the limo with Chilly Q.

Fly Ty: Magic was never crazy about Ace's rapping style. He just didn't get it.

Masta Ace: When "The Symphony" came out, the fans, who had already associated Marley and Magic and others with this "Juice Crew" moniker, they just decided that's everybody that's down. That's really when I became down [with the Juice Crew]. The fans had spoken.

The Blues

Ace wasn't the only one with a bone to pick with the label. While extremely young, many of the recording artists on Cold Chillin' and Prism already had multiple mouths to feed. Roxanne Shanté wasn't the only parent, as MC Shan, Glamorous, Cool V, Big Daddy Kane, and Kool G Rap were among those who had children by the beginning of the '90s and *needed* the money they believed they were owed. Making music wasn't some fun hobby any longer, and many of the artists felt like they weren't being fairly compensated.

Big Daddy Kane: We were in the midst of suing the label [Cold Chillin'], and everybody fell out of the lawsuit except for me. This was just me, G Rap, Biz, and Shanté. It was basically explained to me where if it's all the artists against the label, you got a case; where it's one artist against a label, that's the typical thing that's been going on since the beginning of music. That's something they look at in the courtroom as just an artist who's pissed off because his music ain't selling. It's hard to really win those types of battles. It would have been better if everyone had stayed in with the lawsuit.

Everybody just fell out one by one. Like, "Nah, I'm cool. I'm cool." It ended up just being me trying to sue. In the end, I did end up with a better record deal than everyone else.

George DuBose: When they [Cold Chillin'] got hooked up with Warner Bros., for me that was great, because I was doing the package design and photo shoots for $1,500 or $3,000 maybe for a big project. When Warner Bros. took over, my budget went from $3,000 to $15,000. I was in hog heaven. Also, Cold Chillin' started getting a lot of money for promotion, but unfortunately I don't think they used it for promotion. Lenny had a big sport fishing boat.

Masta Ace: Lenny was a crook who didn't really respect the music, didn't respect the artists, who was just lining his pockets, buying boats and all kinds of shit. It was a multi-million dollar deal they got with Warner Bros. Instead of taking care of the artists the way they were supposed to, instead of spending money on promotion and marketing, they put the money in their pockets.

George DuBose: I don't know what Tyrone did with his money.

Dee Joseph: The whole industry did drugs. From the late seventies through to, I don't know what time, but before I left, certainly cocaine was a very common drug. I could say it now, yeah, it may have not been the best choice to do. There wasn't as much clarity as there could have been. At that time it was like the culture. Everybody was doing it. So we were *all* lacking clarity at that time. Tyrone had a big problem.

Fly Ty: The kids—none of them got high. Me, Magic and Marley and Lenny got high, and we hid it from them. The artists didn't get high. Shan a little bit. But G, Polo, Kane, Shanté, Ace, Craig G, Tragedy—none of them. I'm just gonna say the *adults* got high. Alonzo Brown, Francesca Spiro—*our* generation got high. They might have *maybe* smoked some weed. *Maybe*. Me, Magic, Marley, Lenny—that grown man/woman stuff, *we* did.

Marley's stint with drugs ended during the first Cold Chillin' UK tour in 1988. "It was a rough ride until one year I went to London and seen how famous I was," he told NPR in 2013. "I came home a clean person, and I've been clean ever since that day. No rehab, no nothing—I just saw how famous I was in another country. People knew my name. They was screaming my name. It changed my life. That showed me that there was more to my six blocks where I was living." It was also the beginning of the producer distancing himself from Magic, Len, and Ty, and eventually breaking from his position as the Cold Chillin' staff producer in 1989.

Masta Ace: I remember coming up there [to Cold Chillin'] looking for Ty, trying to get a check. You catch him coming in, you be like, "Ty, I'm supposed to get $1,500 for whatever whatever whatever." He wrote me a check, he wrote himself a check. He's coming in disheveled, dirty clothes, wrinkled clothes, hair not cut, just looking like a street bum. He'd come in, write himself a check, not take any phone calls, and walk right back out the door, go down to the bank, cash it to himself and be gone for the rest of the day. He would literally be in the office less than an hour. He did that on a regular basis.

TJ Swan: It could have been better for him [Biz]. In return, it would have been better for me. He wasn't highly compensated for the stuff he did.

Jeff Smith: In the old soul music days, the managers would kind of take care of them—get them a Cadillac, get them some clothes. It was just like that.

Masta Ace: They bought Biz a BMW, which he crashed the first week. Then they bought him a Nissan Maxima. He didn't know how drive. You can't learn to drive in a $60,000 car. They were paying people in cars. They were paying people in rent. Shan, Kane and G Rap all lived in the same complex in Queens. They were covering those rents. Everybody got a car, and everybody got their rent covered. When I say everybody, I mean Biz, Kane, G Rap. Everything stopped with G Rap. Shan was getting stipend, Shanté was getting stipend from what I remember. They were there every week like they were picking up their check for work. They got money on a consistent basis. That was Lenny's way of keeping the artists from sticking their nose in the books. You're getting these monthly things, but where do you think that money is coming from? "This is your money. We're taking care of you. We're covering your rent. We're covering your car note." Not realizing how much you really are owed. I guess people went along with it. *I* didn't get my rent paid.

Fly Ty: I got the headache with the harvest. They were cool when they were younger, but when they got older they start bitching all the time.

Jeff Smith: The artists had *terrible* contracts. Cold Chillin' was getting paid the lion's share of the royalties. The artists were making four or five percent and Cold Chillin' was making thirteen or fourteen. You'd have to actually see a contract to know, to say with certainty what the numbers were, but the artists had *terrible* deals.

Kool G Rap: I was cool with Lenny. Like any other relationship, you got your high points and your low points. I'm not a bitter dude. I don't forget the reality of shit. If there was no Lenny Fichtelberg, G Rap might have not been G Rap as the world knows today G Rap is, without it happening just exactly the way it happened. And Lenny Fichtelberg believed in me. Bottom line—business with Fly Ty and Lenny Fichtelberg could have been better business. But at the end of the day, these the muthafuckas that put G Rap out. They believed in G Rap. Any time a crisis with personal life matters, G Rap never got left. Like the hospital thing. I'm not one of those dudes to turn around and, "Yo, fuck them!" It just isn't in my spirit to do that.

Jeff Smith: They [Kool G Rap & DJ Polo] did come to me to see if I would manage them, in what was one of the most awkward possible conversations where they described to me the terrible deals they signed. Echoing the old record business way of dealing with guys who aren't terribly sophisticated, they'd throw them some money. They'd get their mother some groceries—little things without ever *really* paying. I don't want to say they were completely dishonest, but there was a level of old-school trickery going on there. Tyrone was the one who was at least as involved in any shenanigans like that as was Len. For sure, there was a certain amount of, "Yeah, here's a car! Here's your rent!" Even at that, they signed for five or six albums, escalating by a half a point per album. When they showed me their contract, I couldn't believe how terrible it was. I said, "We'd have to get you out of your contract for me to be able to afford to manage you." They came to me with Polo with the hat on sideways—kind of a goofy guy. And G Rap, who was big, and physically imposing. These were a couple of tough guys. I don't know how they realized, maybe it just caught up with them, that they weren't getting what they thought they were getting.

"Even Tyrone Williams was in a learning process," said Roxanne Shanté on the *Premium Pete Show* in 2018. "Everyone was in a learning process about it. Should I have been informed on other things? Absolutely. Should I have had a better contract? Absolutely. Should my manager and my record company not have been the same entity? Absolutely. Should my accountant and lawyer, management, and record company have not been college buddies? Absolutely. But also the fact too was, coming from where I was coming from, it was such a different opportunity. Who at age fourteen makes $20,000 a weekend?"

Masta Ace: Ty had more of a relationship with the artists. He tried to be cool with everybody. He tried to speak to everybody on their level. Lenny talked down to everybody for whatever reason. Maybe that was his personality. Maybe that was how he looked at us. He came from a different genre of music, so he probably looked at us as a bunch of street criminals making this music that he doesn't understand, but it's making him money. So he's gonna go with the flow, but he don't really respect these real young black dudes coming up here, dressing all crazy. I never really got to pick his brain, but that's how it came off to me—just a major lack of respect on his part. Fly Ty at least respected brothers.

Big Daddy Kane: It was really more or less a thing where a bunch of young cats is coming to a label. When we came there, Cold Chillin' wasn't with Warner Bros. It was really backed by Len Fichtelberg. So you got young, black dudes coming from the ghetto, looking at the white dude like, "Aight, we got to watch him before he rob us." And confiding in the black dude to hold us down and take care of us, not realizing that the black dude is robbing us worse than the white dude!

Mo Ostin: I wasn't aware of it [fiduciary irresponsibility] if it was going on, nor did anybody tell me if they knew about it. If they were playing games, I might have put a stop to it.

The Ones That Got Away

Masta Ace: Marley didn't want to bring anybody else over there because he didn't like the way Cold Chillin' was getting down. I think he wanted to do other things. He encouraged Craig to go in another direction.

Craig G: It was not legal for me to have a contract. I was fifteen years old. I believe honestly they didn't think it was worth the trouble either, because you know all the stuff you have to go through as a minor to do that. A lot of the songs I was just featured on. I was never really signed to them [Cold Chillin']. When I signed to Atlantic, I was seventeen, and I still had to go to court to do that. Merlin Bobb was the guy who signed me. He was a house music DJ and also A&R for Atlantic. Once upon a time, house music was dope. I made "Turn This House Into a Home" a year before I signed to Atlantic. Marley used to have a house mix show, and he played it all the time. It became like a big song in the city. By the time that album [*The Kingpin*] came out, I was already over with house music. That's why the second album is called *Now That's More Like It*. I think I traded popularity from being on Cold Chillin' and being involved with the Juice Crew, for a better record deal [with Atlantic].

Craig G wasn't the only member of the Juice Crew who ended up signing with a label other than Cold Chillin'. Biz Markie's crooner TJ Swan was recording his solo album *Have No Fear.V*

TJ Swan: In between producing for Heavy D and a whole bunch of different artists at the time, he [Marley] would squeeze me in. I would go to his house and start working at 4:00 in the morning. Big Daddy Kane was featured on it. Craig G actually wrote my rap lyric for "Scent of a Lover." He was part of that. Biz would give me beats and samples. I would sit there and write from scratch. I wrote all my songs and co-produced it with Marley Marl. I also had Force MDs. Incredible! Marley had a track he was working on with them, and they never finished the track, so Marley had the vocals. He was like, "Yo, this is the background vocals." The album was raw, it was hot. He presented it to several heads, and they all was bidding on it. They was like, "Arista don't have nobody. Let Arista have it." Because you had Bobby Brown at MCA, you had Al B. Sure! at Warner Bros., you had Keith Sweat at Elektra—everybody had an R&B, male street singer. Arista came along and that was the perfect opportunity for me. They offered me half a million dollars, I was going to all the parties, I went to an Aretha Franklin party and met all my heroes—Ashford & Simpson, Peabo Bryson. I'm like, "Wow, this is amazing!" Bobby Brown was there. Al B. Sure! was there. They was like, "Welcome to the crew, brother! You got your deal!" Did all the paperwork. All of a sudden my executive A&R had a family tragedy.

Fly Ty: Swan could not really sing that well, but a guy named Eric Mury knew that Swan had been around the country three or four times and girls loved him. He was like a Bobby Brown. Bobby couldn't sing that well either. Eric Mury had his mother and his brother die the same week. He quit.

TJ Swan: He had to leave the project. They appointed me a new A&R guy, but he did not know who I was.

Fly Ty: The new A&R guy came in and said, "This guy can't sing!"

TJ Swan: He did not know my body of work; he did not know my image. None of that stuff. When it was time to sign the last contract, I went to the meeting, and he sat me down. He said, "Listen, I'm the new executive, blahzay blah. This is what I want." He showed me a video of Milli Vanilli "Girl You Know It's True." He said, "This is the direction I want you to go. The more pop-ish." I said, "I can't do that. That's not me. Obviously, you don't know my music. You don't know my background. You don't know my audience. We're not on the same page. Let me go home and think about it, pray about it." I talked to my mother. She told me, "Go pray about it." Then I came back out and said, "I'm not gonna do it. I'm not gonna lose myself based on what somebody else want me to do. I'm not doing watered down pop. That's not my image. I love the strictly raw Hip-Hop and R&B style that was created from love, from my heart and my soul." I just couldn't give that up for that crossover.

Fly Ty: TJ Swan I always thought could have been an Al B. Sure!—he couldn't sing either. Swan could sing just as well as them.

TJ Swan's record deal was terminated and his album lay unreleased. Meanwhile, the careers of Glamorous and Debbie D, the two lesser-known Juice Crew females, ground to a halt. Debbie released a handful of singles on Dutch label Ram's Horn while Glamorous was able to squeeze off one single on Prism in 1988, ghost produced by Howie Tee.

Glamorous: I was Magic's mistress and not happy about that. I was Christian. My mom was not happy about that. I felt sorry for [Mr. Magic's wife] Lisa. He was funny and cool but he loved me. I grew up though in the process of our relationship and stepped off. [Debbie D was with] Ty. That was his girl. She came and then she went.

Masta Ace: There were forces at work to keep her [Glamorous] from ever really coming out with a record. Shanté was looking at it like, "These girls was trying to come in and muddy up the waters, and I'm not having it. I'm the only girl, and it needs to stay that way." She was very vocal probably behind the scenes. Not stuff I've witnessed, but just knowing her personality and seeing her interact with Glamorous now, to this day, it's clear she doesn't want her muddying the waters.

Glamorous: I got along with her [Roxanne Shanté], but she didn't care too much for me. She ignored me. She never said bad things to me. She smiled all the time at me. But her verse in "Juice Crew All Stars" told me what was up. I always reached out to keep the peace.

After recording his tracks for Marley's *In Control, Volume 1* album, MC Percy, aka Tragedy, was sent to prison. Convicted of robbery, the Queensbridge rapper was among the first generation of minors tried as an adult in New York, a practice that was disproportionately applied to African-American youths. Among those who kept tabs on him was ex-rapper Alonzo Brown, who worked his way up from being General Manager of Cold Chillin', to Director of Publicity of Urban Music at Warner Bros. Records, to VP of A&R at A&M Records.

Fly Ty: Everybody wanted something from Cold Chillin' at that time. Alonzo said to A&M, "I can get you this kid named Tragedy." Tragedy had done some records on the independent side, but he was too young to sign at the time [before imprisonment]. He had a rough life. Mother was a drug addict, didn't know who his father was.

"Marley kept telling me to stay focused and hold on," Tragedy told *Vice* in 2015. "And it was hard to do that when you're the oldest of five children, and you got to be the man of the house and help feed your brothers and sisters. So half my life was recording at the time and half of it was trying to get money the best way I could and survive. I wound up doing a robbery. The people whose spot I ran up in, they found out it was me. They ran up on me, they kidnapped me and tortured me for two days. They beat me up, burned me with cigarette butts. You know, sucka shit. After that they threw me in the East River. I couldn't swim either. I don't even know what I thought during those two days. In my mind, I was just trying to ignore the pain, stay focused, hold on, and just believe that I was going to make it out of there. I just remember waking up on the rocks. When I realized where I was, I crawled my way through the park and into the street and passed out there. A car almost hit me. The car wound up summoning the ambulance and I wound up going to the hospital."

Fly Ty: When he came out [of prison], Alonzo [Brown] intercepted him and took him to A&M.

Troy Shelton: Hard rock. Really serious dude. If you was his friend, you was his friend. If you were not his friend, you were not his friend. And he let you know. I love Tragedy.A

Tragedy had changed his name again. He came out of the penal system highly politicized with a new moniker: Intelligent Hoodlum. Released in 1990 by A&M, the album *Intelligent Hoodlum* included anthems more in the vein of Public Enemy than that of any of his Juice Crew peers. “Arrest the President,” “Black and Proud,” and “No Justice, No Peace” were veritable war cries placed over hard Marley Marl beats. The producer was spreading out.

Craig G: I saw what Marley was going through. Marley was having trouble getting money from them [Cold Chillin’]. He was on a salary. He wasn’t getting royalties. Even in that instance, I was a little too young to understand a lot of that stuff. What I did know is even though I was signed to a production deal, I was signed directly to a major and not to an independent through a major. A bunch of people gotta get paid for you to get paid.

Aaron Fuchs: I heard all sorts of stories. There were so many layers. It starts with Warner Bros. Then it goes to Lenny. Then it goes to Ty. Then it goes to Marley. Then it goes to the artists. From what I could see, there wound up being lots of hard feelings because there was so much chipping away at the money, from the time it left Warner’s hands to the time it got to the artists. You weren’t really dealing with people who had a business background, where you could say this guy knew how to take care of business properly.

Letter To the Better

By 1989, Ace got the farm team treatment by Cold Chillin' when they released his debut single "Together"/"Letter To the Better" independently on Prism, just as they had done with Kane in '87 and Kool G Rap & DJ Polo in '88. It was the last Hip-Hop record on the Prism imprint. The artist name on the single was not his own, but rather Ace & Action.

Masta Ace: It was really me trying to steer myself away from being a solo artist, and being more of a group. I was trying to create more of a group vibe. It always felt like groups were more interesting. I stopped that name because it got confusing. People thought Action was Steady. People would always call Steady Pace "Action." "Yo, waddup, Action?" "My name's not Action!" He would get mad. I was like, "This too confusing. People not getting it." So I needed to come up with something else.

When it was time to record his debut album *Just Look Around* for Cold Chillin' proper, this time as Master Ace, the MC brought records to Marley Marl for the producer to work his studio magic on. Things went down a little differently than they did for Biz, Kane, and G Rap however.

Masta Ace: I was the first artist on Cold Chillin' that he [Marley] actually gave co-production credit to. If you look at the credits on *Just Look Around,* it says "co-produced" by me. He gave me some money. His advance was $64,000. That's what he got for producing that record. And out of that $64,000 he gave me $8,000. That's all I ever saw from my work co-producing the record. He worked on every song except for four. DJ Mister Cee got credit for producing four of the records. He actually only produced two.

Mister Cee: "As I Reminisce"—I think I got credit for that, but I don't think I was the producer for that record. I definitely produced "I Got Ta," "Can't Stop the Bumrush," and "Postin' High" solely. If you listen to those records, that's Marley Marl all over. The Marley Marl shakers and the 808s—the production style, that's [influenced by] Marley.

Masta Ace: There were two other records that were produced by my man Uneek from Ice U Rock. He's from my high school. His brother and I were teammates on the high school football team. He produced two of the records, but Marley wouldn't give him credit because he was unknown. [The non-album b-side of the "Movin' On" single] "Go Where I Send Thee" and "As I Reminisce."

Marley's weapon of choice was now the E-mu SP-1200 sampler, and he employed cutting edge studio techniques such as *filtering* bass lines by cutting high end Vfrequencies out of the samples.

Easy Mo Bee: I always like to say the first time I heard a filtered sample in a Hip-Hop beat was "Music Man" by Master Ace. And who did that? Marley Marl.

George DuBose: Ace showed me a Curtis Mayfield cover of Curtis sitting on a beach with projects in the background. He said he wanted that. So I found a place in Coney Island, New York, on the beach, with projects in the background. Ace came. We did the shooting there. I did this design and I sent the design out to Warner Bros. They said, "No. It's no good. We don't like it. It's not rap." I said, "Please take a look at the Curtis Mayfield album *Curtis*. This is what Ace wanted to do." And they said, "Okay." But it was a question of the record company not knowing how the rappers were taking off from their history—what they grew up with. Word got back that they wanted a new cover, but then Ace talked them out of it.

Me and the Biz

Masta Ace: "Me and the Biz" is one of the last records we did. It was supposed to be a duet with me and him [Biz]. It was a beat Marley had. I heard the beat in Marley's collection probably several months before. As soon as I heard the loop I was like, "Ooh, what's this? This is dope. Can I get this?" He's like, "Nah, that's for Biz." I was like, "Aah, wack!" Subsequent to that conversation, he and Biz started to have a falling out of sorts. Biz wasn't gonna be recording at his house anymore.

Towards the end of the making of *The Biz Never Sleeps* album, Biz Markie and Cool V had brought members of New Jersey's Flavor Unit collective and some of their friends, including Flavor Unit manager Shakim Compere, to Marley Marl's new home studio in the Spring Valley/Chestnut Ridge area of New York State, without calling ahead. The intention was to bring the Juice Crew and Flavor Unit together for the ultimate posse cut, but Marley didn't recognize everyone in the entourage, and didn't feel comfortable allowing them in his home. Marley refused to open the door for anyone, Biz included. It was the final straw that permanently severed any kind of working relationship between Biz and Marley. The latter did not mix the album, as originally planned.

Masta Ace: I was like, "I wanna use it [the beat] and maybe I can get Biz on it, because it sounds like a Biz record. It sounds like something he would rhyme to." I wrote the rhyme. I wrote my part, I wrote his part. I recorded it, and then I recorded Biz's parts. I changed my voice so that Biz would know when my parts came and when his parts came. I gave it to Biz. He heard it, he liked it, but he was like, "I'm not recording at Marley's house." Once Biz got his mind made up, there's no changing him. He was like, "If you want me to do it, bring me the tapes, and we record it at my crib." He wanted me to bring the 2" reel to his studio at his house to record it. Of course Marley was like, "Absolutely not." I'm the new guy, so I'm not trying to rock no boat. Marley was like, "Yo, let's just leave it how it is. It's kinda dope how it is. You imitating Biz—people are probably gonna think it's him. Let's just leave it like that." I'm like, "If you say so. I don't think that's dope, but okay." And we left that song how it was. We went to Warner Bros. to decide that was the single. The most playful, most fun record—they wanted that to be the single. And the fact that Biz's name is associated with the record. They were all about piggybacking on other artists that had previous success. I just felt like that wasn't the right move. I wanted to get it on my own merits. I tried to speak up for myself, but I knew that I didn't want to rock the boat too much and have them decide that they didn't want to put the record out. I specifically remember Benny Medina from Warner Bros. in a conference call. I was like, "Let it be the second or third single." He was like, "If 'Me and the Biz' isn't the single, I can't guarantee you're gonna have another single." He basically forced my hand. "If you don't do what we saying to do, we'll just let you die in the water after this record comes out, and not put another dime into it." That was the threat.

"Me and Vthe Biz" was a circumstantial stroke of genius. Adding to the strangeness of Ace essentially rapping a duet with himself in the character of his labelmate, was the Lionel Martin-directed video featuring a papier-mâché marionette Biz Markie doll, sporting the actual rapper's four-finger "BIZ" ring. The duo have coffee together, entertain children on a Brooklyn stoop, drive around in a convertible with Marley Marl, and end up in a love triangle with a real life woman. As undeniably brilliant as this oddball single was, it was totally unrepresentative of the rest of Ace's album.

Masta Ace: Here I am—young, black kid from the projects. I was able to overcome my circumstances, go to college, get a degree. I had so many close friends that had fallen by way of the streets—had gotten into drug selling or using, or gun carrying, and locked up and in jail. I felt like what I wanted to do was send a message to my community that if I could do it, you could do it. There's nothing special about me. You could all do what I did. Just put your mind to it. That was the overall sentiment. The album to me was a little bit preachy when I listen back to it—telling people what to do and how to live their lives. I figured out later in my career that there was a way to do that without making people feel like you're wagging your finger at them.

10
SOMETHING NEW

As African-American families left the boroughs for Long Island suburbs like Roosevelt, Long Beach, and Hempstead in large numbers starting in the 1960s, white families in turn left these communities in droves, taking their business with them. By 1989, many of the same issues that afflicted the city—crime, poverty, the drug trade—had made their way onto the Island. Waiting in the parking lot of a fast food sandwich shop in Hempstead, aka "The Stead," were a handful of young, black men wielding baseball bats and assorted blunt objects.

Smooth Assassin

Grand Daddy I.U.: Biz Mark had a roadie that was from my town, Hempstead. A cat named Jeff. At this time Biz had just got a production deal with Warner Bros. He didn't have enough artists, so obviously he was looking for another dude. Jeff knew I could get busy so he called me on the phone and they met me around my mom's crib at this spot called Blimpie's. We thought it was a joke. We waiting for whoever is going to be up there claiming it's Biz playing a prank, and we gonna whoop his ass. But he *was* Biz. That was it from there.

Fly Ty: Biz was the first person I gave a production deal to. I went to Biz one day and I said, "Biz, if you can produce four acts for me, I'll give you $375,000 an act." He said, "What?" The next day he came to me with a kid named Grand Daddy I.U. I gave him [Biz] $750,000 that same day.

With Marley Marl gone, Mr. Magic off the air, and the Juice Crew brand approaching obsolescence, Cold Chillin' soldiered on into the '90s. What better A&R man/producer to fill Marley's shoes than the person already responsible for bringing the label its two greatest success stories in Big Daddy Kane and himself? Biz Markie

Productions, Inc. was born. Biz was to be the credited producer and Cool V the co-producer on any release by an artist signed to the imprint.
Grand Daddy I.U.: I got a $25,000 advance, and then I got a $100,000 publishing deal with Warner/Chappell. But that ain't have nothing to do with Biz. Fly Ty got me that. Everybody was like, "Who's this muthafucka? Who's this new nigga?" Kane and Biz had fell out for a second.

Big Daddy Kane: Me and Biz used to fall out on the regular, but it was like sibling spats. Nothing major. That type of thing where we stop speaking to each other for a week, and we act like we never had a problem.

Grand Daddy I.U.: I had no idea of that shit, but he [Kane] thought that Biz signed me as some type of a shot at him, because I had "Daddy" in my name. My name was originally just Daddy U. Biz added all that shit to it. I guess Kane thought Biz was trying to make another Big Daddy Kane. He said this to me years later.

Big Daddy Kane: I think what was more or less happening was . . . I.U. was dope, bottom line. Dude is talented. He's a great lyricist. Biz saw that, and I think Ty saw a window. He was trying to find a Kane replacement since I wasn't messing with the label. I wouldn't cooperate. They tried to get me to do songs with other artists on the label, and I'm like, "No." Trying to get me to show up to functions which was for Cold Chillin', and I wouldn't show up. They were trying to find a new Kane.

Masta Ace: He sounded like the second coming of Kane in a way, and I think that's what Biz heard. I think that's why he worked with him. I think Biz was trying to outdo Kane with Grand Daddy. It didn't work that way, but I feel like that was his plan. Grand Daddy I.U. was the replacement, and that's why the word "Daddy" is even in there. I'm sure he gave him the name.

Grand Daddy I.U.: You know how you had something in front of your name like "The *Almighty* Kay Gee," the fuckin' "*Grand Imperial* whoever," know what I'm saying? I had the "Grand." It was Daddy U., but the "Grand" was just the extra part. It was like "*Ladies Love* Cool J." Everybody had a little extra shit in front of their name. They put the whole shit together and put the "I.U." because my [legal] name is Ayub. So I used that as my stage name. So he [Biz Markie] put the whole Grand Daddy I.U. as one whole name on the contract. The day we go to sign, it's either sign the contract as is, or wait for them to fucking change it. It might take a couple of days to get the check, so I'm like, "Fuck that; give it to me right now." I signed it as is, and that's how the "Grand Daddy I.U." stuck.

Dee Joseph: He was very tall. I love Grand Daddy. He was great.

Masta Ace: He definitely had a great album. I thought it was super dope.

Grand Daddy I.U.: Me and my brother [and DJ, Kay Cee] found the samples. DJ Doc [Ivan Rodriguez] was the engineer, and Cool V was like the overseer. He is Biz's right-hand man and DJ, but he was the only one from Biz's team in the studio. It was him in place of Biz. Biz was actually supposed to do that fuckin' album. I looped the stuff I wanted before I got there, but I didn't have no sampler or shit like that. I know what drums I want to match with what muthafuckin' bass line, I know what horn sample I want. And I just tell him, "Yo, put this here, put that there." Biz wasn't even in the studio. He might have came to the studio for three days for a little while, because he was enjoying the money he got from the production deal. He was out buying new cars and enjoying life. We was puttin' that work in, getting the album done.

After breaking away from Marley Marl over issues concerning production credit, Biz Markie's new role as producer for an album that he had very little direct involvement in constructing was ironic at the very least. Recorded at Power Play Studios in Queens, Grand Daddy I.U.'s debut album *Smooth Assassin* was released in 1990 on Cold Chillin'/Reprise, also bearing the Biz Markie Productions logo.

Grand Daddy I.U.: My man Easy Rick the Playa—he was OG. He was from the '70s. He was an older cat, and he always used to rock a muthafuckin' suit and muthafuckin' hard bottoms and all that shit. He was an official gangsta muthafucka from back in the days, so when the record shit came out he was like, "Yo, you can't just wear a muthafuckin' baseball hat and look like a regular muthafucka."

George DuBose: That's not *him* murdering someone [on the back album cover]. It's his pal. *Smooth Assassin.* We knew we had to do a hit just from the title. I talked to Grand Daddy and I talked to my stylist, and we decided that we wanted to do this on the staircase of Grand Central Station in Manhattan. The biggest staircase—all marble. I had to rent Grand Central Station, at least the staircase. I had to pay a big location fee. The stylist got them dressed up as gangsters. I collect knives, and I had a lot of switchblades. The switchblade we used in this picture is quite large and long. It must be almost a foot when it's opened up. We had this whole thing set up where the rich guy is gonna get assassinated by Grand Daddy and this other guy with the knife. I remember we had the whole thing set up and the props, and I realized, "We're missing something! They're robbing this guy—where's the money?" So Grand Daddy looked over at one of his girls who was with him, and said, "Hey honey, give me some money." She must have pulled out about $5,000 in cash. So we did the shoot. I couldn't believe it.

Kid Capri & Diamond Shell

Fly Ty: Then he [Biz Markie] brought me his brother Diamond Shell.

Dee Joseph: Biz had people. He had a stable. He had Kid Capri.

Fly Ty: Then he [Biz] said, "I got Kid Capri." I said, "What!?" I wanted Kid Capri bad, but I didn't want Kid Capri the way they gave me Kid Capri. Kid Capri was a hot DJ.

Monica Lynch: Capri was certainly another guy who became one of the major Hip-Hop DJs—people like [Funkmaster] Flex and Capri, where there was a Hip-Hop DJ hierarchy. Capri was a part of that.

Fly Ty: My idea of having Kid Capri was taking all of my artists' new stuff, give it to him, and make an album with it—like he normally did. I wanted to call it *The Tape*. But Kid Capri rapping was not it. And I fought and fought and fought and fought. I wouldn't put that album out, but by that time Warner Bros. was loving Biz. So they put that album out. He's convinced [Senior Vice President of Marketing & Promotion, Warner Bros. Records] Ray Harris by this time. "It's Kid Capri!" It's Kid Capri, but it's not Kid Capri. People don't wanna hear Kid Capri rappin'! That was that.

TJ Swan: I eventually worked with him [Biz] on his [production] deal that he got. He had his artists like Diamond Shell. I sung on the record for Diamond, I did the Kid Capri record "This Is What You Came Here For." So I was working with him when he got his own production company through Cold Chillin'/Warner Bros. He was like, "Come on, I'll pay you to sing on my brother's record." I was just a hired artist. I didn't know the details of his deal.

Jay Quan: *The Grand Imperial Diamond Shell* was a very good record on Cold Chillin' that was produced by Biz. "Oh What A Night" was a good single. I don't know if it wasn't promoted properly. He never made a follow up.

Both released in 1991, Kid Capri's *The Tape* and Diamond Shell's *The Grand Imperial Diamond Shell* were commercial flops. The biggest success Biz Markie Productions had was one minor hit single by Grand Daddy I.U.—"Something New." Despite Marley's absence, his influence was present.

Grand Daddy I.U.: He [Marley Marl] took a shot at me. I used the "I'm Your Puppet" [by James & Bobby Purify] beat, and he had used it for something ["Live & Direct From the House of Hits" by Intelligent Hoodlum feat. Craig G], but whatever he did with it, he didn't really do nothing with it. I made it a single ["Something New"]. Back then muthafuckas was like, "Yo, muthafucka stole my beat!" You didn't *make* the sample. It's a *record*. Anybody that had that record could sample the shit and do whatever the fuck they wanna do with it. At that time it was more strict. My shit came out better.

The Genius Is Slammin'

Biz Markie wasn't the only one bringing new artists to Cold Chillin' in the post-Juice Crew era.

Easy Mo Bee: On Kane's first album *Long Live the Kane*, at the end of "Set It Off," Kane is doing all these shout outs to different people, and there's a certain part in the shout outs where it's like, "Peace to Mr. Melquan and Shabazz!" I always heard those names, but I didn't know. It was just people he knew he was shouting out. One day, I'm out at some Hip-Hop event, and this tall guy named Melquan walks up to me, and he's like, "Yo, peace G! I love what you did on the Kane album. I want you to work with my artist. I got this artist called The Genius." It goes further and deeper than that. He said, "This is only one of them. There's like eight, nine more. They got this concept, this thing they got called 'The Wu-Tang.' They fusing the martial arts together with the Hip-Hop." Back then Hip-Hop was pretty simple. It didn't have that much deep, intricate concepts to it. He was talking all that martial arts stuff, and in my mind I was like, "Yeah, whatever. Let's hear your artist."

Jeff Smith: The Genius—he could rap. I'll tell you that. The Genius had skills.

Masta Ace: Smart guy, keeps to himself, know how to rhyme, good at it, stays in his lane, don't do a lot of outrageous, outlandish stuff. Just real even-keeled, good dude. Somebody you could rely on. Somebody you could trust. He reminds me of me in that way.

Easy Mo Bee: Genius grew up in Brooklyn. We worked out of different places. I remember Funky Slice in the Albee Square Mall/Downtown, Brooklyn area. We also worked at INS over in the Park Row area of Manhattan. Brooklyn Bridge. Some of it even got done at Unique Recording Studios, and that was probably one of the early introductions to me occupying that place and using it. Because from that point on, I used Unique Recording Studios for almost everything that I was doing, unless other artists and their record labels had other studios set up. After Melquan put me and Genius together, at that point Genius was coming to the crib and we was creating.

Mister Cee: I wish Genius would have been a part of the Juice Crew. I don't like the fact that *Words From the Genius* came out after the Juice Crew went their own separate ways. That was probably the best post-Juice Crew disbandment album that came out on Cold Chillin'. I know Easy Mo Bee produced most of that album. One of my favorite songs on that album is "True Fresh MC." When we [myself and Kane] started going with Rush Management, and started tailing off and being under the Rush umbrella, was Ty and everybody else at Cold Chillin' trying to look for the next Big Daddy Kane? Of course they was. With Genius and Grand Daddy I.U.—yes. But that *Words From the Genius* album is a dope ass album.

Easy Mo Bee: [I was paid] $1,000 a track times ten. I did ten songs on *Words From the Genius*. My brother LG Experience [Patrick Harvey] produced four. Jesse West from the Bronx did the lead single "Come Do Me."

George DuBose: This is again my specialty of taking an artist's concept and making it something marketable. I met with The Genius and his manager Melquan. They had a specific idea. They wanted The Genius at a podium lecturing somebody, with a dozen gold chains around his neck, and gold watches. He wanted to wear more gold than all the other rappers. I said, "Let's do something a little more tasteful, and a little different." I built a gold room. I got thirteen gold art books and put "Words From the Genius" on the spines, numbered one through thirteen. I got a feather, I painted it gold. We had a gold sweater. We had a gold lamé shirt. We had my father's gold bathrobe from Damascus, Syria, 1946 that [had a pattern that] was little black guys hunting cheetahs with bows and arrows, and dogs. Genius loved that. Again, Warner Bros. didn't think it was rough enough. They changed the cover to a headshot of him looking a little more gnarly. They used that picture with a different color treatment for the second version of that album. They thought the cover was too smooth.

Dee Joseph: He [The Genius] was pissed off, I'm sure. I'm sure. He didn't get promoted the way he thought he should get promoted. It didn't get the promotion he deserved or wanted or thought he deserved. I don't think that the Warner Bros. machine probably understood The Genius who went on to form Wu-Tang Clan. Are you kidding? These guys out here in sunny California think they understood The Genius? He probably didn't get the shake that he deserved.

Kool G Rap: I don't think his album wasn't strong enough. I think there's a way for everybody. I don't think the time he came to Cold Chillin' was the perfect time for him. If he was there toward the mid '80s when most of us came there, like me, Kane, Biz, and Craig G, he would have been more affiliated with Juice Crew, and he would have had a better shot. He was just on the label, so he didn't get none of the momentum that Juice Crew would get. When Juice Crew drew all the attention to them and its group members, he wasn't included in that. He pretty much had to struggle on his own with a roster of already established artists.

Mister Cee: In '90, '91, Biz and Kane was at the tipping point. It came to the point where Cold Chillin', if it didn't have Biz or Kane's name on it, nobody wanted to listen to it. And I'm just keeping it funky. The fans or radio DJs didn't want to hear who it was. You had a couple records that came through that had some moderate success, not as much as Kane and Biz, but Kane and Biz's impact on Cold Chillin' was so huge it was almost like they became the label.

Masta Ace: In '91, after Cold Chillin' got their Warner Bros. money, they decided to sign all these artists. Kid Capri was one. The Genius was one. Diamond Shell, Grand Daddy I.U. There was about five or six artists they signed when they got that deal. They decided to embark on their own tour. I was like, "Cool, this is cool. Now finally, Cold Chillin' trying to do something." They got two tour buses. But they said, "This is a *promotional* tour." That means your hotels will be covered when you sleep in a hotel—because we were sleeping on the bus a lot. "You'll get a per diem." Back then it might have been $25 a day. "You're gonna do these shows." We went around the country. I remember New Orleans, a couple of weird southern cities, somewhere in Florida. We were all through the south. East coast too. It was probably eight to ten shows that we did. Biz wasn't on every show. He was on the shows in the big cities. It was Kid Capri, myself, The Genius, Grand Daddy I.U., Kool G Rap, and maybe one other act.

Easy Mo Bee: I still have to this day cassette demos with Genius, and a lot of early rhymes he did on those cassette demos are some of the same rhymes that ended up on [Wu-Tang Clan's debut album] *36 Chambers*. And every time they would come to the crib, they would bring somebody else different with them. I remember a young Raekwon coming tagging along. He also brought this guy name Ason. He called himself "The Ol' Dirty Bastard."

Masta Ace: The very first date was in south Jersey. Ol' Dirty was Genius' hype man. I wanted to watch Genius' show, so me and Steady was out in the crowd. Ol' Dirty comes out first and he immediately starts insulting the crowd. People started booing because he was like, "Fuck New Jersey cats." He was drunk, and he was being outrageous like he always is. He was screaming at the people and cursing them out. I was like, "Damn, this is not a good way to set the table for your man who's about to come out and perform. This is not good." Genius eventually came out. It didn't go that great. After that, a riot almost damn near started. Fly Ty told Genius, "Your man can't come on the tour. He's done," and kicked him off the tour after the first show. We're having a good time, cracking jokes, getting girls, doing all that stuff. Then at the end of the tour, the very last show, we wound up in the room with the promoter. No Fly Ty or anybody around. We find out that these guys, Cold Chillin', Fly Ty, had been making like $60,000 a night on this tour. It was almost a coup. We had to have a big conversation about, "Do we do this last show or not?" Because we was gonna straight up not do the show. I believe we wound up doing the show, but when we got back home it was like a shit storm. "We should go up there and fuck everybody up!" There was a big conversation on what to do—how to go about it. It solidified for me that I was trying to get as far away from Cold Chillin' as possible at that point. That was when I knew that I needed to move on. I think The Genius felt the same way.

Wu-Tang Clan Ain't Nuthing Ta Fuck Wit

Not unlike the situation Ace found himself in with "Me and the Biz," the single and accompanying music video chosen for The Genius was totally unrepresentative of the rest of his album. "Come Do Me" was new jack swing through and through, but lacking the production expertise of Teddy Riley that Kane had for "I Get the Job Done." Simultaneously, Genius' cousin Robert Diggs, aka Prince Rakeem [later RZA], was going through a similar situation at Tommy Boy.

Easy Mo Bee: When I first started to work with Genius, mind you, I produced RZA too in 1990 on Tommy Boy Records. He had a single, a-side "Ooh I Love You Rakeem," and the b-side you had "Sexcapades." That right there, which was a hot second even before Genius, I would say that was the first true entry of a member of the Wu-Tang. You had RZA with the single deal on Tommy Boy, and then following that, '90 to '91, you have The Genius popping up on Cold Chillin.'

Previous to having any record deal, RZA, The Genius and their cousin Ason Unique (aka Ol' Dirty Bastard) had been in a group together called Force of the Imperial Master, which changed its name to All In Together Now. Having left their fruitless situations at Cold Chillin' and Tommy Boy around the same time in 1991, RZA and The Genius (who would soon go by GZA) teamed back up with Ol' Dirty Bastard, initially adding five more members to the group, turning their Wu-Tang Clan concept into a full-fledged rap group. Keeping Melquan and Shabazz as their managers, Wu-Tang Clan pushed the kung fu angle harder than anyone had done previously. They had grown up going to see the same Bruce Lee films in Times Square and had watched the same TV program that inspired Kane to name himself, but they constructed a universe around their obsession. Wu-Tang Clan's home base of Staten Island where many of them lived was re-christened "Shaolin," and they lyrically blended Eastern philosophy filtered through kung fu movies, Five-Percenter terminology, and the hard realities of street life in New York. Wu-Tang Clan was the Juice Crew in reverse—instead of being free floating solo artists who cliqued up for an occasional posse cut, they would instead introduce (or in RZA and Genius' case, *reintroduce*) themselves to the world as a group, and then split off to do solo albums between more group releases.

Wu-Tang Clan's self-released 1992 single "Protect Ya Neck" featured a verse by The Genius that could not be interpreted as anything other than a scathing indictment of Cold Chillin'. He cited stingy, career killing business practices as well as the label's recent inability to produce hits. The tables had turned—Wu-Tang was hot and Cold Chillin' was cold.

Cut Chemist: The first version of "Protect Ya Neck" and [b-side] "[After the Laughter Comes] Tears" were really poorly mixed, in the best way. Distorted and fucked up. It sounded like a Marley record. Something happened where they were like, "Let's buy some broken gear and record on it so it sounds like shit. *Now* we got something!"

Grand Daddy I.U.: Me and him [The Genius] didn't get along too good. We never was beefing, but he took a jab at me on that "Protect Ya Neck" about suit-and-tie rappers. So who on the Cold Chillin' label was wearing a suit and tie? Muthafuckas ain't put it together, so he took a little shot because at the time he had a song called "Come Do Me," and they was pushing my shit over his shit, and he was mad about that. Rather than saying something to me, he went and made that little sneak diss. I seen him after, and we talked about it.

Movin' On

Cold Chillin' pled with Marley Marl to deliver a sequel to his successful 1988 album, in a work-for-hire arrangement. 1991's *In Control Volume II (For Your Steering Pleasure)* on Cold Chillin'/Warner Bros. produced no hits, despite all-star appearances by Chuck D of Public Enemy (rapping with Tragedy), LL Cool J, Heavy D, and a reprise of "The Symphony," which included the original posse of Master Ace, Craig G, Kool G Rap, and Big Daddy Kane, plus Kane's younger brother Little Daddy Shane. Marley was not proud of the album and he learned a valuable lesson: don't do something just because the money is right. This time the split between Cold Chillin' and Marley Marl was permanent, and he wasn't the only one.

Masta Ace: Something came down from Warner Bros. They sent a list of everybody Cold Chillin' had signed. They drew a line. I saw the paper. They said, "Everybody above this line you can keep. Everybody below this line has to go." I was the name *right* below the line, which was actually fine by me. I had already decided in my mind that I didn't want to be there anymore. I saw Grand Daddy I.U. above the line and I thought, "Wow, he's up there, but I'm down here. Okay. It's time for me to go." Fly Ty was like, "Don't worry about it. We gonna put your album out on Prism." I was like, "What? I don't wanna put no album out on Prism. Prism is a singles label. I did my Prism thing. I ain't trying to do no album on Prism. Nobody ever did that before. I ain't trying to be the guinea pig." I had been talking to this new manager a little bit. He said he might be able to get me a situation over at Delicious Vinyl in LA. He was able to create an opportunity over there, and I was out the door. When I moved to Delicious Vinyl, I changed the "Master" to "Masta." I didn't want any connection to that time period [at Cold Chillin']. I viewed the label as a boat with a hole in it.

It Don't Mean a Thing

The avalanche of Cold Chillin' releases in 1990–91 by established artists Big Daddy Kane, Kool G Rap & DJ Polo, Biz Markie, and Marley Marl, Biz Markie Productions artists Grand Daddy I.U., Kid Capri, and Diamond Shell, as well as new signees 2 Deep and The Genius proved to be largely fruitless.

Jeff Smith: I don't know for certain, but my hunch was Warner Bros. said, "Do you think you could give us more hit records? Because the economics are now not working in your favor." I think there was some amount of reading the riot act. MC Shan was one. MC Shan did that video ["It Don't Mean a Thing"]. Record companies are strange places. Somebody identifies something as a hit, and then it starts to take on the aura of being a hit. I guess they came in and really felt strong about the song by MC Shan. It had a real pop moment to it. [Senior VP of video for Warner Bros. Records] John Beug saw it. They had this gorgeous girl named Carole Davis, who made a record for us. She was really hot. She had great tits, great hair, great skin. She was *hot,* okay? They got her in the video, and they wound up spending a *fortune* on this video. Hip-Hop videos only had one place that they could play. The Hip-Hop show was one hour a week on MTV. Maybe I'm overstating the case a little bit, but they spent a fortune, and most of the videos getting on there were not a fortune spent. Maybe Run-DMC was an exception and LL was in that group, but most of them were pretty down and dirty. The Warner Bros. approach was always, "Let's throw some money at it!" I think that that was the beginning of a reckoning that they had to look more closely at this. They weren't all going to be hits. It was also largely a singles-driven business. With the exception of the flukey thing with Biz and I guess both of the first two Kane albums made it to gold. They weren't going platinum. All of a sudden this idea, "We've got product!" "Yeah, but it's not all hit product." Shan was one of the guys who was definitely on the list [of artists who were cut].

MC Shan's trouble with Warner Bros. extended beyond the poor sales of his 1990 album *Play It Again, Shan,* a largely G-rated affair masterminded by Benny Medina. Medina was in the process of casting for a new television show based loosely on his own rags-to-riches life story. Shan told *HipHopDX* in 2012, "Know why I really got messed up with Warner Brothers? Like I said, I was a wild boy back then. I was real wild, just straight hood. So, I was up for that part of *The Fresh Prince* [*of Bel-Air*] because I was signed to Warner Brothers where Benny Medina was. And why I didn't get that fuckin' part was because I called Benny Medina a faggot. I was just wild. That's probably why I had no juice with Warner Brothers or their backing because I was crazy like that."

Shan wasn't the only MC who got in hot water for homophobia. The Beastie Boys' 1986 debut album *Licensed To Ill* was originally going to be titled *Don't Be a Faggot* before their label made them change it. In '89, both Big Daddy Kane and Kool G Rap & DJ Polo felt push back for lyrics in their songs "Pimpin' Ain't Easy" and "Truly Yours" respectively.

Big Daddy Kane: That got me into a whole lotta trouble. You're not thinking about how someone else might get offended because this is what we do: we play the dozens. Talking about each other's mother and finding faults. In my mind, what I'm thinking is all that I'm saying is, "Hey baby, you gonna get some of this hardcore, real dick." I'm thinking that's what I'm saying, but I'm offending a whole community of people, which I didn't really mean to do. At that point in time, you hear the word *faggot* on TV shows—*Sanford and Son* all that stuff, the movie *Which Way Is Up?* You heard it a lot. I didn't mean it that way because I don't have anything against anybody gay. It was a bad time because a lot of people were offended.

Kool G Rap: They pulled my album from the shelves because of that. They boycotted the station K-DAY, which was a real hot station for Hip-Hop in Cali back in the days. I heard they boycotted the station because of one line that I said. I wasn't really intending to gay bash or nothing like that, but you had people that took it that way, and it caused a bunch of ripples behind my album. And they ended up pulling my album off the shelf. I didn't hear anything about it being a particular group. I just heard that it was gay rights activists. Not a particular group.

Fly Ty: G Rap always got caught up in politics. There's some line there about being gay, AIDS and whatever. Society of Gay Men or whatever protested and marched in front of Warner Bros., and they had to drop that too.

Masta Ace: The same sorts of comments would pop up pretty prevalently in comedy, Eddie Murphy comedy and some of the other bigger names. It was spoken about more publicly in a more derogatory way with very little filter back then, because you could just blurt stuff out. If it was against gay people, you would get away with it; everybody would just laugh it off, definitely more then than now.

Jeff Smith: Gay rights groups were getting upset about a lot of things. Sam Kinison. They were upset *a lot* at that time.

Fly Ty: What would Shan's career have been like had he been the Fresh Prince? He might not have done as good of a job. He might have done a better job. We'll never know. That's where he's coming out on that—at the beginning of a brand new album that Benny got Shan to do, that type of music, to soften it up a little bit. He had a song called "It Don't Mean a Thing" where he has a white suit like Cab Calloway. Shan was the golden boy that Benny was gonna make, and it didn't happen.

Will Smith was a fellow alum from Philadelphia's Pop Art family, having originally been on the Goodman-owned Word Records as one half of DJ Jazzy Jeff & The Fresh Prince. He got the gig and on September 10, 1990, *The Fresh Prince of Bel-Air* hit the airwaves, becoming an immediate sensation. Smith rocketed to superstardom, becoming an A-list actor for many decades to follow. The extent of MC Shan's acting work was a cameo part as a rapping waiter at the fictitious restaurant L'Idiot in the 1991 Steve Martin film *L.A. Story*.

Livin' Large

Fly Ty: Livin' Large came about because when Benny dropped Shan, I created Livin' Large for Shan.

George DuBose: Livin' Large was a sub-label of Cold Chillin', and it was not distributed by Warner Bros. MC Shan and Shanté wound up with some records on that label. So maybe that was coming down the back slope.

Dee Joseph: It was nothing other than, "Let's have another label for some other acts," I think just to have the option of getting more air time. You can only go on so many times with, "This is Cold Chillin'. This is Cold Chillin'." We were a small, independent label at this time. And distribution-wise, I think it was a benefit to put it on Livin' Large, or to have two separate entities.

Aaron Fuchs: Everybody likes to give the impression of growth, and the way you do it is by forming a second label, whether it's an imprint or not.

Tom Silverman: I talked to Ty about it because I was a fan, and I'd like to do something with it. We knew that it was kind of a second look deal. Warner was supposed to get the best stuff, and we'd put the other stuff out. I always knew that you never knew what was going to be a hit. So maybe they would give us something that would get lucky. It never really worked out that way. You know I mean the stuff they gave us at Livin' Large was . . . they had already stopped putting up most of their hits at that point. Shanté, YZ,

[Kane's dancers] Scoob & Scrap, MC Shan. We tried. We released those records, but none of them connected. All of them were '92 and '93, so only two-year span that we released those records.

Mo Ostin: Tommy [Boy] was their distributor for a while. We didn't have the expertise to do it.

Tom Silverman: We were pretty much just distributing it. We didn't have interaction with the artists at all. We're getting the records out, and we would meet with them and talk to them about their marketing plans and how they could do things, but none of the stuff that we had ever had enough . . . I hate to use the word "hooks," but marketing hooks or sparks that we could ignite and take them further. We would love to step in and bring any of the things further once they showed their potential. There has to be some story to take the record further. You got to have a story to tell.

Masta Ace: I thought it was corny. The logo was terrible. I didn't like anything about it. I was pretty much long gone by the time that got up and going.

Grand Daddy I.U.: I don't know what the fuck they were doing with that. They had a little fuckin' cubbyhole at the label that was dedicated to that Livin' Large shit. You had YZ on there, and he dropped some Shanté shit on there. I don't know what that was.

Big Mama

Shanté's 1989 debut album *Bad Sister* on Cold Chillin'/Reprise wasn't commercially successful, despite having Marley Marl production, and the rhyme writing expertise of Master Ace, Kool G Rap, Craig G, Big Daddy Kane, 2 Deep's Jae Supreme, and the bad sister herself. Marley recalled Kane recording scratch vocals for "Go On Girl" so Shanté would understand the cadence of his lyrics, and then she would record her own vocals for the record. Released a half decade after her first single "Roxanne's Revenge"—a virtual lifetime in a genre that was only in its tenth year of recorded output—there wasn't enough momentum left behind her to make an impact.

Mister Cee: She had a baby. She was dealing with somebody that was not treating her right, and the person who was not treating her right couldn't get along with Tyrone [Williams]. That was during the height of her career. That was during "Roxanne's Revenge" and "Go On Girl," and "Have a Nice Day." All of those trials and tribulations she went through . . . and remember she broke as a teenager so all the stuff she was going through, that was the reason for the delay of her first album. It had nothing to do with anything musically. It was about all the stuff she was going through with having a child, raising a child, and dealing with a dude that was doing stuff he didn't have no business doing to her.

Jeff Smith: Roxanne Shanté didn't really do very much once she got to Warner Bros. Her biggest hit happened [earlier] when they were still an independent label.

Masta Ace: Shan had already run his course. He had done what he was gonna do. Shanté had done what she was gonna do.

By 1992, Shanté had dropped the "Roxanne" from her name (her rival The Real Roxanne shortened her own stage name to Roxanne by that point), and her sophomore album *The Bitch Is Back* was out on Livin' Large.

Mister Cee: Fly Ty was always a good guy to me. He always treated me with respect. I never had any issues with Fly Ty. Never. I remember specifically during '91, '92, '93, when Cold Chillin' wasn't as popular as we was in the late '80s—the Livin' Large era. I was doing a little bit of A&R at the time with Livin' Large, I produced some songs for Roxanne Shanté's second album *The Bitch Is Back,* which allowed me to make money. It allowed me to still have an income. Ty always took care of me. Him and Lenny and Dee, they always made sure that I was working and doing something to keep an influx of income. I produced damn near half of Shanté's *The Bitch Is Back* album.

Cut Chemist: Shanté put out some *really* good records on Livin' Large. "Big Mama"—that song's fucking dope, man. Great production.

Grand Daddy I.U.: Fly Ty asked me to produce and write some shit for Shanté, so I did that. Then they told me, "Yo, I want you to do a diss song dissing all female rappers." So I did that "Big Mama" shit. Then all the DJs were scared to play it.

"Big Mama" was the hardest diss record from the MC who invented the diss record. The first female from the second generation of MCs, Shanté held the door open for newcomers Queen Latifah, Monie Love, MC Lyte, Yo-Yo, and Salt-N-Pepa, and was being forgotten about in the process. Verse by verse, she dismantled these women in the least politically correct way possible, and it didn't win her any fans. The backfire Shanté and lyricist Grand Daddy I.U. received was immense and turned the two into pariahs within the growing Hip-Hop community. Queen Latifah was part of the Flavor Unit collective, as was Naughty By Nature, led by Treach. One night Treach and his entourage, which included a rising star named Tupac Shakur, confronted I.U. to defend Latifah's honor. The extent of the violence was Treach throwing a bag of Styrofoam peanuts at I.U.

Grand Daddy I.U.: That was the whole Treach and Tupac shit that went back and forth between his crew and my crew. That was his man. That's what you're supposed to do. Nothing ever happened. It was thick for a minute. [When he threw Styrofoam at me, I was like] "Come on, man. For really real? And you got me outnumbered crazily? Come on man. *That's* what you do?"

MC Shan Discovers Snow

MC Shan released two singles on Livin' Large ("Hip Hop Roughneck" and "Pee-Nile Reunion") around the time he was introduced a white reggae artist from Toronto by their mutual friend Martin Prince. Born Darrin Kenneth O'Brien, Snow grew up in the Allenbury Gardens housing project and was exposed to the sounds Jamaican immigrants brought with them to Canada. Shan introduced Snow to producers Steve Salem and David Eng (the latter of which had ironically worked with KRS-One and Scott La Rock's early group 12:41), and the three produced his 1992 single "Informer" on EastWest Records. Shan, Snow, and a man named Edmond Leary co-wrote "Informer," which went on to sell 8 million copies, and sat at the top of Billboard's Hot 100 chart for seven consecutive weeks. Just as Shan's solo career was grinding to a halt, this great white hope from the Great White North came into his life.

Dr. Butcher: We was actually all producing an album for him [MC Shan] right before Snow released his record. G Rap was writing, and Large [Professor] was producing. I was doing all the DJing and scratching and stuff, and helping Large with some of the beats, like co-production. It never came out. Next thing you know, Snow came out and took off. Shan didn't need nobody no more. He made a ton of money from Snow. and he disappeared.

"I made a conscious decision not to do no more music with Cold Chillin'," MC Shan said in his 2012 interview with *HipHopDX*. "Now, if you look at the timeline, I produced Snow at that point. I was getting millions of dollars with Snow. I got jerked for every other album that I had before, so why would I go and continue [releasing solo albums]? Who knows how many more albums I had left with Cold Chillin'? I didn't care. I was out on tour with Snow just rappin' one verse and making money on the production side, the publishing side, and everything. So I didn't really care about [my solo career], especially to do another record with Cold Chillin' to get jerked. For what?"

The Tommy Boy-distributed Cold Chillin' sub-label Livin' Large proved to be a failed experiment, and its 1993 dissolution also marked the beginning of a long hiatus in the recording careers of MC Shan and Shanté.

The early '90s was a highly competitive period in Hip-Hop as new labels were springing up all the time, and the genre was turning into a worldwide phenomenon. Ty and Len's company was slipping. If anyone could save Cold Chillin' it would be its marquee artist. Antonio Hardy, aka King Asiatic Nobody Equal, had a clear direction he was going to take his career and all eyes were on him.

11

IT'S HARD BEING THE KANE

"There are a lot of rap artists that are into graffiti, and that look, that fashion. I'm one that's not. To me it symbolizes . . . as if, 'That's what rap is. Here's this place for rap. Put it over here with the graffiti and this dancing and the violence.' I feel that rap is music. I felt like the set I should be on is the same set that Quincy was on," Big Daddy Kane said on *The Arsenio Hall Show* in 1989. Kane was unpleasantly surprised that the entire backdrop of the studio at KCOP in Los Angeles had been transformed into a gritty urban streetscape. Hip-Hop had been marginalized and stereotyped—packaged in a graffiti-covered box, but that year's leading MC felt it needed to break out of that box in order to be on equal footing with Patti LaBelle, Quincy Jones, and the plethora of black entertainers who had garnered the nation's respect before rap came along.

Big Daddy Kane: It wasn't that I was against it. That *is* Hip-Hop. That's Hip-Hop in its truest form, so I'm not against it. It's just that it's not Hip-Hop in that Kane form. Like how the cats from the Bronx come up there b-boy style, and they breakdancing and what not. In the '70s in Brooklyn, we be like, "You going to the jam?" We throwing on some British Walkers, we throw on some straight jeans with the permanent crease in them, a mock neck sweater, Kangol, some fresh Cazals or Yves St. Laurent. That's how we rollin' on some ghetto sexy stuff. We had that type of look because we pretty much got our swagger from the pimps and pushers that we saw riding around in the Sevilles and the deuce and a quarter Buicks. It was like, "Do you see this here silk shit I'm about to come on stage with and these brand new fresh Ballys out the box?" That graffiti stuff and them trash cans don't work with that. I need that sexy stuff that was here when I was here with Quincy Jones. Bring that back out.

Back On the Block

Quincy Jones wielded a lot of power at Warner Bros., where he had his own imprint Qwest Records. He saw something more in Kane than a good looking guy who could rap well. There was musical greatness in him.

Mo Ostin: Quincy Jones had signed with us after he left A&M. He had three albums to go with A&M. He wanted to leave the company for whatever reason—he was disillusioned with Herbie [Alpert] and Jerry [Moss of A&M]. I think I know the reason. What happened is they started a label called Horizon Records, which was a jazz label. They made Tommy LiPuma the head of it, and Quincy felt it should have been him. For whatever reasons he decided to make a change, but getting them to allow him to leave, he made a deal with them where he was to do one album for them, and then we were going to pay them *x* amount of dollars, and he'd be free. So he did *The Dude* as his last album there, which was a huge success, then came to us and started producing Michael [Jackson] and all sorts of other things. We signed him [as a solo artist] I think in '80. He didn't make an album with us until '89. But the first album he made included a lot of rap. He used Big Daddy Kane a lot. *Back On the Block*—that was the one.

Big Daddy Kane: Quincy scared the hell out of me one day, talking about how much I look like Otis [Redding]. Quincy is one of those "Let's go the book! Let's go to the tape!" Digging for information. One of those dudes. He did this one time at a cookout at his house. It was just me, him, Ashford & Simpson and someone else. He was like, "When was you born?" I'm like, "September 10." He was like, "Otis Redding was born September 9. What year were you born?" I'm like, "1968." He's like, "Otis Redding died in 1967. You was born a day after him and born a year after he died. You might be the reincarnation!" For years upon years I wouldn't take no flight around December 10.

Mo Ostin: It [*Back on the Block*] did win a Grammy and it was a terrific album. Quincy's Quincy—he's as good as they come. At that time, because I didn't have a smidgen of what that music was about, he said to me, "Mo, this is the future of bebop." He felt that strongly about it then, so he had a great sense of what the future of music would be and how it would change, and rap, which he called "the new bebop," would become a very, very important part of music. He had real insight.

Released in 1989, the title track for Quincy Jones' *Back On the Block* was a posse cut with Kane, Melle Mel, Kool Moe Dee, and Ice-T. By 1990, the album had gone platinum. In 1991, it won the Grammy Award for Album of the Year, and the "Back On the Block" single won in the Best Rap Performance by a Duo or Group category. The show's producers had refused to televise the brand new Best Rap Performance award two years previous, but by '91, Quincy figuratively kicked down the front door, bringing Big Daddy Kane in with him. The box was coming apart. With one platinum album and three gold albums (*Colors* soundtrack, *Long Live the Kane, It's a Big Daddy Thing*) under his belt, and a Grammy on the way, Kane entered the new decade with an aura of invincibility.

Taste of Chocolate

Ife Kiara: Me, [Kane], and Ice-T were out on a promo tour, and one of our stops was Chicago. We did an in-store in Chicago at a one-stop. Along with the security, we had Chicago PD as security. One of these was a female cop. The next day we had to go to the suburbs, an hour outside of Chicago to do another in-store. When we finish that in-store, I look up and that female cop and her partner, still in uniform, came to *that* in-store. I know that's way out of their district. I didn't say nothing about it. Then I had to put Kane in a limo to go take him to the airport, because he was going somewhere else. It had to be about twenty, twenty-five minutes [later], and I just happen to walk outside, and I see the limo is still there. And I was like, "Why is the limo still here? He's got to catch a plane." I see the store owner, the store promotion people, we had some off-duty cops, all these guys, and they were all standing around and looking in the window. I was like, "What's going on, guys? He needs to get out of here." So they hit the car, and out comes the lady cop fixing her clothes.

Grand Daddy I.U.: I seen Kane beat a guy up. The muthafucka kept talking to him. He had a party, and I guess the nigga was coming to Kane, "Yo yo yo!" all crazy groupie'd out. And he's trying to talk to this nigga, but Kane is having a conversation with a young lady, and the dude keeps interrupting, so he just turned around and threw the muthafucka over the railing. He on some old James Cagney shit. Fucked the nigga up and tossed him over goddamn the railing, and turned around and continued the conversation like that shit never happened.

Big Daddy Kane: Me and Benny [Medina], we were real good at one point. I think we had the same vision, just different paths of getting there. I wanted the commercial success, I just didn't want to sell out to do it. I liked what Heavy D was doing. I always admired Whodini's music. But I didn't want to transform from what I was doing to what Benny wanted, which was Hammer. I remember dude invite me to the crib, and I'm seeing Beverly Johnson and Iman swimming in his pool, telling me to get in. The water's warm. Marvin Gaye stuff is playing. "You like that Marvin stuff, right right?" His chef bringing out lobster and this here. Now I'm a little uncomfortable; I'm like, "Where this here going. What's really good?" Then we get to the point. He wanted to convince me to use Rick James "You and I" since Hammer had just won with "Super Freak." I thought Benny had saw my vision, but now I don't think so as much.

Mister Cee: They [Warner Bros.] saw the success of "Smooth Operator" and "I Get the Job Done," and they wanted Kane to stay on that path. This happens to a lot of artists who become successful off of one or two records, and your record label is gonna say, "We need another 'Smooth Operator'! We need another 'I Get the Job Done'!" Even though Kane had the power to say no, he wasn't gonna say no. At that time, the leverage of power from the artist wasn't there. Later on in the '90s when you had a Roc-A-Fella and you had a No Limit and you're owning your own label, and you can say no to the distributor, and say, "We not doing that. We going this way."

Big Daddy Kane: We [me and Benny] kinda started getting at odds with one another. When something happened on *It's a Big Daddy Thing* album, I just was like, "You know what? Let me hurry up and get out here these last three albums so I can get the hell up out this deal and move on with my life." I went in and rapidly did *Taste of Chocolate*. "I'm a Barry White fan, I'm a Dolemite fan, Barbara Weathers is fine as hell"—it was that type of thing. It was really my autograph book—People I looked up to or wanted to smash.

Jeff Smith: That was a big departure for him. Here he had done *Long Live the Kane* and *It's a Big Daddy Thing,* which was *great*. Unbelievable. And then he did *Chocolate.* I remember driving him somewhere and said, "So Kane, everybody tells me you're a big fucking pussy now." He said, "No, Jeff Smith. It ain't like that, man. See you gotta be hard for the fellas, but you gotta be soft for the ladies." He did one song with Barry White. He was just *enamored* with Barry White. Everybody loved Barry White to begin with, but when you saw Barry White with the fur coats, he was like a real pimp. He *was* hard for the fellas and soft for the ladies. He could do all that crooning.

Andre Booth: He [Kane] said he was looking for something for Barry White, and I told him, "I got the perfect joint." I played it for him and he said, "That's it." We went on out to LA, booked this studio, and went in and cut it. Me coming in doing my thing with Kane and Barry, they had a respect for musicianship. They was asking all kinds of questions. "Who's playing the horn?" I would say, "No, that's me. That's all keyboards."

Jeff Smith: Kane was looking down the road at Hip-Hop as a young man's game, but it was a reckoning for him. And it didn't work out well. It's not that it was bad. It didn't connect. Maybe people weren't ready for it yet. I don't know exactly.

Mister Cee: *Taste of Chocolate* come and we do "Cause I Can Do It Right." Our core fans was starting to rebel against us. And then he does a record with Barry White called "All of Me," which is a straight up ballad. Our core fans didn't want to hear that from Kane.

Cut Chemist: He leaned a little bit more towards the ladies kind of thing, and things got a little sexier. A little less b-boy and little bit more pimp. My shit was hat to the back, tough rhymes. Then when you start putting on silk, and start wearing too much shiny purple . . . the music reflected that too. The subject matter got to something I didn't care about as much. *Taste of Chocolate*—that's really the one where I was like, "Ah, there's really not much on here."

George DuBose: One of the comments I heard about that [album] cover is that Kane's arms are too skinny. They said his arms looked like chicken wings. The concept was a rip off for me. He told me the name of the album was going to be *Taste of Chocolate,* and the first thing that came to my mind was Ohio Players' *Honey,* back in the '70s. And I remember the cover of that record being a naked woman covered in honey, so it wasn't too far of a stretch for me to pour chocolate all over a black girl and call it *Taste of Chocolate.*

Eugene Shelton: He started wearing suits and silks and all that before Jay-Z and all these other guys. You dressed down, not up. But Kane dressed up. I think there was a backlash because not everyone was doing that. And there was this talk of him being too R&B and not rap enough, not hard enough. But he was just being himself. I saw an image. I saw someone with a very dynamic personality, someone my sons looked up to very much.

A foot-long Tootsie Roll holder was created as a promotional item for *Taste of Chocolate.* Printed on the packaging was the phrase: "Ain't Nothin' Vanilla About It"—a thinly veiled swipe at Vanilla Ice who had become one of the biggest rap stars the world had ever seen up to that point, and had appropriated the notches Kane had shaved into his own eyebrows. Much like *It's a Big Daddy Thing, Taste of Chocolate* exhibited a diverse musical palate with production by Prince Paul, Cool V, Mister Cee, Andre Booth, and Kane himself. The guest stars were even more diverse, ranging from comedian Rudy Ray Moore trading insults with the MC while in his Dolemite character, to Malcolm X's daughter Gamilah Shabazz rapping with Kane about black consciousness. *The Source,* the magazine that was quickly becoming the gold standard for Hip-Hop record criticism, gave *Taste of Chocolate* a rave review, but due to the paucity of hits, the album failed to go gold like its predecessors. Kane always had ballads on his albums, going back to "The Day You're Mine" on *Long Live the Kane*, but the decision to make the Barry White duet a single with a video (ridiculed a few years later on *Beavis and Butthead*) pushed that side of his music front and center.

Prince of Darkness

The following year, Kane released *Prince of Darkness*, continuing on with his "Blackanova" image and doubling down on the ballads. Kane self-produced the lion's share of the hard rhyming tracks, one of which featured Q-Tip from A Tribe Called Quest and Busta Rhymes from Leaders of the New School—two fresh-faced MCs whose stars were on the ascent. These uptempo songs were interspersed by syrupy love raps produced by Michael Stokes, who had taken the place of Andre Booth.

Big Daddy Kane: He called himself "Music Mike"—great keyboard player that was deep into jazz and new jack swing, but he had played stuff on some of Eric B's songs a year or two prior. So he had a Hip-Hop influence as well, so he could get it when you explain stuff. He don't get too technical, he don't get too musical. He knew how to stay in pocket. He was a real talented dude. I ain't gonna lie, it's songs on there that I like, but I wasn't too crazy about it [*Prince of Darkness*].

Jeff Smith: He [Kane] was really like a king, he was so beautiful. I know. Listen, I was in love with Kane, but everybody was! When he made the *Prince of Darkness* album, they got some photographer who comes to LA, and they're gonna shoot this thing. He's all up in this Barry White thing. He's got this chocolate brown suit, and he's ready to go into it. He had broken his arm. He had some kind of motorcycle accident I think it was. So he had the suit cut so the left arm had buttons on it or it was slit open. But he couldn't tie his tie. That would be a complicated thing to do with a broken arm. So he says, "Jeff Smith, can you tie my tie?" I got up on a chair looking in a mirror. Of course it was a photographer's studio, so they had the three-sided mirror so I could see every angle to it. In order to do it you have to get your face right up alongside of his face. I remember tying his tie, and I was just about to leave the company. I had a wonderful time there, but I had gotten another opportunity. I was gonna go to Ticketmaster. And it reminded me of the final shot of *All About Eve,* where you're looking in the mirror and you see all the different angles of it. I thought, "If they could see me now." It was a very happy moment for me; very bittersweet because I was leaving these guys. Who knew which way they were gonna go or which way I was gonna go? I had a wonderful run with them; I loved them all and wanted them to do better than they did. To a degree, there wasn't much more we could do for them because we didn't know how to help them . . . His hand was broken and they had to shoot it at an angle, and they had a beautiful girl in the foreground, who was kind of covered and very mysterious.

Big Daddy Kane: The one where Mister Cee is dissing me called "DJs Get No Credit"—I wrote that. I never wrote for Scoob or Scrap though. Mister Cee was highly upset at me at one point about stuff that was going on on the road. Once he complained about it all, I wrote it all in song, and I said, "Tell the world."

Mister Cee: I used to always complain about stuff I was going through on the road like carrying the DJ cases. I would have to carry everything back to the hotel by myself. When the show was over everybody got broads, and they done took the van back to the hotel, and I'm still at the arena by myself with the records and the cases lugging these shits back to the hotel by myself. But I would never complain to Kane directly. I would always complain to the road manager or to security, anyone that wanted to hear my gripe. They would always go back to Kane. "Yo, your man is bitching about carrying cases. Why we not helping him?" A couple weeks ago, Kane brought this up and was like, "Yo, I just want to apologize to you because you was right back then. I should have got people to help you." I'm like, "Yo Kane, it's 2018!" He was like, "Nah man, I should have helped you out more. Everything that you was saying that you was going through, you was right."

Sex

Around the time of the *Prince of Darkness* album cycle in 1991–92, Kane's public image took an interesting turn, with the help of Benny Medina and Warner Bros. publicists Eugene Shelton and Liz Rosenberg.

Big Daddy Kane: *Playgirl* was me and Gene Shelton. We sitting around getting drunk one night after getting into *Essence Magazine*. He was like, "[*Essence* editor] Susan Taylor said you're the second rapper to be in this." We accomplished pretty much everything. I was like, "Shit, ain't nothing left but *Playgirl!*" He was like, "I know you don't want that." I just looked at him. He was like, "Well shit, let's go get it!" That's how it started, just from us having a few drinks and a joke.

Eugene Shelton: That was his idea. I just said, "Okay," and I picked up the phone and got him in it. It was as simple as that. It opened the door. That led to an article in *USA Today,* it led to an appearance on Rick Dees' late night talk show. Rick Dees asked him, "Why did you do this?" He turned around and said, "That man right there. My publicist." I'm on national TV with Big Daddy Kane. He said I'm responsible for putting him in *Playgirl,* but that was his idea. Burt Reynolds, Jim Brown, a number of other celebrity males [were in *Playgirl*]. It was the craze at the time. It was a very tasteful photo shoot. Big Daddy Kane had sex appeal, so that was his calling card. Women loved him.

Liz Rosenberg: I had been working with Madonna since late 1982. I was representing a variety of acts. I was representing Color Me Badd. I think I mentioned Kane to Madonna. I must have liked him or his music. Madonna would do an annual visit to the hospitals to give out toys for the holidays. Somehow I assembled this group of people all together at New York Hospital. We all assembled and Color Me Badd sang a lot. Lots of times you visit for the parents more than the kids because it's kind of a nice distraction for them. These kids are all pretty sick. Madonna sort of led the way, as she does. It was all very harmonious. Everybody knew what they were there for.

Big Daddy Kane: It was white kids who knew who Color Me Badd and Madonna was, who didn't even know who I was.

Liz Rosenberg: This thing stuck that in my mind was when a mother came over to me and said . . . this is Madonna, not Kane, but she said, "This is the first time my son has smiled since he's been here." That particular moment helped me stay with Madonna for a really long time through lots of other things, because I remembered that parent telling me that.

Big Daddy Kane: Madonna talked to one of the kids and said, "Do you know who that is? That's Big Daddy Kane! He's a famous rapper. Say, 'Ain't no half-steppin'!'" I'm sitting there like "*Oh my God*." I'm like, "Yo, Madonna know my music." I'm sitting there freaking out. Buggin.' I'm like, "Thank you. Thank you." Then she tells me that she thinks I'm attractive, and she's doing this book and would love to have me in it. I'm like, "I'd be honored to be in a book with you." She said, "Just so you know, it's gonna be nude photos." I'm like, "Well hey, even better, baby!"

Liz Rosenberg: I think Madonna's message was sexual liberation, mostly for women, and not to keep these conversations and the whole concept of sex in the closet. It's not a bad thing. It was so revolutionary at that time. She got endless amounts of criticism for doing it, not that she cared. There was a whole buildup about it, and she got tons of shit. Of course it [*SEX*] was a huge best seller and did really, really well. There were very few defenders of her vision and what she was trying to accomplish with the book.

Big Daddy Kane: As sexy as she looked in the nude, she was just so down to earth and so humble. I was still in that fan place where I can't believe this is happening.

Published in October of 1992 by Warner Books/Maverick Callaway, Madonna's photo book *SEX* came sealed in a giant condom-style wrapper and contained multiple images of herself, Kane and Naomi Campbell in various stages of undress, engaged in posed sexual acts. The only other rapper who appeared in the book was Vanilla Ice. It sold half a million copies in its first week of release.

Big Daddy Kane: Benny Medina reached out to me one time and said Patti LaBelle needs a favor. I'm like, "Excuse me?" "Her son is a big fan of yours and wants you to autograph a poster for him." So I'm like, "Okay, cool." I swung by Benny's office and signed it, then I said, "Yo, do me a favor. When you give it her, tell Patti don't be scaring me like that, because I got excited thinking that we doing a song together." Then Benny hit me a few days later and is like, "I gave Patti your message, and she said y'all can do that too. She said she's working on her new album now." I had a vision and Benny had the same vision. He saw the big picture, and he knew I was willing to go there. I think the path he wanted me to go was a path where there's no return.

Cut Chemist: Kane wasn't gonna let his style and his bravado slip. Whether he's wearing his shirt or not on the cover, he's spitting rhymes. That's his thing. He knows that. He's not gonna ever let up on that, even if he does a couple songs for his pimps and ladies or whoever.

Big Daddy Kane: Back then, with a diehard Hip-Hop fan, one good thing you can count on is they gonna test you. Even though you might see me half naked in this magazine, or dressed in some shiny ass stuff over here, you're gonna run up on me backstage when I'm at the Apollo. Or you're gonna run up on me at some corner store somewhere and test me. And what you're gonna do after that is go back to your people and be like, "Nah, that nigga still nice. He still a beast."

"Once the undisputed King of the Rap hill, Kane has received sharp criticism from the hardcore rap audience for his collaborative commercial R&B efforts," *The Source* wrote in its January 1992 review of *Prince of Darkness*. "Whether he'll create other impact classics such as 'Set It Off,' and 'Ain't No Half Steppin' remains to be seen as Kane tries to find a balance between a streetwise smooth-operator and a love drenched crooner. R&B is Black music and it can coexist with Hip-Hop, but on this album the results are uneven."

Big Daddy Kane: After *Prince of Darkness,* I'm still hanging at parties with Quincy Jones and rubbing elbows with the best of them, getting drunk with Gerald Levert. I'm doing my thing, but after that album I'm seeing it in magazines—"Kane fell off."

Mister Cee: The success of Heavy D was so powerful in the '90s, with his crossover records. They both had the same element—the rapper/dancer, they had two dancers—had the same package, same element. They both had the sex appeal. The only difference—Kane's a slim, dark-skinned dude; he's a fat, light-skinned dude. Overall, Heavy had a couple more better records that extended his recording lifespan more than Kane did as far as those big radio records.

Looks Like a Job For . . .

Big Daddy Kane: With *Taste of Chocolate* and *Prince of Darkness,* really I was trying to rush albums. I got one or two good songs and everything else just be trash, that way we ain't gotta focus on three or four singles. After the first single, maybe the second single, we can focus on the next album. And I think Benny caught on to what I was doing, but then he made me wait a year. "Nah, you gonna sit this one down before you bounce." Now I'm hearing people saying, "He fell off." I'm like, "We gotta take it to the streets then. We gotta do it right." Then I'm reaching out to famous producers. Now all of a sudden they too busy. I'm like, "Oh, okay. I see what it is." At that point in time I'm like, "Yo, we need to take it back to *Long Live The Kane.*" We brought it those type of producers that had that, and really went in that direction—Trackmasters, Easy Mo Bee, and Large Professor I believe. That's what we was trying to do with that particular album [*Looks Like a Job For . . .*].

Easy Mo Bee: At the time, the innovators of the SP-1200 [sampler], or just sampling period, that I looked up to and influenced me was Marley Marl, then you got Ced Gee from Ultramagnetic MCs, you have Hurby Luv Bug, you have Howie Tee, Jazzy Jay, Skeff Anselm. The things that they were doing in sampling is what inspired me to do my thing. I think everything that we did following all of those names that I was inspired by,

I think we all trying to emulate that [on *Looks Like a Job For . . .*]. We all wanted to be the Marley Marls and Ced Gees and Hurby Luv Bugs and Howie Tees.

On his final album for Cold Chillin'/Reprise, Kane dispelled a pervasive rumor that he was stricken with AIDS ("Give It To Me"), and also expressed a distaste for the gangsta rap that had been sweeping the Hip-Hop world for the last few years, before launching into his own crime rhyme ("The Beef Is On") to prove to his naysayers that he had topical versatility. An Easy Mo Bee remix of his Bomb Squad-produced song "'Nuff Respect" from the *Juice* soundtrack was included. The film that made a movie star out of Tupac Shakur also marked a turning point, as rap's third generation (represented by Cypress Hill and Naughty By Nature) was beginning to supplant the heavyweights of the late '80s. No more sexy record covers—*Looks Like a Job For . . .* featured a black and white photo of a hooded Kane with a gritty cityscape in the background. There was only one love song—a duet with Salt-N-Pepa DJ Spinderella. Benny Medina's decision to delay the release (completed in the summer of 1992) for a full year after it had been recorded only exacerbated the contrast between the '88 rap style found throughout on the album and that of the rapidly evolving Hip-Hop sound of the early '90s.

Big Daddy Kane: I think that album failed because of me. Even though I think I was spitting incredible rhymes on there, at that point in time MCs weren't ahead of the beat like [they had been] during the Kane/G Rap/Chuck D/KRS/Rakim era. This was the weed smoking era of the '90s, and everybody was behind the beat, going a lot slower. I think my flow was real dated. I was too aggressive. So I think what I did hurt the album, not the production. It was a five-album deal, and once I did *Looks Like A Job For . . .* I was getting the support I needed from Warner Bros. and I thought me and Benny was starting to come back. Even he was like, "Yo, you need some street stuff," and he tried to put me with Kay Gee from Naughty By Nature. I was actually gonna stay with Warner Bros. I knew I had to do at least one radio joint, so I did the "Very Special" joint with Spinderella. As soon as the album was done, that's what Benny wanted to put out first. At that particular time, Ty had to fight for me, like, "Yeah, that can come down the line. We need to get the street edge back for Kane." Benny agreed, but they didn't promote the first single "How U Get A Record Deal." We had to get a cheaper video director than we wanted to use, and they didn't really promote it at all. It was out for maybe a month or so, and then Benny moved on to hurrying up to getting "Very Special" out. I was like, "You know what? I'm done. I'm done." This lawyer I had named Paul Marshall was cool with whoever was running MCA at the time. Warner was offering me $800,000 to stay. Paul was like, "I can get you a million plus over here at MCA." That's my man. He made the deal happen just on the strength. It had nothing to do with Kane popularity.

Big Daddy Kane, the flagship artist of Cold Chillin' Records, was gone. He released five albums for the label in as many years—more than anyone else. After he signed with MCA, he made one album (1994's *Daddy's Home*) and eventually moved to a short-lived Mercury imprint called The Label for one album (*Veteranz Day,* 1998).

In the maelstrom that was the 1990s, slow record sales weren't the only concern Cold Chillin' would have. Two unforeseen circumstances almost brought the label to its knees, both of which challenged the very essence of Hip-Hop.

12
F.G.O.S.

Biz Markie was at it again, and another album of his was in the works for Cold Chillin'/ Warner Bros. It was 1991 and *I Need a Haircut* had a lot to live up to, being that his previous album *The Biz Never Sleeps* went gold and contained the platinum hit "Just a Friend." From the George DuBose cover shot depicting Cutmaster Cool V as a barber, standing behind his cousin Biz with a chainsaw held up to his head, to the Biz/Cool V co-production (with Ivan "DJ Doc" Rodriguez behind the boards), and lyrical topics ranging from girl trouble to bathroom humor, Biz's third full-length was spiritually in line with its predecessors.

I Need a Haircut

George DuBose: The idea was his hair is so tough; it broke all the clippers, so they had to use a chainsaw to cut his hair. Warner Bros. had given me $15,000 to do a package—including the photo shooting, the stylist, the hair and makeup, clothing if there was any, designing of the whole project. Dee Joseph, who was the project manager at Cold Chillin', had a house in upstate New York. She said when the shoot was over, she wanted that chainsaw. After the shoot, I saw Cool V walking off with the chainsaw, putting it in the trunk of his car. I said, "Hey Vaughan, I gotta have that. It's for Dee." He says, "No, I want it." We got into this tug-of-war. Literally. I got my hands on it, he's got his hands on it, tugging back and forth. I said, "Dee says she wants it!" He says, "I want it!" Finally Biz came out and says, "I'm paying for it. I get it." He was right. Warner Bros. was paying for it, but it was Biz's money so to speak. Vaughan [Cool V] got the chainsaw.

Dee Joseph: Apparently he needed to do some trimming in New Jersey.

Alone Again . . . Naturally

Biz's awfully/incredibly sung choruses of recognizable songs had become his trademark, and could be heard on "Road Block" (The Guess Who's "American Woman"), "Kung Fu" (Gregory Isaacs' "Lonely Soldier"), and another song towards the end of the album called "Alone Again," in which he belted out the chorus to Irish singer-songwriter Gilbert O'Sullivan's 1972 hit "Alone Again (Naturally)" over a long sample of the same tune.

George DuBose: I was doing the graphics for *I Need a Haircut*, and I remember reading the packaging text that came from Warner Bros. with the lyrics and credits and everything they typed up. I had to mark this typewriter paper up with a special code for the typesetter, so he knew what font to use and how big to make the fonts. I remember seeing, "All lyrics by Biz Markie." Of course he did a cover of "Alone Again (Naturally)" by Gilbert O'Sullivan and didn't give Gilbert any credit at all.

Jeff Smith: I told them they shouldn't do it. I called Len and Ty. I was screaming bloody murder. I said, "You don't understand. This isn't some small sample. You stole the *whole* hook, and you're singing the chorus. And this guy [Gilbert O'Sullivan] only had one hit. I think this is going to go badly." And that was the moment that sampling as an issue was really coming to the fore. You really had this whole thing of, "When are you borrowing and when are you stealing?" If you pick up a bass line from here or you borrow from sounds there, and make a pastiche, that's one thing. That's a musical collage. That's totally defensible as far as I'm concerned. And especially since it's become a very prevalent thing. There was no doubt in my mind when I heard it. I went running to Fred Brown who I think was doing the legal. From my perspective, it was clear that this was more than borrowing. It went to the core of the song. He was singing over the lyric. It was very clearly a problem to me and they had it scheduled as a single. "You can't put that out! If *I'm* thinking that way, imagine what the publisher is going to think."

Ife Kiara: When he [Biz Markie] did his album and the pop department took him out, he was supposed to go for a thirty-day promo tour. I think there was some problems with sampling. He was told not to sample something, and there still was the sample on the album, and they had to pull the whole album, and then pull him off the road. That just squashed all of that.

Jeff Smith: This is exactly at the time that I was leaving. One of the last things I said on the way out the door was, "Kane, you look like a big pussy," and "Biz, you really shouldn't put this record out. You're asking for trouble with it." I left, and the trouble followed him. It's not a surprise at all. It was just so *blatant* to me.

Aaron Fuchs: To this day, I don't know what matters to people in the music business and when it matters. For me, as somebody who was looking at the broad context of things, rather than setting a legal precedent, it showed me that Lenny Fichtelberg wasn't somebody I was gonna make a very long term bet on, because he put himself in a position of being sued willfully. That's when you make yourself vulnerable. He went to Gilbert O'Sullivan and said, "Can we do this deal?" He said no, and they put it out anyway. I'm much more micro at that time. I'm going, "Wow, I don't know what this guy is thinking."

Cut Chemist: I don't think at that point it was really on peoples' radar about how this music was being made. In the exec's office they were like, "Yeah, this is cool. Hey yeah you used that. Whatever." As long as no one is saying anything; but then someone said something. But clearances I think go back to "The Adventures of Grandmaster Flash On the Wheels of Steel" [Sugar Hill, 1981]. He had to clear "Good Times" [by Chic] and so did "Rapper's Delight." They didn't get away with just using those records.

Road Block

On November 11, 1991, Gilbert O'Sullivan's publishing company Grand Upright Music Limited filed suit against Warner Brothers Records, Inc., its distributor WEA International Inc., Marcel Hall ("*known professionally as Biz Markie*"), Biz Markie

Productions, Inc., Cool V Productions, Inc., Cold Chillin' Records, Inc., Bizmarkie Music, Inc., Cold Chillin' Music Publishing, Inc., Tyrone Williams, and Benny Medina. The plaintiff's cause was listed as Copyright Infringement. On December 19, U.S. District Court Judge Kevin Thomas Duffy ordered the defendants to "notify all wholesalers, consignees, retailers, and other entities to which the Biz Markie album has been distributed that the Biz Markie album, entitled 'I Need a Haircut' . . . must be immediately withdrawn from display and must no longer be offered for sale." By December 23, the defendants were to furnish the plaintiff's counsel and file with the court a report of their compliance, "and the report shall include the identities and addresses of the entities from whom the Album was recalled and the number of Albums recalled from each entity." The Turtles had recently sued Tommy Boy recording artists De La Soul for using a piece of the 1969 song "You Showed Me" on the 1989 song "Transmitting Live From Mars," but it was settled out of court, and the De La Soul album *3 Feet High and Rising* was never pulled. Biz Markie's case was unprecedented.

Tom Silverman: They had to actually pull the records out of the store. Only time anybody was such a dick basically that they forced that to happen.

"We said no to it because it was a comedic thing, but they still did it," said Gilbert O'Sullivan on a television interview.

Fly Ty: I'm gonna tell you exactly what it was—they didn't want this black guy using his music.

"I used to listen to 'Alone Again' when I was little," Biz Markie told actor Tommy Davidson in a tape recorded conversation for *The Source*. "I still listen to it now—but he [Gilbert O'Sullivan] broke my heart trying to sue my motherfuckin' ass."

Dee Joseph: Warner Bros. had never been sued for anything like this. "What do you mean? What do you mean you stole somebody's song? What do you mean you're using other people's music?" Their legal people, I think it like kind of flipped their heads out. I don't think they had been in that position. But everybody was doing it—biting beats from other people, using other people's music. That was how they made their music. And here Warner Bros. makes a nice deal with Cold Chillin' and it gives them a lot of money, and then they're being told that they can't sell this particular product because they ripped somebody else off and they owe a lot of money. That didn't sit well with everybody at Warner Bros. I think there was a lot more attention paid from that point on. You had to really find out where the music was coming from, and get your clearances together, and pay the people that are supposed to get it.

Monica Lynch: I think part of it was that everybody knew that song "Alone Again (Naturally)." It was a big, fat pop record that even back in '91 was still a record that was in the pop classic milieu. I would just say it was the magnitude, the hugeness of the fact that it was "Alone Again (Naturally)"—a song that everybody fucking knew. I don't think that everyone would say, "Oh yeah, the Turtles 'You Showed Me.'" Well that was a little, earlier, '60s, hippie. I don't know that every kid whose sister had a record collection or whose parents had a record collection were as familiar with that as they were with the Gilbert O'Sullivan song. There were all sorts of sample issues with De La Soul, and it served a cautionary tale. This was uncharted territory. You can say any number of James Brown songs were sampled ad nauseam in the '80s by Hip-Hop artists, and I'm sure there was probably money that some parties never received for these usages. When the big fussy, wussy rockstars started getting involved . . ."It's our art! They're stealing!" the labels and the publishers were responsive. On Facebook not very long ago when homeboy from Steely Dan died, I posted the letter that we had received from I guess it was MCA Music Publishing. It was a cease and desist for the usage of a Steely Dan song on De La Soul. What was funny is they didn't even spell Donald Fagen's name right in the letter, dated Feb. 23, 1989.

Tom Silverman: In the early days, we didn't understand sampling. The Turtles was just that their daughter heard a sample in one of the interstitial pieces and they said we want to get paid for that. But I think Gilbert O'Sullivan wanted to stop it. He just didn't like the idea. I would say artists in those days really didn't understand sampling and didn't like it. The economics hadn't developed, and the people didn't know what it cost to sample a record. To me sampling is really near and dear—the fifth pillar of Hip-Hop.

Hip-Hop could not probably have broken without sampling. Every single Hip-Hop hit from '79 to '90-something has had a sample or replayed sample. I can't really name a big Hip-Hop record that doesn't have some interpolation or sample in it. It was the re-contextualization of old music in a new way that's part of the genius of Hip-Hop.

Kenneth David Freundlich (lead attorney for Warner Brothers Records, Inc. and WEA International Inc. in *Grand Upright Music v. Warner Brothers Rec*): Cold Chillin' got made an example of, for something that was already widespread. That set the tone for the future of music and the future of monetizing sampling.

Arthur Baker: I wanted to be the test case. When I did "Put the Needle To the Record" [by Criminal Element Orchestra on Criminal Records, 1987], I sampled Prince and I sampled all this shit right in front. But you need to have a hit record. Where there's a hit, there's a risk, as they say. My thing did okay, but it wasn't a big hit, so no one came after me to sue me. To me, being the test case was gonna be really important. Everyone remembers the Gilbert O'Sullivan case. It could have been an interesting thing to have as part of your history, that you have the test case for sampling.

After Warner Bros. settled for an undisclosed sum, it scared labels into employing people specifically to find samples in recordings before being released, as a precaution to avoid future lawsuits.

Bill Bentley (VP Media Relations, Warner Bros. Records): Sherwin Strull was a fanatic music listener who kind of knew every song ever recorded more or less, and they put him down in a little room in the Warner basement. I think they locked him in there, and he went through every rap/Hip-Hop record to pick out the samples. It actually drove him insane.

Mama Said Knock You Out

The future of sampling—the very art form that Marley Marl had mastered in the mid '80s by jerry-rigging delay units to a drum machine—was now being called into question. Marley's own work wasn't immune from the hailstorm of lawsuits either.

After befriending LL Cool J when he was invited as a guest on the *In Control* radio show and having success reappropriating Biz Markie's beat as "Jingling Baby (Remixed and Still Jingling)" for LL, Marley was commissioned in 1990 to produce what was to become *Mama Said Knock You Out*. LL Cool J's Grammy-winning double platinum album was a triumph for himself, his label Def Jam, and his new producer. However, trouble stemmed from those same drum sounds that had been the source of so much controversy during the Bridge Wars several years earlier.

Aaron Fuchs: I had left the multi-track to "Impeach [the President]" with Marley because I had the bright idea, again being of an older generation and having these textbook ideas like, "Hey, let's cut Spoonie over a funk track instead of a Hip-Hop track!" It would be something somebody older would think, instead of chopping up the funk and creating Hip-Hop out of it. I had left it with him and while it was in his possession, he ran off the drum track and he used it for *Mama Said Knock You Out* [by LL Cool J]. And I sued. I got a settlement. How long does it take for the business to learn something? How many times does something have to happen before somebody gets the message? Some people say, "How could you do that to the guy who made 'Take It Off' [by Spoonie Gee] for you?" I didn't name him [Marley] in the suit. It didn't cost him a dollar. I got the money out of CBS and Def Jam.

Here's a Sample

Monica Lynch: A lot of stuff was a pain in the ass to clear, but it also took money out of the artists' pockets. If they had to give up a lot of their publishing for a sample, there's a big incentive there to not sample, or to skate along that very thin line where it sounds like, but it's not quite . . ..

Easy Mo Bee: When Biz went through the sample lawsuit thing, that totally changed what I did. I can remember clearly, because I was managed by Rush Producer's Management. Big Daddy Kane was managed by Rush Artist Management, but they created another department for producers. Rest in peace and shout to one of the greatest managers that I ever had before, Francesca Spero. One day she called a meeting over at 298 Elizabeth Street in Manhattan. She called all of us producers together and she passed out a memo that she typed up. It had a list of all of these names. Steve Miller Band was on there, Prince, Anita Baker. She said, "Okay, you see that list?" We like, "Yeah." "You see those names?" We all said, "Yeah." She said, "Stay away from them! Don't touch them." And we was like, "What do you mean?" She was like, "Don't *ever* sample or touch these artists." Mind you, this was right after what Biz went through, and De La Soul had went through it too with *3 Feet High and Rising*. This is the reason why now, part as the production manager for a roster of producers, she had to actually call up a meeting with this list. I remember leaving that meeting and going home and getting in my car. Yo, I was depressed because I actually felt like, "Yo, what I'm gonna *do?*" You don't know how many names was on that list and how many different plans I had for like touching up certain samples. That's probably one of the greatest things that could have ever happened to me, because it challenged me to take what I do to a higher level. In other words, stop relying on just loops and be a bit more creative than that. After I got past the depression of not being able to sample this or sample that, I went home and I just really did some serious thinking. I said, "You know what? Why don't you *play* samples?" In other words, when you cut on a keyboard, all keyboards have a bank of sounds—factory sounds that are already in the keyboard. You cut the keyboard on, you run the click, you get a rhythm going, and with all the factory sounds that's in the keyboard, you sit and you play something that's original. In my mind, I was like, "Why you can't take a bass, some strings, horn, guitar, put a band into the SP-1200 and *play* that shit?" That meeting, that depression, that memo changed my life. It changed my style, and that style became to this day a habit. Or the habit became a style. From avoiding samples, I started playing what I call "playing samples." To this day, by mistake, it wasn't even planned, that habit became my style. The style we talking about, you hear it in so many of the songs that I did for Big Daddy Kane. I'm talking about on his later albums. You hear that style in particular on "Flava In Ya Ear" by Craig Mack and "Everything Remains Raw" by Busta Rhymes. "It's a Party" featuring Zhane. All the guitar is in "Flava In Ya Ear" is just two notes transposed, that's it. It's one guitar that's transposed in two different notes. And just keep repeating. Add drums, add other elements and voila! Records like "Poison" [by Kool G Rap & DJ Polo] and "Duck Alert" by Craig G—what I'm talking about is the same concept. Marley put instruments into the machine and played back something original. It's just about being original, man. We love the samples, but you can't just always rely on a loop. That challenged me to take myself to a higher level.

All Samples Cleared!

Biz Markie's final album for Cold Chillin'/Warner Bros. was released in 1993—it would be his last for a decade, as he began to concentrate more on live DJing. The full-length bore no hits, but it lived up to its title.

Tom Silverman: They called the album *All Samples Cleared!,* which is great. Classic.

George DuBose: I had to wind up building a courtroom. This is before computers, so I had to take one picture with the camera on the tripod of Biz as the criminal with Cool V [as a lawyer], and another picture of Biz as the judge, make two big prints, cut them together with a razor blade, then copy that print with a camera, then use that for the cover. So I had my own assembly there. If you look really closely on the [cover art for the] vinyl, you can see on the court document with Cold Chillin' letterhead, it says in big letters at the bottom: "F.G.O.S."—"Fuck Gilbert O'Sullivan."

The majority of the full-length records on Cold Chillin', most of which were released in partnership with Warner Bros./Reprise between 1987 and 1993.

Left: *Rap Attack* radio show host Mr. Magic would often host performances by his hand-selected Juice Crew All Stars, including this 1987 show in the Bronx (flyer courtesy of Cut Chemist).

Right: Mr. Magic, aka "Sir Juice," whose taste and ability to break records (figuratively and literally) formed the basis of the Cold Chillin' label (photo by George DuBose).

Roxanne Shanté was discovered at the age of fourteen by producer Marley Marl and became an immediate sensation with her diss records. "Have a Nice Day" photo shoot, 1987 (photo by George DuBose).

MC Shan (left) and "super producer" Marley Marl (right) changed the way Hip-Hop records were made. At the shoot for Marley's *In Control, Volume 1* album, 1988 (photo by George DuBose).

Biz Markie (left) and DJ Cool V (right) enjoying some Diabolical Crunch™ at *The Biz Never Sleeps* shoot, 1989 (photo by George DuBose).

Original Hip-Hop crooner TJ Swan (left) and Biz Markie (right) at "Make the Music With Your Mouth, Biz" shoot, 1986 (photo by George DuBose).

(L-R): DJ Mister Cee, dancers Scrap Lover and Scoob Lover, Big Daddy Kane at "I'll Take You There" shoot, 1988 (photo by George DuBose).

Scoob Lover adds the finishing touches to Big Daddy Kane's "Cameo" hairstyle, modeled after Larry Blackmon from the funk group Cameo, 1989 (photo by Al Pereira).

Kool G Rap & DJ Polo with their posse, including airborne dancers TCF Crew, at *Road To the Riches* shoot, 1989 (photo by George DuBose).

Marley Marl and most of the Juice Crew at Republic Airport in Farmingdale, NY, for *In Control, Volume 1* shoot, 1988. Opposite (L-R): Master Ace, Craig G, Big Daddy Kane, Marley Marl, MC Shan, DJ Steady Pace, Biz Markie, Kool G Rap (photos by George DuBose).

BIZ MARKIE

Master Ace with Biz Markie doll at "Me and the Biz" shoot, 1990 (photo by George DuBose).

Master Ace at *Take a Look Around* shoot, 1990. The cover art was modeled after Curtis Mayfield's album *Curtis*. After leaving Cold Chillin', Master Ace permanently changed the spelling of his name to Masta Ace (photo by George DuBose).

Right: Craig G and Marley Marl at "Droppin' Science" shoot, 1988 (photo by George DuBose).

Below: Grand Daddy I.U. on the steps of Grand Central Station in Manhattan for *Smooth Assassin* shoot, 1990 (photo by George DuBose).

The Genius, clad in photographer George DuBose's father's Syrian bathrobe, at *Words From The Genius* shoot, 1991. The Genius co-founded Wu-Tang Clan, whose debut single was released the following year (photo by George DuBose).

Above Left: Cold Chillin'/Warner Bros. letterman jacket (courtesy of Dee Joseph).

Above Right: A mouse-sized promotional plastic toilet for Biz Markie's "T.S.R. (Toilet Stool Rap)" (courtesy of Warner Bros. Records).

Bottom (L-R): Cold Chillin' co-owner Tyrone "Fly Ty" Williams, VP Dee Joseph, VP of promotion Earl Sellers, co-owner Len Fichtelberg in their Broadway office on the day of signing the partnership deal between Cold Chillin' and Warner Bros. Records, 1987 (courtesy of Dee Joseph).

13
LIVE AND LET DIE

Kool G Rap: I was so into hardcore rap. I lived, ate, shit, and breathed hardcore rap. I'm N.W.A, I'm Geto Boys, I'm G Rap personally, and I'm so into other artists—Slick Rick and all the multitude of other artists that was out that had that hard edge. I didn't wanna hear nothing else. I didn't wanna do nothing else. If it wasn't a gangster movie or something about some gangster shit, I wasn't really into it.

Kool Is Back

Kool G Rap was a survivor—he had survived his brain surgery and he was determined to survive Hip-Hop's changing atmosphere. By the turn of the decade, the sub-genre dubbed "reality rap" by Ice-T and "gangsta rap" by the media began capturing the general public's imagination. Cassettes, compact discs and records by west coast juggernaut N.W.A (Niggaz Wit Attitudes), their lead MC Ice Cube who had recently defected to start a solo career, and a slew of three-initialed disciples such as CMW (Compton's Most Wanted), ATL (Above The Law), and SCC (South Central Cartel) flew off the shelves with very little airplay and oftentimes no major label backing. It was a ground up movement, and Kool G Rap & DJ Polo, who had already been releasing *street shit* since 1986, were there to catch the wave. With Marley Marl out of the picture at Cold Chillin', the duo got another Queens native named William Paul Mitchell, aka Large Professor, for the majority of production duties. At only sixteen, Large Professor was a wizard on the E-mu Systems SP-1200 sampler, which had become the go-to machine for Hip-Hop producers. While recording demos for his own group Main Source, he was taught about the secret menu built into the SP-1200 by another Paul–

producer/engineer Paul C, who had also worked on *The Biz Never Sleeps* and with Ced Gee's group Ultramagnetic MCs.

Ced Gee: Paul C was dope. He was more technical with the SP-12[00]. I taught him little tricks like how to create echoes and stuff like that. Paul C taught me stuff like how to truncate fast. He was the wizard technically. I had guerilla tricks. He had technical stuff that wasn't in the manual. For instance, when you are sampling, like when you chopped it, there was a process where you had to use the resolution to truncate the sample. That would take time. Paul showed me how to do that instantly with a trick. Sometimes it would take you ten minutes to truncate a drum precisely because you have to get it right on top. You can't have a little space, because then it would be off beat, and you can't have it too much in, because then it would start too fast. He showed me how to do it instantly and get it on the money. That took Hip-Hop to another level. It took it to where you can just go in the studio and do stuff. You didn't have to pre-do it at home. Before Paul's tricks, you would have to do everything at home because of all the time it took. Now you can just go in the studio and do the samples and the whole thing in like ten minutes. Paul C was deep.

On July 17, 1989, Paul C was murdered in the basement of a house he shared with his mother and brother. He was only twenty-threee, and his killer (or killers) was never apprehended. Large Professor immediately went into overdrive, filling the shoes of his sensei and beginning production work on Main Source's debut album and Eric B. & Rakim's third album *Let The Rhythm Hit 'Em*, in a work-for-hire arrangement with the duo. Towards the end of '89, Eric B got him the gig to produce *Wanted: Dead Or Alive,* the second full-length by Kool G Rap & DJ Polo, and second for Cold Chillin'/Warner Bros.

Kool G Rap: Eric was telling me that Large Professor was signed to his [Eric B's] production company, but Large Professor wasn't making that clear to me. He telling me he just Large Professor. He not saying, "I'm doing this under Eric B's production." So I had one person saying one thing, I had another person saying another thing. Large Professor was in the studio *producing* the album. Large Professor [picked the samples] straight up and down. I would have Dr. Butcher come in and do some cuts. Dr. Butcher was a way better cutter and shit like that. He did cuts and scratches phenomenal.

Dr. Butcher: G was like, "Yo, I need somebody who can light up the turntables." His girlfriend, who was like a sister to me, asked him, "Why don't you get Drew to do it?" He was like, "What are you talking about?" He only knew me as a rapper. He didn't know I could DJ. When he came to my house he started laughing. He was like, "You're gonna be Dr. Butcher! Nothing else to be said." I was quiet—nobody knew. I came up with Cut Creator, who was probably one of the best DJs I had seen. I had a couple of guys I seen who were extremely incredible growing up who mentored me. I kind of kept the DJ thing quiet for a while. Dudes didn't really know what I could do. I was studying all of those dudes, and I was just as good or better than the people I looked at, but I didn't tell anyone. I didn't go around bragging, "I can battle you and beat you." I didn't say that to anyone. He [Kool G Rap] brought me in the studio. I ended up working on the album. I was just kind of scratching on top of "Kool Is Back," and they actually kept the performance. It became part of the record.

Kool G Rap's longtime neighborhood friend Dr. Butcher ended up being a *ghost scratcher* of sorts by doing all the DJ work on the album. DJ Polo had no qualms about it, especially being that Marley did most of the scratching on their first album. Relased in 1990, the finished product was a critically lauded sleeper, and its sub-gold sales didn't reflect the level of fanaticism associated with it. Between Large Professor's work layering samples by the Fatback Band, Syl Johnson, Bob James, and even Tom Jones, Dr. Butcher's cuts, and G Rap's astonishing lyrical wit and focus on crime-related subject matter, *Wanted: Dead or Alive* helped define the sound of the early '90s pre-Gilbert O'Sullivan lawsuit era. The crown jewel of the album was the very song the MC wrote after his brain surgery as a way of proving to himself and the rest of the world he still had it, and then some. "Kool Is Back" was all the evidence anyone needed to know Kool was back.

Cut Chemist: That's some rhyming couplet shit all day. "Kool Is Back" is maybe my favorite rap song of all time.

Dr. Butcher: Everybody thought he would never come back to make a record. To walk in the studio and hear "Kool Is Back," it was like, "Did they give you some extra brain power or something? Where did *this* come from?" His rhymes seemed like they got ten times better! I was like, "Yo, this is crazy!"

Fly Ty: I was a G Rap fanatic. To me, he was the best rapper ever.

Erase Racism

Kool G Rap: Biz wanted to do a track on my album. I was open to it. Him and Cool V came through and did that track, and we made "Erase Racism." And Kane came and jumped on it. Dee Joseph: They [Cold Chillin' recording artists] trusted me I think because I was always there for them. If they needed something they could count on me helping them figure it out, whether it was Bizzy [Biz Markie] saying, "Come downstairs and get me a cab," because at that time, as crazy as it sounds, Biz would tell me, "I can't get a cab. Come down and get me a cab." I was really a little protective of them in that way.

Kool G Rap: In cases of being with a group of other blacks, there's probably been situations where a whole car might have got pulled over, guns was drawn on us. And other times it was expected because I was on a drug block and police pull up, or they ride by, just scoping out shit. For me doing a lot of shit I did, I was fortunate not to ever really get caught doing nothing. And I done pushed my luck. That's why first time going over to Marley's house I never went back to no drug block again.

Masta Ace: Sheepshead Bay [High School] was a predominantly white school that had been integrated. [It took an] hour and forty minutes to get out there every day. Two buses. By the time I got there it was maybe thirty percent black. In the years leading up to going to Sheepshead Bay, I would hear all these stories about black kids getting beat up at this school and others out there—getting beat up, getting chased home by groups of white kids with baseball bats and pipes and chains. They were literally like, "We don't want you in our neighborhood." When I stepped into Sheepshead Bay in 1980, I was right at the tail end. It was still going on, but it wasn't as crazy as it was in the late '70s. There was still incidents. I remember one specific incident. This white girl, this Italian girl got her chain snatched by somebody in the school. At the end of the day there were probably fifty to sixty Italian dudes parked outside in front of the school, sitting on the roofs and hoods of their cars waiting for this girl to point out the guy who snatched her chain. At some point, she pointed him out. They chased him to the bus stop. The kid made it to the bus. They surrounded the bus. The bus driver locked the door and they were rocking the bus, trying to tip it over. Eventually he got away, but they would have killed that kid if they caught him. Killing did happen. Howard Beach is one example. Definitely chasing, definitely terrorizing. Because we were in their neighborhood, there was a sense of fear on our part. You saw that shift from '80 to the time I graduated. The fear shifted from us to them, because our numbers grew. All of a sudden, *they* felt outnumbered. You started seeing white families fleeing the school, fleeing the neighborhood, putting their kids in private schools.

"My boy Rich Luke, he got killed by the police," said MC Shan on VladTV in 2016. "His mother called for an ambulance because he was having an asthma attack. And when the police got there, they're talking about 'he's not being cooperative' and this, that, and the third. And they choked him out. And so I made that song 'Time For Us To Defend Ourselves' back then. The cops hated me in the projects. It was all in the name of Rich Luke to show the violence that's going on in the projects. Hip-Hop has been the voice of the hood to tell the story of what's going on in our neighborhood that the people just don't see."

"The most recent New York case under scrutiny involves the death in police custody of a twenty-five-year-old black man, Richard Earl Luke," the *New York Times* reported in 1989. "On May 22, two housing police officers, responding to a 911 call at a Queens housing project, were assaulted by Mr. Luke, who was unarmed, the police said. Only after a violent struggle at the entrance to a building, the police say, were officers able to restrain Mr. Luke, who was then taken to a nearby holding cell. There he stayed, handcuffed, for more than thirty minutes. The police said that after Mr. Luke began to bang his head wildly against the floor and walls of the cell, Emergency Services Unit officers and an ambulance were called. The officers from the emergency unit wrapped him in a restraining blanket and put him in an ambulance bound for the City Hospital Center at Elmhurst. But he died along the way. The autopsy attributed the death to an overdose of cocaine."

Home Sweet Home

For all the power the police wielded in the streets and in the courts, young, black Hip-Hop artists carried immense power in the words contained on the records making their way into households across the nation, and eventually the world. Those two forces would soon collide. Work was beginning on Kool G Rap & DJ Polo's third album *Live and Let Die.*

Dr. Butcher: Him [Kool G Rap], a guy named Naughty Shorts, and the [rap group/production team] Beatnuts started *Live And Let Die* in his house. Marley had got a lot of money, I forget where it was from, LL or somebody made a lot of money, and he got rid of his in-house studio. G bought it from him and put it in his house. It was just a basic 16-track Tascam board. He thought he could save a lot of his money, his budget, if he made it at home. We started working on the album early, and luckily my uncle was an avid jazz collector and funk collector. He was sick and he knew I was into music, so he gave me all his records, which was like thirty or forty crates of records. I wasn't heavy into production; I was just getting into it at the time. But I took all those records to G's house. We just had a wealth of material there. Then I brought the Beatnuts in, and they came in with a lot of crazy stuff too. Those recordings were *monstrous*. Just monstrous. I was like, "Oh man, this is gonna be G's best album ever. This is incredible." Everybody was like, "Yo, when you hear this album, it's gonna blow you away."

Kool G Rap: I wanted to work with [producer Sir] Jinx because I thought Jinx was dope. I thought the shit he did on Ice Cube's album was dope. My label Warner Bros. hooked that up and made that happen. I went out to Cali, and me and Jinx got to working.

On the Run

Dr. Butcher: G Rap caught up with what the west coast was doing, and what Ice Cube was doing. Polo was getting upset. He was like, "We're wasting mad money out here." In the meantime, they met Sir Jinx. Him and [Dr.] Dre are cousins or something. He was like, "Yo G, I can do all that Dre stuff man." To me, Jinx didn't produce on Dre's level musically, but he could do all those interludes. Fancy stuff. And G got caught up in that. He took all of the reels out there, and Jinx remixed everything that we had done.

Kool G Rap: A lot of things I already had produced before I got to him. "I Ain't Trickin'" [released on *Rated XXX*, Cold Chillin', 1996], "Edge of Sanity," "On the Run"—the original version that's on the album—"Great Train Robbery" I already had produced by myself. This is when I was first producing strictly by myself, working the machines. I think I was second guessing myself even though I had other producers like Trackmasters saying, "Yo G, that's hot!" But I was still not sure of myself as a producer, because I'm working the equipment myself. But I guess it was good, because Jinx wouldn't have put his name on it, because all Jinx did was produce on top of what I produced already. So he would add elements.

Fly Ty: Trackmasters—Tone and Poke—were OJ's [Wedlaw] friends from high school. They used to come to our office all the time. Tone wanted to be a rapper, but he couldn't rap. But I always liked his tracks. His tracks were slammin.' I said, "I'm gonna give you a production deal. You can produce *anybody* on Cold Chillin'." I convinced G Rap to let them do a song called "Ill Street Blues," and that blew completely up. When that happened, *everybody* wanted Trackmasters!

Kool G Rap: Trackmasters didn't do nothing on the album, but they did singles when it was too late for me to add it to the album. I had heard their production and I wanted to work with them, but I think the album was wrapped up already. But I wanted to work with them that bad, that I did singles with them. That's why "Ill Street Blues" wasn't on the *Live and Let Die* album. And that version of "On the Run."

Crime Pays

One of the songs on *Live and Let Die,* "Crime Pays," addressed the racial profiling Kool G Rap and many of his peers were targets of by the police over the years. The victimization of black communities by law enforcement agencies wasn't a concern confined to New York. In March of 1991, a black motorist named Rodney King was beaten mercilessly by four LAPD officers in the Lake View Terrace neighborhood of Los Angeles. A bystander videotaped the event, and the video made its way onto television sets throughout the nation. Thirteen months later, every officer was acquitted by a mostly white jury in Simi Valley.

Kool G Rap: I was right at the end of recording it [*Live and Let Die*], and the Rodney King verdict came out. I was in the studio with Jinx. Tupac was in another room in the same studio. When we left the studio, we left in the same car. We were riding with my man Gooch. Gooch had a convertible BMW. The shit was crazy. I remember leaving the studio and by the time we got to the more inter-LA LA, it was just cars riding around, people going crazy, dudes poppin' off they guns in the air. You could just see the frustration of everybody in every direction. We was in the car shooting guns and all that. Me, Jinx, Tupac, Gooch. We was all expressing our anger with that verdict. Every black person in America, and probably around the world had thought this is gonna be the time when it's different, because this the first time when this shit has actually been caught on tape and presented to the world. Everybody knew it was gonna be a different outcome for sure, and by not being that, it was a clear indication of bias, racism and a double standard in this country. It was a clear example of that. And then you would get to that frustration years later again with the OJ Simpson trial—white America being upset that he got acquitted, and there was *no* taping of it. So it was a clear double standard. I'm not talking in technical terms of this piece of evidence or that piece of evidence, but the point is nobody was able to *see* what happened. But the Rodney King verdict, you got to *see* what happened. So you had to believe if that wasn't police brutality and excessive force, you have to not believe your own fucking eyes, plain and simple. Ain't no ifs, ands, buts about it. No way around it.

Go For Your Guns

Two years previous, Ice Cube had flown to New York with Sir Jinx to work on his debut solo album *Amerikkka's Most Wanted* with Public Enemy's production team the Bomb Squad. It was a crash course in cutting edge production techniques for Jinx. Now Kool G Rap, a New York MC, was working with Jinx on his home turf, and the result was a testament to the power of cross-coastal pollination. G Rap's cinematic lyrics ranging from double-crossing the mafia in a drug deal to hilarious scenarios of being "cock blocked" were complimented by Jinx's trademark interludes and white noise. This was going to be the one. The cover art for *Live and Let Die* depicted two white cops with nooses around their necks, standing on chairs, with Rottweilers tied to the chairs, being taunted with raw steaks held by Kool G Rap & DJ Polo. It was classic George DuBose, albeit far darker than any of his previous album cover designs.

George DuBose: One guy had "TNT"—Tactical Narcotics Taskforce, and the other guy had "DEA" painted on their Army jackets. Warner Bros. made us take it off. Also for the booklet, we made coffins, and the two narcs are laying in the coffins surrounded by a black posse—Kool G Rap and Polo, and about ten of their pals, and a couple of white guys I knew to stand in. Everyone's wearing suits. I don't know if this is in the package of the CD. Warner Bros. put a nix on it. The two narcs in the coffins had silver dollars on their eyes, which was a Greek custom to pay the boat man when you go to Hades. When people die they put coins on their eyes to 1) keep their eyes closed, and 2) to pay the ferryman when you go to Hell or Heaven or wherever. At one point everyone cracked up, so you see the dead guys laughing. They're howling with laughter. Warner Bros. nixed that too because they were white guys killed by black guys.

Cop Killer

That same year, there was another song written by a black man fantasizing about killing cops, released under the Warner umbrella, which sent shockwaves through the entire music industry, and involved the *actual* bomb squad. The fallout would be devastating to Kool G Rap & DJ Polo's careers.

Bob Merlis (Senior Executive Vice President of Worldwide Corporate Communications, Warner Bros. Records): In a way, Warner Bros. dumb lucked into the rap business when Sire signed Ice-T. He was a truly personable guy and despite the gangster overtones on his records, he wasn't seen as a threatening guy in any real way. It was a surprise when he came up with *Body Count,* a metal album [by his band Body Count] that was a stylistic departure. Long after it had been released and run its course in terms of sales, I was called into Warner Bros. Records President Lenny Waronker's office where he showed me a pile of letters that had come in protesting the release of "Cop Killer." I'm sure that I jokingly said, "Where were these people when the album was first released? It's kind of over." Nonetheless, pressure built and it was clear that there was a well-organized letter writing campaign to denounce us for having released the album. Soon thereafter press inquiries started to come in and those were directed to me. I did my best to correct quite a few incorrect assertions—that it was a) in fact, a rap album, and that b) we had released "Cop Killer" as a single. It was clear that those protesting had never heard it. I used what I euphemistically call "the Randy Newman defense" with most of media asking about the imbroglio. Ice-T was as much advocating killing police as Randy Newman was advocating that "Short People" be dispatched in his song. I suggested that Ice-T was describing a harsh reality that might exist but wasn't suggesting that listeners go out and kill cops. Very few picked up on the nuance I felt was there, and things proceeded to get worse. There were threats and the bomb squad detonated a suspicious package. It contained someone's demo tape.

Eugene Shelton: Ice-T was very meticulous in explaining to the public the difference between art and life, and that it was just a song. And there was an overreaction to it. Besides, "Cop Killer" was a Body Count song, not an Ice-T song. When you have a police association calling for the boycott of anything Bugs Bunny, that's a lot of money. It was a huge overreaction.

Dee Joseph: You started getting a lot of backlash from that. Once they realized that these guys are writing about violent stuff and killing cops—not good.

Mo Ostin: We took a lot of heat. We had a stockholders' meeting here in LA and Charlton Heston got up and actually read the lyrics to "Cop Killer," and then they had like twenty-five police people speak—chiefs of police and top executives in that community. And everybody opposed it.

Bob Merlis: While all this was going on inside the grand ballroom, Ice-T himself cruised by in his Rolls Royce as if to taunt the protesters—or at least those of them who actually knew who he was.

Monica Lynch: "Cop Killer" was at fever pitch, and all these police organizations had sent in members to attend the shareholders' meeting, including, very visibly, law enforcement officers who had suffered paralyzing injuries and were in wheelchairs. It was at this event that Charlton Heston rose like Moses on the mountain. He was sitting towards the back of the room and got up and started reciting the lyrics to "KKK Bitch" [by Body Count], which was a pretty singular performance. I wish there was videotape of it. "Oh my God! There's Moses! He's doing 'KKK Bitch'!"

Troy Shelton: People were perpetuating a fight based on political wants. People were trying to look for a scapegoat for something that had nothing to do with anything. Violence wasn't caused by music. Drug addiction wasn't caused by music. These were things they were trying to pin the tail on the scapegoat on.

Mo Ostin: We had a lot of dealings in Washington. We were a cable company and we were a movie company in addition to being a music company. It was important that we maintained relationships with Washington. The corporation felt that it was a threat to our relationships there if we continued with putting out rap records, so they insisted that we censor the records. And we refused. We put out "Cop Killer" anyhow because we were standing on the Constitutional right of free speech. All that bullshit. There was so much heat that they wanted us to drop Ice-T. We refused to do it. They made me go before the board of directors, and they gave me a real talk. They were really tough about this, and I still held my ground. Then Ice, who happened to be a gentleman, saw all of the pressure we were getting, and he said, "Look, I don't want you guys to end up getting hurt because of this. I'll leave the label voluntarily." He left himself. We did *not* drop him. "Cop Killer" wasn't even necessarily a rap record. It was more rock 'n' roll. The corporation was fantastic. I don't think there was a better corporation supporting a record company than Warner Communications. [Time Warner CEO] Steve Ross was phenomenal in terms of giving us almost anything we wanted. But they were very pragmatic. They dealt with Tipper Gore and all kinds of other people who were talking about censorship. They felt, "This is hurting the corporation, and there is a bigger picture we have to address than just the music business, as important as the music business is to our corporation."

Bob Merlis: The album, which had stalled and was dropping precipitously in the charts when the protests started, actually came back to life and wound up achieving gold record status, which I'm quite convinced would never have happened if the protests hadn't materialized.

Operation Cock Block

As a result of the "Cop Killer" controversy, major record labels went into panic mode, pressuring rappers to remove songs from their albums or dropping Hip-Hop acts entirely. Violent lyrical content, which had been an asset up to this point, was quickly becoming a liability. A&M president Al Cafaro asked Tragedy to drop a song about killing cops called "Bullet" from his sophomore album or find another label. Tragedy went with the option *A*. Samoan-American rap group Boo-Yaa T.R.I.B.E. wrote the song "Shoot 'Em Down" in response to the shooting of two Samoan youths by the LAPD. Their label, the Disney-owned Hollywood BASIC, distributed by Elektra, got them to drop it from their EP *Rumors of a Dead Man*. FU2 released a single with a b-side entitled "No Head, No Backstage Pass" on the MCA-distributed JDK Records. MCA chairman Al Teller had the record pulled from store shelves, and refused to release the group's album. The Boston Police Patrolman's Association pressured Tommy Boy to drop Boston group Almighty RSO because they objected to the song "One In the Chamba." Live Squad squeezed off one single ("Murderahh") on Tommy Boy before they were dumped. Donald D, who was signed to Sire through Ice-T's own Rhyme Syndicate Records, made a music video for his single "I'm Gonna Smoke Him," only to have Warner cancel its release. The song was on the *Trespass* soundtrack, a film co-starring Ice-T and Ice Cube that had undergone a name change when its original title *Looters* was deemed inappropriate in the wake of the LA riots. Paris, another Tommy Boy artist, was dropped after a new employee stole the cover art of his soon-to-be-released second album depicting the San Francisco MC about to assassinate President George H.W. Bush, and showed it to her family members who were in law enforcement. It was a witch-hunt of epic proportions, and Hip-Hop got the brunt of it, but not exclusively. Gwar, on the Warner-distributed Metal Blade label was told to remove the song "Baby Dick Fuck" from their album *This Toilet Earth*. Gwar and Metal Blade flat-out refused, severing ties with Warner Bros. in 1993, releasing the album independently the following year ("Baby Dick Fuck" intact). Cold Chillin' wasn't immune to the wave of paranoia. Kool G Rap & DJ Polo was yet another act that was hung out to dry in an attempt to save face for the corporate overlords who were terrified of potential boycotts.

Kool G Rap: They [Warner Bros.] didn't want to put out the album because they was getting a lot of flack for gangsta rap, things of that nature. They had C. Delores Tucker speaking out against gangsta rap, and Reverend [Calvin] Butts. All these people creating a circus around gangsta rap music because of Ice-T's "Cop Killer" record, that it had a ripple effect. It affected my deal structure, with my next album release with Warner Bros. There was this emphasis on this new form of rap. I say "new" form because this is the explosion time of so-called gangsta rap. After groups like N.W.A, it started this whole trend of dudes expressly saying they gangstas and shit like that. I wasn't expressly saying I'm on some gangsta shit when I did "Road To the Riches" or "Rikers Island" or any of those records. Now it became a trend to do that. All these things got lumped up in the same "gangsta rap" bucket. It affected everybody.

Fly Ty: Mo, having the personality he had, he didn't just say, "We're not distributing it." He said, "How much is it gonna take for you to do it properly?" And he gave me the money. He didn't just say, "Get outta here, we're not doing it." We did it independent.

We didn't do a major. We did it the way we did Shan's first album. That's why we were able to kinda get away with it.

Kool G Rap: I think my record got a bad break because of that. It didn't have the major label machine behind it. I got a bad break with my first album, and a bad break with my third album. I guess for me to exceed the level that I been on for pretty much my career, it wasn't meant to happen.

Mister Cee: "Ill Street Blues" and "On the Run" and "Talk Like Sex"—those are records that came from G Rap later on in his career. It's weird with G. Some of his biggest sounding records came later on. He still didn't have the overall commercial success. By the time they came, Cold Chillin' as a label wasn't as powerful as it once was, and that's where the disconnect comes in at. "It's a Demo," "Poison," "Road To the Riches," "Streets of New York"—that's when Cold Chillin' was *popping,* but Kane and Biz was smothering G Rap. Not on purpose. They was smothering them with the hit records. Biz and Kane's hit records were so much bigger than G Rap's records. As a program director, listen, if I got "Smooth Operator" and I got "Just Rhymin' With Biz" and then you're giving me "Road To the Riches," I can't get all of them on.

George DuBose: I only saw one instance of any promotion expense, and that was when *Live and Let Die* was released by Kool G Rap [& DJ Polo], and Warner Bros. paid for two billboards—one on Flatbush Ave. in Brooklyn. I drove out to Flatbush Ave., and I see this big billboard on top of a building with the cover graphic for *Live and Let Die,* and then I drove up to 125th Street in Harlem, looking for the other billboard. I'm driving down 125th Street, and first I see a billboard on top of one building that said, "Cop Shot. If you see a policeman getting shot and report it, you can get $10,000." Across the street was the billboard from *Live and Let Die,* with Kool G Rap & DJ Polo hanging two narcs. I thought that was real . . . I don't know what you'd call that. Not a coincidence, but something.

Epic (Street?)

After the dust on the great "Cop Killer" purge had settled, 1993 saw the breakup of two duos: Cold Chillin'/Warner Bros. Records and Kool G Rap & DJ Polo. The major's distribution term with the indie had expired, not to be renewed. Controversy aside, Warner couldn't justify continuing with a label that hadn't had any significant hits for three years. G Rap soldiered on as a solo artist with Cold Chillin', which still had Grand Daddy I.U. on the roster.

Kool G Rap: Me and Polo parted ways because I felt it was my time to separate. Polo had brought me in the game, so I gave Polo three albums and seven years of my life. For it to not be a group where we're contributing to the group evenly—50/50—then I felt like it was time for us to eat off our own plates. There was nothing Polo was contributing that would make up the group Kool G Rap & [DJ] Polo.

Fly Ty: Dave Glew [Atlantic Records 1975–94, President of Epic Records 1994–98] comes to me. I felt like a mafia guy. Michael Corleone. Trying to get out, but they won't let me out. Dave Glew was at Sony. They had just taken over Epic. He comes to me and he says, "I'll sign Kool G Rap only if I can have the whole thing." Like Warners did.

Kool G Rap: Pretty much Epic had wanted to sign me. The head of the A&R department Awanda Booth wanted to sign me. I was about to leave Cold Chillin'. Ty didn't want me to leave. I wanted a different contractual structure. I wanted to renegotiate. Me getting ready to leave is what would make us all come back to the table and renegotiate. I was basically gonna bounce because Epic wanted to sign me, and I was gonna sign with them direct. But I ended up working something out with Ty. I was happy, he was happy. Epic put out who they wanted to put out. I don't think they deal was obligated to put out whatever artists through Cold Chillin'. I think it was structured in a way where they pick particular artists that they wanna put out that was on Cold Chillin''s roster.

Fly Ty: Sony was the worst. Not record-wise, but people-wise. Mo and Warner Bros. had the same kind of personality that I did. Sony was strictly business. It was too much negotiation to get anything done. Too many people to talk to. With Mo . . . it took me two years at Warner Bros. to even realize I could talk to somebody else. I knew there was senior VPs, but I always dealt directly with Mo to get what I wanted. At Sony, there was so much backstabbing. The executives were backstabbing one another. That threw me for a loop. Every department hated each other.

Lead Pipe

Grand Daddy I.U.: We getting kicked out of the muthafuckin' studio. We can't even record because they [Cold Chillin'] owe all studios across muthafuckin' New York. You go to the studio, and in the middle of a session muthafuckas is kicking us out. This is like '93, '94. [My second album] *Lead Pipe* came out in '94. The shit was already done a year and a half before they put it out. It had to be like the end of '92, '93. Stylistically it was all the way different. This fucked my whole shit up because when I came out people was trying to say that I sound like Rakim. It bothered me so much that I changed everything the next go around, and that wasn't beneficial. That wasn't the shit to do. Muthafuckas was riding the wave. You have the yes men in your corner when you poppin.' OJ [Wedlaw] was a promotion cat from Cold Chillin' and when they got the deal with Epic, they took OJ to be the promotion dude, because they didn't know what the fuck they was doing with Hip-Hop. I was like the fucking guinea pig. They had some shit called Epic Street. I was the first muthafucka offa there. OJ did some wack shit. He was supposed to look out for us because he was down with us, and he went and worked for them. We thought, "Okay, you got our man in there. We good." He started promoting everything but our shit. He was Fly Ty's nephew, and he got him the job at Epic. And he was over there and didn't promote none of our shit. We on the road and shit, my shit ain't even the stores. We doing a promo tour and my shit is not being promoted. I'm like, "What's going on?" And he acting like on some brand new shit, so I threw a chair at the muthafucka. But it was a lot of reps that was around. I don't know who these people are, and I'm young and I don't give a fuck, and I feel like people doing me dirty right now, so this is my reaction. But they like, "Yo, we can't work with this muthafucka. This nigga unruly." I got a little reputation for being wild, or hard to work with. What I'm supposed to do? This muthafucka supposed to be my man, and he's out there promoting everything but our shit. When I asked him about it, his response wasn't what I was looking for. This was some type of rap convention shit, where a bunch of fucking label reps was.

4, 5, 6

Dr. Butcher: A little incident happened that got G [Rap] involved in some street stuff, with some serious street dudes. They kind of threatened him. They put a contract on his life. So the label had to move him around a lot. We were being moved around a lot from studio to studio.

Kool G Rap: That's something I'm not gonna really put out there like that.

Dr. Butcher: He didn't trust many people, but he brought me in to remix one of his songs and when the label heard it, the A&R, Awanda Booth said, "He has to be on this album. He's gotta do your whole album." I didn't do the whole album. I probably did half of it, but she was persistent that I do it. Me and him [Kool G Rap] were like brothers, so he didn't have a problem with that whatsoever. [The other producers were] Todd Ray [T-Ray], Naughty Shorts, who worked on the other album [*Live And Let Die*] initially, Buckwild, and I think that was it. He [Kool G Rap] moved to Arizona right after *4, 5, 6* was completed. He was living in Staten Island. He moved around, but apparently they found out where he was and somebody put a call in to say, "Hey, tell G to leave. They know where he is and they're coming for him right now." So he just stopped and left. Me and him was working on music and I drove out to his house. I was there the day before. When I pulled up to his house the following day, there was a moving truck in front of his house moving all the stuff out. I was like, "What the heck is going on?" He was gone. I didn't hear from him for a few weeks. At the label, people had to tell me what happened. He didn't tell *nobody* he was gone, not that he didn't trust me. He didn't even tell his girlfriend where they were taking his child. The record label didn't know. He just said, "Send me money." In his own mind, he knew he wanted to go to Arizona for some odd reason. He got a flight to Arizona and took his family with him, and stayed quiet for a while. Nobody knew where he was. He was shook. He was paranoid.

Kool G Rap's first solo album *4, 5, 6* was released on Cold Chillin'/Epic Street in 1995. Darker in tone than anything that had come before, it was the second of only two albums in the doomed partnership between the two labels, and also the last album consisting of entirely new material on Cold Chillin'. Timing-wise, it was disastrous for the MC, as he was literally on the run, not just rapping about it. The label that had begun almost a decade previous, returned to its independent roots and went into reissue mode before eventually closing its doors.

It's a Shame

Fly Ty: I got out and went back to radio. I got with HOT 97 and became a consultant. I stayed there until 2004 and I was retired basically.

Dee Joseph: I had a child in 1994 and I was only working part time at that time. The label was kind of in its final stages. I worked from home at times so I didn't even go into the office, so I missed a lot of this era, like the *end* end. I knew at the end of '94 that things were rocky. He [Len] was concerned records weren't selling; things weren't happening the way they had hoped, and they put out stuff that really wasn't very good. There were deals being made, and somebody wasn't saying no.

George DuBose: In the Cold Chillin' office . . . there was a sign under the receptionist's window: "NO DEMOS." I thought that was really fucking weird—a record company that didn't want to hear new music. Evidently, they thought they had so much of the right shit; they didn't need to listen to anything else. I thought that was really stupid.

Dee Joseph: I don't know what door George was looking at. I don't remember ever putting putting a sign "NO DEMOS." No, I don't remember that ever.

Grand Daddy I.U.: They closed the fuck down! They downsized from Broadway to some bullshit ass office. They couldn't even afford that no more. They went out of business and that was it. They folded. Boom. This is '97 or some shit. I don't know.

Monica Lynch: I think that when you look at labels at large, especially when you're looking at independent labels, there are all these variables that factor into the mix. A lot of labels really only had a hot run for a short period of time, and then they sort of petered out or went on to do other things in other genres. Sometimes it's kind of an ephemeral thing. Who is at the helm of the label? Who is producing? Is there a primary artist that they're reliant on, and they run out of gas? There are all sorts of factors for that. To have a run of a good six years or something, that's more than some labels get. So I think that maybe the way to look at it is there are labels that actually defied those odds. It's not unusual to have a short-lived burst of hotness, and then, eh, you know.

Tom Silverman: A lot of people are wearing blinders and they just see that it has to be one thing. The problem with Cold Chillin' and Livin' Large is they weren't great at marketing. Their business is really about A&R—finding artists and making records. But even there they didn't really find it. You know they never found a Tupac or Treach or somebody who would break through. And they rarely had big hits. They had like three or four that were sort of mid-chart hits, and was the biggest they got unfortunately. I don't really think they thought out of the box that much. They didn't do anything new. They represented a few cool artists, but weren't able to find any other new ones. I understand that. We [Tommy Boy] ran into parts where we couldn't do it either. Sometimes you just have to get lucky.

Mister Cee: Cold Chillin' was not the same label [towards the end]. Great records, but the label wasn't as strong. Because then Bad Boy comes in, Def Jam is even stronger, Death Row. These labels came in and they was taking over.

Almost poetically, Len Fichtelberg's other *Cold Chillin'*—his boat—met a similar fate as the label.

George DuBose: Lenny bought this sport fishing boat. It must have been well north of $100,000. I'm a sailor, and Lenny was this motor boater. We both stayed in the same region in the summer time. I remember meeting him some years later in a restaurant, just coincidentally, and he said, "Join me at my table." And I did. His motor boat had exploded. It was a gasoline powered sport fisherman. Probably forty- fifty-feet long. When they were were filling up the fuel tank in Martha's Vineyard, they probably didn't ventilate their engine room enough, and when they started, the whole boat exploded. Luckily nobody died, but one guy had his leg completely shattered, and his wife was blown into the water. It was a pretty big disaster.

Cold Chillin' was history. What is not reflected in the sales figures is the immense influence its acts had on the next generation of rap artists. Hip-Hop's third wave pushed Ty and Lenny's label into obsolescence while simultaneously using the production techniques, lyricism, and diss record template pioneered by the Juice Crew as a foundation to take rap out of the Golden Era and into the Platinum Era.

(Epilogue)

IT WAS ALL A DREAM . . .

Kool G Rap: I think everybody had to have some sort of influence of Juice Crew, because that's the impact Juice Crew had. I think it touched a lot of people.

Contained within Kool G Rap's *4, 5, 6* album was "Fast Life"—a duet between him and a Queensbridge MC named Nas who had been on the rise for the last few years. Although not by design, "Fast Life" represented a figurative passing of the torch to Hip-Hop's next generation, as Cold Chillin' gasped its final breaths. He was one of many superstars-in-the-making who were influenced by the Juice Crew.

Nasir Jones

Craig G: Nas is from the other side of Vernon. Me and Nas went to the same junior high school. I didn't know he rapped back then, but of course I knew him.

"Back in the days Roxanne Shanté was getting a name as this big rapper in the neighborhood and she came to my building one time, and she heard us in the hallway trying to rap," Nas recollected in the documentary *Time Is Illmatic*. "Shanté said, 'Look, I want y'all to come perform.' It was like some Queensbridge park jam that was gonna happen and we heard about it. She wanted to bring us on as a crew. It was like, 'Oh wow!" So we talking about this every day, working on it. That's when we start to realize we not really *good*. She asked us to spit for her. This a different time. We try to rap and we started laughing because it wasn't coming out right. She didn't laugh. She said, 'Listen, if y'all don't have your routine next time I see y'all, I'm fucking both of y'all up.' She's older than us and taller than us, and we believed her."

Dr. Butcher: When Large [Professor] was doing [Kool G Rap & DJ Polo album] *Wanted: Dead Or Alive,* I think Joe Fatal introduced him to Nas. Large took a liking to him and started bringing him up to the studio. DJ Premier was coming into the studio every single day. Premier hung out with me all the time. Nas was just kind of a student. Not knowing where his career would ever go, he would come to the studio and sit there quietly. Having somebody like Nas to just have that fire and that desire inside of him to be a great rapper, to get to experience being in a G Rap session while he's working on an iconic album . . . I think that motivated him and inspired him.

Large Professor gave Nas a guest verse on a posse cut at the end of his own group Main Source's debut album *Breaking Atoms* in 1991. The Hip-Hop community took immediate notice of the seventeen-year-old's rhyme, which employed florid language reminiscent of Tragedy and off-color metaphors one would expect from Kool G Rap.

Craig G: I was at a show in the City watching Main Source, and he came out. "Oh shit, that's Nas. This kid is dope." He was doing "[Live At] the Barbeque."

Dr. Butcher: When G had the studio he would let him record songs there. He didn't get his deal through G, but G was definitely influential and played a pivotal part in his career, and took interest in him.

Kool G Rap: He [Nas] makes mention of me on recordings he did. I'm not saying I'm the *only* influence, because there's a heavy influence in Nas from Rakim as well. But I know I'm one of the influences on him.

Kool G Rap tried to help Nas get a record deal in the early '90s, bringing his demo to Cold Chillin' and Def Jam. Nas reminisced in his 2007 song "Surviving the Times" that the former didn't have the contract he wanted, and G Rap has since said that the latter didn't want to sign the budding MC because they thought he sounded too similar to G Rap himself. In retrospect, this was tantamount to Decca and Atlantic passing on The Beatles 20 years previous, as Nas ended up signing with Columbia Records (with the help of MC Serch) and selling over 13 million copies of the records he released between 1994 and 2004. Large Professor, DJ Premier, Q-Tip, newcomer L.E.S., and

Marley Marl disciple Pete Rock all contributed to the production on his debut album *Illmatic*. The title was named for a piece of Queensbridge-specific terminology, coined by a local who went by Illmatic Ice, and used by Tragedy on "The Rebel" from Marley's *In Control, Volume 1*. If the legacy of Shan and The Bridge appeared to be tarnished by his loss to KRS-One in 1986–87, it was now restored tenfold by Nas' constant promotion and endorsement of his neighborhood idols throughout the years. In 2000, he put together a collective called QB Finest and released *Nas & Ill Will Records Presents: Queensbridge The Album*, which featured "Da Bridge 2001," a sequel to Shan and Marley Marl's 1986 anthem. A posse cut that represented multiple generations of Queensbridge Hip-Hop artists including Nas, Tragedy, his protégé Capone, Cormega, platinum-selling duo Mobb Deep, Nature, Millennium Thug, Shan, and Marley, the song was the ultimate homage to the housing project that launched dozens of rap careers.

In 2014, while filming for the documentary on his *Illmatic* album, Nas laid it out. "I never saw that I'd be having this day to look back and think about where I come from, and made it to where I'm at. It was a story that needed to be told. It was already told by MC Shan and Marley Marl, Craig G, Shanté, the Juice Crew, Tragedy. It was already told, so I was just an extension of that. They paved this way. They made this happen."

Then there was Brooklyn.

Shawn Carter

Kool G Rap: Jay-Z came up from under Kane.

Shawn Carter grew up in the Marcy Houses in Big Daddy Kane's neighborhood of Bedford-Stuyvesant. One year younger than Kane, he actually got on vinyl first, as part of a group called High Potent with his mentor Jaz-O (Jonathan Burks). Released in 1986 on micro-label Get Live Records, "H.P. Gets Busy" made no impact, but Jaz-O, now going by Jaz, had a contract as a solo artist with EMI America by the end of the decade, and some of his songs featured Carter, who was going by Jay Zee (later spelled "Jay-Z," and named for the J and Z subway lines that passed under his neighborhood). It is around the turn of the decade that he met Kane.

Big Daddy Kane: When I was on the road with Patti [LaBelle], I'm noticing she just leaves the stage and her background singers do a gospel song, then she come back out in a different outfit. I was like, "That's dope! Do anybody in Hip-Hop do that? I gotta try this." At the time I was taking Jay-Z and Positive K in the studio to work on material to try to get them a deal. So I was like, "Yo, why don't you come out on this tour with me? I got an idea." I do the first half of the show by myself. So in the middle of the show, I would introduce Pos and Jay-Z, and let them freestyle on stage for the crowd while I go back, change outfits, and me, Scoob, and Scrap would have on the same outfit. Then I would come back out and finish up the rest of the show.

Fly Ty: Jay-Z—that was Kane's man. Kane started taking him on tour with him. A lot of these acts—the big ones, the great ones—came through us, because we were the place to be.

Eugene Shelton: Through Kane, I met Jay-Z for the first time. Jay-Z drove down from New York with Kane to do BET. Kane was booked on *Rap City*. He said, "Gene, listen to this guy. His name is Jay-Z." I had never heard anybody rap that way. He said, "He's gonna be a star." I'm thinking when Jay-Z becomes successful he's taking Kane with him because Kane opened the door for him in so many ways. I think they still have a great relationship.

Big Daddy Kane: I thought he [Jay-Z] was a great lyricist, but Jay was always so quiet. I'm not gonna lie. I believed in him as a great lyricist, but I felt that we gonna have to really package this right. When I played his stuff for Lyor Cohen [at Def Jam/Rush Management], Lyor's exact words were, "Kane, I get it. He's a great rapper. But he'll never sell records."

Cold Chillin' wasn't even a consideration for Jay-Z, being that Kane himself was trying to leave the label, and Def Jam struck out yet again. Jay's ascent to superstardom was a slow burn; he would occasionally pop up for guest verses on the records of others throughout the first half of the '90s, including Kane's 1994 *Daddy's Home* album on MCA. After co-founding his own label Roc-A-Fella, he teamed up first with Priority to release his debut album, a full decade after High Potent's single dropped. The following year, Roc-A-Fella partnered with Def Jam in an ironic twist, and between 2004 and 2007 he served as president of the label that was originally dismissive of him. Jay's first 13 albums all went platinum or multi-platinum, and he started venturing into businesses outside of music, buying a minority stake in the New Jersey Nets. Becoming the public face of the NBA team's move to Brooklyn's newly built Barclays Center in 2012, Jay-Z performed for eight nights at the arena. Just as Kane had Jay come out during his sets more than twenty years earlier, Jay now returned the favor to one of his greatest influences.

Big Daddy Kane: He did the same thing that I used to do with him. He had me come out in the middle of his show. There's a song that he has "Do It Again." On tour, when he would perform that song, when he got to that part, it would switch to the "Ain't No Half-Steppin'" beat and he would finish it off that beat. So people were accustomed to him using my beat during the middle of that song. So I guess they would think that he about to finish that way, but when "Half-Steppin'" drop, I came out and performed it. I brought my dancers out, and we did "Warm It Up." Then he came back out and finished his show.

Christopher Wallace

Another Bed-Stuy MC came up in the early '90s, whose career was intertwined with the Juice Crew. Christopher Wallace grew up on St. James Place in what is now the Clinton Hill neighborhood of Brooklyn, approximately two miles west of his favorite rapper Big Daddy Kane. Born in 1972, he was raised on the Hip-Hop of the '80s before rechristening himself Biggie Smalls, and alternatively BIG and The Notorious B.I.G.

Mister Cee: He was definitely a humongous Big Daddy Kane fan. When I first heard Kane in our old high school, I thought that Kane was incredible, and I got that same reaction when I first heard Big. When I heard Big I was like, "This is the second coming. It's like I'm hearing Kane all over again." Doesn't rhyme like Kane, but I just felt like it was that same reaction when I first heard Kane. It was just like something I never heard before. Something different. I'm the man behind the man. I discovered him. I met him through his first DJ 50 Grand. 50 Grand was a guy who I grew up with in Bed-Stuy, Brooklyn. That's how I met Big. I get George DuBose to take his photo around the corner from my house, and he [Biggie] did a basement demo with 50 Grand, but the basement demo was very distorted. We recreated the demo at my house. I lived right around the corner from 50 Grand at the time. One of the records that Biggie was rhyming to was the actual sample that me and Kane used for "Ain't No Half-Steppin.'" It was a song called "Blind Alley" by The Emotions. Biggie rapped off of that, which is so ironic. That freestyle that he kicked blew my mind.

Easy Mo Bee: He [Biggie] never mentioned that he wanted his records to sound like Kane, but he definitely was inspired by Kane. I know that he loved "Ain't No Half-Steppin.'"

Mister Cee: We redid the demo at my house. The first person I *ever* let hear Biggie's demo was Kane. When I redid the demo, Kane, Scoob, and Scrap are the first people I let hear it. Kane thought he was dope. I wanted Kane to work with him, but Kane was already working with Positive K and Jay-Z at the time. Kane felt like he had too much on his plate. We submitted it [the demo] to Matty C to *The Source* magazine, to this *Unsigned Hype* contest that they were doing. He loved the demo. If they like it, they give you a record deal with Relativity Records. Relativity Records was the same record label that Common was on. They offered us a record deal, but it was a shitty deal. It was just horrible. So I just turned it down and was like, "Nah, we not gonna go this route." And then next thing I know, P. Diddy, Puff Daddy contacted Matty and was like, "I know you doing this *Unsigned Hype* thing going on. Who's the best rapper you got over there? Matty told him, "Notorious Biggie Smalls & The Hitman 50 Grand." The first thing Puff asked Matty was, "Yo, how does he look?" Matty told Puff, "He's not the best looking rapper, but he can rap his ass off." Puff asked him, "How do I contact him?" Matty said, "Get in contact with Mister Cee." That's when we had 1–800 SkyPagers. Puff hit me and said he wanted to meet with us. I took Big to Uptown Records to meet with Puff, and Puff asked Big to rhyme right on the spot. No demo. He just wanted to hear him rhyme in the office, and Big kicked a rhyme. Puff was like, "Yo, I could have a record out on you by the summer. You be cool with that?" Big was like, "Talk to Cee. Cee will make everything happen. Talk to Cee." One thing led to another and we did the deal. Biggie was originally signed to Uptown Records.

Dee Joseph: When Biz had "Make the Music" when he first started, Puffy, P. Diddy, Puffy, whatever his name is now, Puffy would call me like on a regular basis to try and book Biz for one of his shows because he started out as a promoter. He was doing these shows and he called *begging* for Biz, begging for him to do a show for him.

Fly Ty: I used to call Puffy "The Shan Man" before he got the name Puffy. He was just an MC Shan fan.

Mister Cee: We started the recording process for [The Notorious B.I.G.'s debut album] *Ready To Die,* and next thing you know Puff gets fired from Uptown, and starts the Bad Boy label with Arista. What Puff had to do was buy the masters. Half of *Ready To Die* was already done. He had to buy the masters from Andre Harrell. In the midst of all of this, Biggie gets dropped from Uptown/MCA after making the song "Dreams of Fucking An R&B Bitch" [released as "Just Playing (Dreams)"] because he's talking about fucking Patti LaBelle and fucking Raven-Symoné. And these artists was on MCA at the time. The chairman of MCA asked Andre to drop him. If I remember correctly, he had asked Andre to drop five artists from the label. On top of that, Biggie had made this record, so it was a double whammy. "I need you to drop five artists, but one of them got to be the Biggie guy, because he can't be making these type of records about fucking our labelmates." I wouldn't be surprised if Patti LaBelle complained about it herself. And Patti collaborated with Kane.

Released in the fall of 1994, *Ready To Die*—partially produced by Cold Chillin' alumni Easy Mo Bee and Poke of the Trackmasters—went platinum six months later, making Biggie the biggest MC on the east coast. The lead single "Juicy" was both a Horatio Alger rags-to-riches story and an homage to the rapper's Hip-Hop heroes of the '80s. One line mentioning *Rap Attack,* Mr. Magic, and Marley Marl solidified the legacies of the New York radio show, its host, and its DJ on an international scale for decades to follow.

Tupac Shakur

The Juice Crew continued to influence the influencers. On the other side of the country was rap's other biggest star. Tupac Shakur grew up in New York before moving to Baltimore and then Oakland where joining the rap group Digital Underground as a dancer and occasional MC. Like Biggie, Tupac looked up to Kane, and they found themselves on tour together in the early '90s.

Big Daddy Kane: Pac used to hang around. There was times he'd come by, getting girls in the room and stuff like that. When we first met, we talked for almost an hour about him being an MC. He's telling me he's getting ready to do his own thing solo. He was like, "Yo, it ain't gonna be like this Digital shit. I'm spittin.' I'm trying to do what you do. I'm spittin' some real stuff." On that tour, him, Scoob, Scrap, and Mase from De La Soul were hanging most of the time.

Mister Cee: In October of 1993 at Madison Square Garden there was the *Budweiser Super Fest*. We [Big Daddy Kane] was like the only Hip-Hop act on the show. You had Patti LaBelle, After 7, and I think Bell Biv Devoe was on that show too. We only had like ten minutes. They didn't give us a lot of time. I was telling Kane about Big. Big was coming to the show. Kane's like, "Aight, aight." I told Kane that Tupac's coming with Big, and that's what really kind of lit Kane's eyes up, because Tupac was so huge at that time. *Poetic Justice* had came out in theaters a couple of months before that concert, so Tupac wasn't even just a rapper—he was a movie star at that time. Kane's like, "We should put them on." Once I got the confirmation from Kane that he was gonna put Pac and Big on stage, I went straight to the soundman. I was like, "I need to record this show." He was like, "Yo, we don't allow that." I was just begging him. I went to the store and I got a 120-minute cassette. I was like, "*Please* let me record this." He was like, "Yo, we don't do that. It's against the law." I'm like, "Yo, I'm not gonna tell nobody. Nobody's gonna know." I just begged him. I stayed on him. He's like, "Yo, you cannot tell *anybody*." And he let me record it off a cassette. I had the 120-minute cassette and I didn't wanna miss nothing. I didn't know what that moment was gonna be, but I just knew it was gonna be a moment. Tupac, Biggie, Kane. Big was so huge in New York at that time.

Cee's cassette containing the cipher between Scoob Lover (who had recently changed his name to Big Scoob), Biggie, Tupac, thirteen-year-old Wu-Tang Clan associate Shyheim, and Big Daddy Kane captured a narrow sliver of time when the Golden Era and Platinum Era overlapped, just before coastal turmoil drove a wedge down the middle of the map. In November of 1994, Tupac was shot and robbed in the lobby of Quad Recording Studios in Manhattan. Biggie had been in the studio several floors above the lobby at the time of the event, and was accused by Tupac of setting him up. Soon the two rappers and their respective labels were engaged in a feud—Tupac's LA-based Death Row headed by Suge Knight, and Biggie's New York-based Bad Boy headed by Sean Puffy Combs—replete with diss records from both sides. Blown out of proportion by the media, the beef was presented as an east vs. west war, hearkening back to KRS-One and MC Shan's borough-based beef, only with much more serious implications. On a flight to LA while entertaining the prospect of signing to Death Row himself, Kane attempted to quell tensions by convincing Tupac to put an end to his personal war with Biggie. It didn't work. On September 7, 1996, Tupac Amaru Shakur was shot again, this time in Las Vegas. He died six days later. On March 9, 1997, Christopher George Latore Wallace, Biggie Smalls, was shot and killed in Los Angeles. Like Scott La Rock and Paul C before them, the murders were never solved, making it impossible to establish motive. However, it was treated as a wake up call to the Hip-Hop community to end the geographic grudge match that had so many engaged. Rap's two biggest stars were dead.

Marshall Mathers

Marshall Bruce Mathers III was an MC out of Detroit who went by Eminem and was eventually discovered by west coast producer Dr. Dre. He would go on to become one of the highest selling recording artists of all time, in what was gradually becoming the highest selling genre.

Masta Ace: I found out about him [being a fan of mine] around early 2001. He was already pretty much a big star. He wasn't headlining tours yet, but he was definitely one of the bigger names in Hip-Hop. I met his road manager, this guy Marc LaBelle. Marc put another friend in touch with me and basically told me, "Yo, Em loves you." He was like, "I want to invite you out to a show." It was the *Up in Smoke Tour* with Dr. Dre, Ice Cube, Snoop. Eminem was one of the opening acts. I thought he was ill. Jazzy Jeff was the first person who played him for me back in '99 or 2000. Now he's on these giant tours and he's selling all these records. I met him backstage and he told me my album *SlaughtaHouse* was one of the important albums in his life. It was a time when he was broke and driving around Detroit with his D12 crew in a beat up car, and they would just play *SlaughtaHouse* all day. The tape popped, they bought a new one. That was their album in the summer of '93. We talked briefly. We connected that day. Later on, he received a Grammy and he mentioned my name among a list of people that were big influences. A lot of people were like, "Ooh, wow! That's crazy!" But I had already known that and spoken to him. So I already was aware.

"I made me a little list of MCs that I wanted to name off that inspired me to bring me where I am today, because honestly, I wouldn't be here without them," stated Eminem during his acceptance speech for *The Eminem Show* winning Best Rap Album at the 45th GRAMMY Awards in 2003. "The list is this: Run-DMC, the Beastie Boys, LL Cool J, Kool G Rap, Masta Ace, Rakim, Big Daddy Kane, Dr. Dre, all of N.W.A, KRS-One, Treach from Naughty By Nature, Nas, Tupac, Biggie, Jay-Z. Thank you, 'cause I learned from all of you."

Masta Ace: As far as what he borrowed from me, I don't know. We all borrow from each other. Just the idea of being as clever and as slick as you can with your wordplay. I think we all feed off of each other. I think he would say some of the storytelling stuff. For me it goes back to Slick Rick, so it all passes down.

The main hook in Eminem's 2017 song "Untouchable" included lyrics from Ace's "Born To Roll"—an homage to his elder. Ace wasn't the only Juice Crew alum to have involvement with the Detroit recording artist. When Eminem starred in *8 Mile,* a film loosely based on his own experiences as a struggling rapper, Craig G was employed to write rhymes recited by Em's fictitious rival MCs in its now famous battle scenes. Craig, at this point an accomplished battle rapper in his own right, also aided in 50 Cent's semi-autobiographical 2005 film *Get Rich or Die Tryin'*.

Tariq Trotter

"When I saw Big Daddy Kane and Kool G Rap and Rakim sort of rapping in iambic pentameter, it had a huge impact on me as a young writer," said Black Thought (né Tariq Trotter) on NPR in 2018. The lead MC in Philadelphia Hip-Hop band The Roots, which became the house band for *The Tonight Show* in 2014, explained that Shakespeare often wrote using the same meter as his rap idols, and were equally influential on his own rhyming. "It sort of opened up a world." Later on in the program, Black Thought rapped the first verse of Kool G Rap & DJ Polo's "Men At Work" over the record, and explained that the song was the basis for The Roots' 2003 song "Thought @ Work."

Calvin Broadus

Biz Markie's "Vapors" was covered by Long Beach rapper Snoop Doggy Dogg in 1997 with modified lyrics. TJ Swan, Kane, Cool V, and Biz's stories were swapped out for Snoop affiliates Nate Dogg, Daz Dillinger, Warren G, and "Tha Doggfather" himself. His album containing the cover went double platinum, introducing the early work of Biz to a much broader audience. Snoop was so enamored of the Juice Crew that he covered "The Symphony" two years later, again altering the lyrics but keeping in the original's posse cut tradition. In place of Master Ace, Craig G, Kool G Rap, and Big Daddy Kane, Snoop had himself, C-Murder, Fiend, Goldie Loc, Mia X, Mystikal, and Silkk The Shocker taking turns on the mic.

Kendrick Lamar Duckworth

On June 17, 1987, a newborn child in Compton, CA was being driven home from the hospital. His mother got into an argument with his father, behind the wheel. "Pops was playing this really loud, and my moms was like, 'Turn that shit down!' He was like, 'No. Let him hear it. This is music and it's good music. Big Daddy Kane.'" Kendrick Lamar's retelling of the story to Nardwuar decades later based on his parents' recollections became an interesting footnote to the career of a rapper who went onto win multiple Grammys, record several chart toppers and sell millions of albums. During the 2010s, the MC defied trends by emphasizing lyricism and subject matter relating to social justice, over sample-based Hip-Hop music. Raised from his infancy on a foundation laid down by Kane and his contemporaries, Kendrick Lamar's career was a testament to the lasting influence of the music of Cold Chillin', now spanning several generations.

Miles Dewey Davis III

Wu-Tang Clan, co-founded by The Genius, proved to have such a far reaching impact on Hip-Hop in terms of sound, iconography, business, and even fashion (launching their own Wu-Wear clothing line in the mid-1990s), that it is difficult to even point to a handful of recording artists as evidence of the group's influence. The Genius' shortlived career as a solo artist on Cold Chillin' has largely been thought of as a footnote in the story of this much larger phenomenon, but that tiny blip inspired perhaps the most beloved musician in the history of jazz to find the right person to produce his final recording.

Miles Davis called Russell Simmons in 1991 with an idea to make an album combining jazz with Hip-Hop. Simmons' employee Francesca Spero at Rush Producer's Management had a cassette delivered to the trumpeter, containing one track by each producer they represented at the time. Miles took a liking to Easy Mo Bee's track. "She [Spero] is the one who set up the initial meeting between me and Miles that took place at his Upper West Side apartment on Central Park West between 88th and 89th Streets," recalled the producer on Instagram in 2018. "It was then and there that I first played him the cassette tape with a skeleton of what became 'The Doo-Bop Song.' It was also then and there that I played him The Genius' 'True Fresh MC' and he asked me, 'Would you do that for me?' Of course, I replied, 'Yeah Miles.' It's almost like he didn't believe me, and he asked me one more time. I laughed and said, 'Yeah let's do it Miles.' The album was recorded, and he gave me full responsibility in titling every song, including the title of the album."

Miles Davis recorded six tracks with Easy Mo Bee as producer before passing away on September 28, 1991. Completed by Mo Bee with a few previously unheard Miles performances, *Doo-Bop* was released in June of the following year on Warner Bros. Records. The album earned a Grammy Award for Best R&B Instrumental Performance and was an early example of the burgeouning intermingling of jazz and Hip-Hop—two art forms with distinctly African-American histories.

Forever Diss

Roxanne Shanté, the Queen of the Juice Crew, may have had more of an impact than anyone else in all of Hip-Hop. Having introduced the concept of the diss record in 1984 at the age of fourteen, she opened a door that could never be closed. Whether it was Kool Moe Dee vs. LL Cool J, Jay-Z vs. Nas, Eazy-E vs. Dr. Dre, Ice Cube vs. Cypress Hill, Foxy Brown vs. Remy Ma, or Pusha T vs. Drake, Eminem vs. Machine Gun Kelly, talking shit about one's rival on a record simply never went out of style. It is difficult to fathom that such an integral part of the rap landscape didn't always exist.

Respect the Architect

Marley Marl continued having success well into the mid 1990s, producing records by LL Cool J, Heavy D, and New Jersey group Lords of the Underground. When his name no longer carried marquee value, beats he created several years earlier for records such as "Make the Music With Your Mouth, Biz" began showing up on several R&B singles by the likes of Mary J. Blige on through to the twenty-first century with Ariana Grande. His direct influence as a pioneer of Hip-Hop production techniques also played a huge role in the music that was becoming the soundtrack to the '90s and beyond. World-renowned producer DJ Premier continued using the structure of "Nobody Beats the Biz" as the template for his work. Marley's *In Control* radio program live DJ Pete Rock had massive success with his own group Pete Rock & CL Smooth, and many others into the 2000s. Large Professor, Easy Mo Bee, Wu-Tang Clan's RZA, and Just Blaze were all fundamentally using Marley's template as a blueprint, as were two DJ/producers from California—Cut Chemist, a founding member of Los Angeles group Jurassic 5, and Peanut Butter Wolf from San Jose. The latter worked with a charismatic

MC named Charizma up until his murder in 1993, and then went on to found the Stones Throw label.

Peanut Butter Wolf: Before I "discovered" Charizma in 1989/1990, I was working with a gang of different rappers, trying to make my own compilation album where I did all the beats, and it was all different rappers from San Jose that were influenced by New York "keep it real" Hip-Hop. The only rappers in San Jose with records out were MC Twist and Chris & Ray, and they were both more of a dated Miami Bass, party rap style. My comp idea was inspired by Marley Marl *In Control*. After meeting Charizma, who was supposed to be part of my comp, I liked him better than the others on a personal level. I enjoyed hanging out with him, whereas the other rappers just came in and did their rhymes and bounced. I scrapped the comp idea, but put it out over 20 years later as *Straight To Tape,* and I focused on being in a group with Charizma. After Charizma died, I did an album of instrumental tracks I made influenced by 45 King's break albums, then made *My Vinyl Weighs a Ton,* which again was a bunch of different rappers and influenced by Marley Marl *In Control*.

Cut Chemist: I think everybody was [influenced by Marley Marl]. All these people making records at that time, myself included, grew up on all of Marley's records. Whether they admit it or not, that crept into their psyche at some point. Marley got us into wanting to make rap records, plain and simple.

Easy Mo Bee: Whatever happened in the past, everything from Lightnin' Hopkins, B.B. King, all the way to Kool & The Gang, Earth, Wind & Fire, all the way to a disco group, music made its way into Hip-Hop by way of sampling. In my opinion, in the Cold Chillin' era of Hip-Hop, a lot of that music continued to embody some of the most important forms of black music. And it's always happening through sampling. And it's always happening with producers like Marley Marl.

As I Reminisce

After being diagnosed with multiple sclerosis in 2000, Masta Ace pushed himself harder than ever before. Without knowing what the future of his health would hold, he ramped up his recorded output and touring schedule, developing a large and loyal following, especially overseas. The Genius/GZA continued to thrive as a member of the massively popular Wu-Tang Clan, and also as a solo artist. Kool G Rap continued making albums and making guest appearances on the records of countless others. Big Daddy Kane continued to tour relentlessly, as did his old friend Biz Markie who had rebranded himself a live DJ and a personality on children's show *Yo Gabba Gabba*. Roxanne Shanté mentored high school kids in New Jersey and was the subject of the 2017 biopic *Roxanne Roxanne*. Marley Marl's career came full circle when he got a gig doing exclusive remixes for LL Cool J's *Rock the Bells* channel on SiriusXM in 2018, just as the producer had done for *Rap Attack* in 1983. Core Juice Crew members Kane, G Rap, Craig G, Shanté, Marley, Ace, and Biz reunited for a series of shows in the U.S. and Europe starting in 2016. There is a general acknowledgement that those formative years in the '80s and early '90s helped define them in the public consciousness.

Kool G Rap: I believe I got exactly what I wanted. You manifest your strongest desire. My strongest desire wasn't to be the richest rapper. It was never that. I wanted money—of course. Everyone want money. But I didn't have a desire to be the richest rapper. I really just wanted to be acknowledged for my skill capability, and I think I achieved that. I may not have achieved that in the mass mainstream audience, but the mass mainstream audience is not entertained by the quality of lyrics in the first place. They're entertained by shit they could dance to, or something that's simple enough to sing along to, and G Rap was never that type of artist. G Rap was an artist you *listen* to the shit he's saying. I'm a rapper for listeners and fans that appreciate lyrics. Years later I would learn there's a big difference between being that type of artist and the type of artist where you really want to entertain.

Big Daddy Kane: I didn't get into this to buy Bentleys and Maybachs, to be flossing and all that there. This is something I got into because I love *Hip-Hop,* but I always understood the dynamics of it. I always wanted to be that lyrical dude, but at the same time I'm that type of person that was like Marvin Gaye was—just this stand out, phenomenal dude. Smokey Robinson, Kris Kristofferson—they had amazing pen games, and they could make other people sound better as theyself. James Brown was this incredible performer. Prince—amazing vocalist and performer. I wanted to really raise the bar. I wanted to be respected as a lyricist, but at the same time take what's normal to a whole other level. I think I did, but I probably won't get the credit because I did it too damn fast. Had I came out during the Bad Boy era, I would have probably been the greatest thing ever. Someone like a Puff that saw my vision.

Masta Ace: I definitely want to be remembered as a contributor and somebody who tried to be lyrical at a high level, who tried to entertain fans and people with my music, with my albums, with the way that I put them together. I want to be remembered as a writer, a storyteller, and somebody who made music that made people *feel* my music, as opposed to just hearing my music. I was continuing to try to prove myself. I felt like I never really proved myself because I was on that label with all those big stars, and great artists, and super lyricists, and for some reason never really got what I feel like was proper recognition. Because I never felt like I *made it,* it's always kept me hungry, and kept me recording and rhyming at the highest level possible. A lot of my peers, they *made it.* They did it. They got the accolades. They got the flowers. People list them on their top 10 and 20 and 50 lists. I'm always left off those lists. Because I'm always left off those lists, it pushes me. You know what I compare it to? Tom Brady was a sixth-round draft pick. There were six quarterbacks picked before him in that draft in 2000. He sat there and he watched the draft days go by one by one—all these cats getting picked by teams. Every moment that he sat there watching quarterbacks getting drafted, and him still sitting there with his parents, it just built up this fire in him, this determination in him that, "If I get this chance, I'm gonna show *everybody.*" I feel like my career is Tom Brady sitting there, waiting to be drafted. I got something to prove and I just continue to work that way.

Grand Daddy I.U.: [I want to be remembered as] underrated. The real time muthafuckas know I get it in. I just want to be remembered as just a cool muthafucka, man. That shit don't mean nothing to me. The best part about it is a muthafucka can't say I did nothing dirty to them, muthafuckas can't say I jerked them, I stole nothing from them, or none of that shit. A standup muthafucka.

Craig G: I just want to be remembered as a guy that just did what he did. Everyone has their purpose and their lane. I just want to be the guy that I grew up with the people that listened to my music and made the music accordingly. That's pretty much it. There's no bells and whistles with me. I rap well and that's it really. I feel like I made history already. Now I just do it because I like to create. The whole business side is a mess sometimes. I just love performing still.

Mr. Magic & "Kool Ass" Lenny

Fly Ty had been mentoring an inner-city marching band, when in 2009, Mr. Magic, aka Sir Juice of the Juice Crew, got the opportunity to reignite his radio career on WBLS. Ty was to be his producer. It felt like 1982 all over again.

Fly Ty: He had been off radio. WBLS called me. Charles Warfield. They wanna put Magic back on the radio. All day Thursday I'm calling Magic. Can't get him, can't get him, can't get him, can't get him. He calls me Thursday night. I said, "Remember tomorrow we gotta be at BLS at 10:00 A.M." "I'm ready, I'm ready, I'm ready, I'm ready." When I wake up that morning, I see all these missed calls from a number that was strange to me. This other artist I had named King Sun, and Just-Ice—they used to call me all night. I thought it was one of them. I go in the shower and come out. The phone's ringing again. Same number. I pick it up. It was Magic's girlfriend at the time. Her name is Crystal. She's twenty-two. She said, "Are you up?" I said, "Yeah." She said, "Are you sitting down?" I said, "I'm alright." She said, "Magic is gone." I thought she meant he left to come to me. I said, "Why he have to come this early?" She said, "He's gone. He's gone." I'm still not catching on. I'm like, "Okay, okay." She said, "You don't understand. Your brother is *dead*." Because we always called each other "Brother." I'm *still* not thinking dead. I was thinking when Magic gets hot, by hot I mean popular, he can be a handful. He can get a little arrogant. So I thought he got arrogant because he knows he's going back on the radio. I said, "Don't worry, baby. When he get here I'll talk to him." At that point, her mother, who I had never met, takes the phone. "I'm Crystal's mother. Magic died at two o'clock this morning." I'm still not hearing this. I'm thinking they got the wrong person. You might have thought it was him, he went out. I kept saying, "Nuh uh, Magic's on his way here." She said, "Ty, the city morgue just picked him up. He's not coming there." I dropped to my knees. I couldn't believe it. "You and his sister need to come identify the body. It's at Interfaith Hospital." I just sat there with a wet towel. Now I got to call WBLS before I go to the hospital. I said the same thing Crystal said to me. "Are you sitting down? Magic died this morning at two o'clock." They could not believe it. Magic was Catholic. He would go to mass every day. His mother passed three years before that. After his mother passed, he changed. Him and his mother were very close. He didn't want to be around entertainment. He changed his life. He was working for American Express. He was happy with that, going to a 9 to 5. I'm buggin.' I'm like, "What did he die from?" His girlfriend said, "He was supposed to get a double bypass, but he didn't get it." I said, "What do you mean he didn't get it?" "He was afraid. He told me not to tell you, because if I told you, you would make him get it." "*Yeah* I would have made him get it! *Yes*." If the alternative is death, yes, I would have made him get it. An older woman would have said something, or made him do it. Then my grandmother passed. I had three deaths of people who were close to me back-to-back-to-back—Magic, my grandmother who I loved like he loved his mother, and Lenny. He was like my Jewish brother. Magic died abruptly. Lenny went downhill. He had chemo. Lenny was my son's godfather. He told me he didn't want my son to see him anymore. "Don't bring him. Don't bring him." Then it got to the point when you called, his wife would have to talk on the phone for him. He aged *extremely* fast and he died in November of 2010. I had to deal with that. Within a year, everything close to me was gone. That was rough for me, but I had my marching band kids to keep me busy, to keep my mind off it. I put everything into work.

Mr. Magic, the first Hip-Hop radio show host, was gone at the age of fifty-three. Len Fichtelberg, the founder of Prism Records, and co-founder of Cold Chillin' passed away just before his seventieth birthday. How will Cold Chillin', the label of his creation that grew out of Mr. Magic's *Rap Attack* be remembered?

Monica Lynch: I think that they should be remembered as a really vital part of Hip-Hop history. When you look at the label pound for pound, they had a lot of hits. It's great to see that Biz Markie has become a huge star DJ who's booked every night of the year. It's great to see Big Daddy Kane is still doing shows. They're a huge part of the New York Hip-Hop story. Nothing but love for the Cold Chillin' folks as far as I'm concerned.

Masta Ace: I think Cold Chillin' should be remembered as the label that could have. Cold Chillin' should be looked at as the biggest underachieving label in Hip-Hop history. There should be *countless* platinum records that came out of that stable, but because the leadership was severely tainted and were basically crooks, it led to the label not achieving its greatness. And that's unfortunate.

Dee Joseph: I think that it was one of the precursors to what's happened in Hip-Hop and rap now. These guys were pioneers. They started it. I think if nothing else they should get some kudos for at least laying the foundation. Sowing the seeds. You look at the success of everybody now and rap is so acceptable. It's everywhere. It's so recognizable. You've got awards on the Grammys, but we never even had a rap award at the Grammys. They should be considered pioneers. Some of these guys are still looked up to by some of the younger guys who have come after them. From a historical standpoint I would say they were forebears of rap.

Grand Daddy I.U.: At one time that was like the hottest shit ever. When I first got my deal muthafuckas was like, "What? You on Cold Chillin'? No fucking way." They couldn't even believe it. It was like a fucking miracle. That was the American Dream to some muthafuckas at that time. The way the shit fell off was like . . . it never lived up to the potential. They should have been in the same conversation with Def Jam and whoever else because at one point they was. How you got Kool G Rap, MC Shan,

Biz Mark, Big Daddy Kane, all these muthafuckas at one point? They was *all* poppin'. And then nobody give a fuck about that shit no more. Cold Chillin' was a force to be reckoned with, and they fucked it up.

Dr. Butcher: Cold Chillin' was pivotal in the game. You had Big Daddy Kane; you had Master Ace, Craig G, G Rap. They brought the lyricists to the table. You had Marley with the beats. They really brought that New York Hip-Hop to the forefront. MC Shan, Roxanne Shanté. You just had a legacy of good music there early on that kept the crowd excited, kept the fans excited.

Eugene Shelton: I think that Cold Chillin' should be remembered as a trailblazing label that brought an element of east coast rap to the world, mostly through Big Daddy Kane. It had its high point with Biz, and somewhat with Roxanne Shanté. It should have been more successful based on what music was being created and what was being done. I don't know where it failed. It was just a very positive experience. All my years working with Warner Bros., and working with Ty, Dee, Alonzo was just a very positive experience. I can't think of anything negative. Unfortunately they lacked the success needed. And that was always the big question. Why? Why can we not do more?

Mo Ostin: They were an early harbinger of the future. Rap evolved to the point where it exploded and became the dominant genre. It's certainly one of the early labels that had some sort of modicum of success.

TJ Swan: Cold Chillin' should be remembered as an innovator. You talking about the first crew, the first multi-talented crew with individual artists that made a mark in this game. Kool G Rap made a mark. Craig G made a mark. Master Ace made a mark. Tragedy made a mark. Big Daddy Kane, Biz, TJ Swan—we all made our mark. We set the freaking level of success when it comes down to have a crew of individual talent. Everybody had talent out the yin yang. To this day, everybody's still eating off of they talent.

Easy Mo Bee: I think Cold Chillin' should be remembered as one of the most breakthrough, innovative Hip-Hop labels to ever happen inside of the music business. Especially because what it showcased in the beginning was the crew thing, a family of MCs. I think Cold Chillin' should also be remembered for showcasing some of the most innovative sampling techniques.

Kool G Rap: [Cold Chillin' should be remembered] as a classic, independent label during the explosion of a new genre of music, that would surpass the running time of many other genres. I'm not saying jazz ain't still around or blues still ain't around, but I'm talking about a genre that is at the forefront of music even to this day that's considered mainstream. Like what Motown was in the '70s.

Dee Joseph: I think it started out as a way of expression for these young kids who really had hard lives. They grew up in the projects, so this was a release for them. This was an outlet. This was a way for them to talk about their angst, their anxieties, their feelings of rejection or disappointment, or their feelings of elation—whether it was boasting or braggadocious. This was their music and this was their expression of themselves, pure and simple.

"Hip-Hop was a way of us in the projects getting our message out to the world," MC Shan declared on Instagram in 2018. "News reporters was not paying attention to the struggles and strifes of the hood. Nobody cared. My friend got killed by the police. Many people have gotten killed by the police . . . This was our way of taking our message out to the world and letting people know that hey, we exist. You just can't ignore us. It was our form of entertainment. It was our form of news. It was how we spread what the hell was happening in New York with our brothers and sisters in LA and everywhere else."

Craig G: They had a collection of some of the greatest MCs and some of the greatest albums. As you get older, you get more mature, and you look back and you go, "We made history together."

"That about wraps things up for yours truly, Super Rockin' Mr. Magic . . . Super Listeners, you got an extra day off, so make sure you do your homework to the best of your ability, but *always* remember, Super Listeners: *any fool can learn from his own mistakes, but it takes a wise man to learn from the mistakes made by others*. Till tomorrow night at two in the A.M., this is Mr. Magic for my crew, and WHBI FM. We'd like to say adios amigo. Ciao!"—Mr. Magic, 1981

CAST OF CHARACTERS

Arthur Baker: Producer/DJ. Produced Soulsonic Force, New Order, and popularized the Roland TR-808 drum machine. Founder of Streetwise and Partytime Records. Mentor to Marley Marl.

Bill Bentley: Vice President of Media Relations for Warner Bros. Records 1986–2006.

Big Daddy Kane: MC/Producer/Lyricist. Member of the Juice Crew, recording artist for Cold Chillin'/Prism 1987–1993. Wrote rhymes for Roxanne Shanté, Biz Markie, and others.

Biz Markie: MC/Producer/DJ. Member of the Juice Crew, recording artist for Cold Chillin'/Prism 1986–1993. Signed and co-produced recording artists signed to Biz Markie Productions through Cold Chillin' 1989–1991.

Boogie Down Productions: Rap group initially consisting of KRS-One, DJ Scott La Rock, and D-Nice. Rivals to the Juice Crew, specifically MC Shan.

Andre Booth: Producer/Songwriter/Keyboardist. Co-produced Dimples D with Marley Marl, introduced Marley to Arthur Baker. Wrote many ballads for Cold Chillin'.

Ced Gee: Producer/MC. Produced records for Juice Crew rivals Boogie Down Productions. Rapper in Ultramagnetic MCs.

Stu Cohen: Senior Vice President of promotion for Warner Bros. Records 1973–1999.

Craig G: MC/Lyricist/Producer. Member of the Juice Crew, on many Cold Chillin' releases including "The Symphony" and "Droppin' Science."

Cut Chemist: DJ/Producer. Member of Jurassic 5, worked with Big Daddy Kane and Biz Markie.

Cutmaster Cool V: DJ/Producer. Member of the Juice Crew. Biz Markie's cousin and DJ. Co-produced many records with Biz Markie.

DJ Polo: DJ. Member of the Juice Crew, recording artist for Cold Chillin' 1986–1993 as one half of Kool G Rap & DJ Polo.

Dr. Butcher: DJ/Producer. "Ghost scratcher" on Kool G Rap & DJ Polo album *Wanted: Dead or Alive* and produced much of Kool G Rap album *4, 5, 6*.

George DuBose: Photographer/Designer for vast majority of Cold Chillin' releases.

Easy Mo Bee: DJ/Producer. Produced Big Daddy Kane, The Genius, Prince Rakeem, Tupac, The Notorious B.I.G., Busta Rhymes, Craig Mack, and the last Miles Davis album ever recorded.

Len Fichtelberg: Founder of Prism Records, co-owner of Cold Chillin'.

Fly Ty (Tyrone Williams): Co-owner of Cold Chillin', manager for many Juice Crew/ Cold Chillin' artists. Producer of Mr. Magic's *Rap Attack* radio show.

Kenneth David Freundlich: Lead attorney for Warner Brothers Records, Inc and WEA International Inc. in *Grand Upright Music v. Warner Brothers Rec* court case.

Aaron Fuchs: Owner of Tuff City Records. Employed Marley Marl for many productions.

The Genius/GZA: MC. Recording artist for Cold Chillin' 1990–1991. Co-founder of rap group Wu-Tang Clan.

Glamorous: MC. Member of the Juice Crew, rapper in Glamour Girls, Juice Crew All Stars. Recording artist for Prism in 1988. Employee of Cold Chillin'.

Grand Daddy I.U.: MC/Producer/Lyricist. Recording artist for Cold Chillin' 1990–1994. Wrote rhymes for Roxanne Shanté, Biz Markie.

Grand Dragon KD: DJ for Philadelphia rapper Steady B/A&R for Pop Art Records.

Dee Joseph: Vice President of Prism/Cold Chillin' 1979–1994.

Ife Kiara: Artist Relations for Warner Bros. Records 1987–1996.

Jay Quan: Hip-Hop historian for The Foundation.

Kool G Rap: MC/Producer/Lyricist. Member of the Juice Crew, recording artist for Cold Chillin'/Prism 1986–1996.

Monica Lynch: President of Tommy Boy Records 1986–1998. Employee of Tommy Boy Records 1981–1998.

Marley Marl: Producer/DJ/Engineer. Member of the Juice Crew, engineer/DJ for *Rap Attack* radio show, host of *In Control* radio show, DJ for Roxanne Shanté and MC Shan, primary producer for Cold Chillin' roster 1986–1989.

Masta Ace: MC/Producer. Member of the Juice Crew, recording artist for Cold Chillin'/Prism as "Master Ace" 1988–1991.

MC Shan: MC/Producer/Lyricist. Member of the Juice Crew, recording artist for NIA Records (1985), MCA (1985), Bridge Records (1986), Cold Chillin' 1986–1991, Livin' Large 1992–1993. Main rival to Boogie Down Productions. Discovered platinum recording artist Snow.

Bob Merlis: Senior Executive Vice President of Worldwide Corporation Communications for Warner Bros. Records. Head of publicity department 1975–2001.

Mister Cee: DJ/Producer. Member of the Juice Crew, DJ for Big Daddy Kane 1985–1994. Produced many records on Cold Chillin'. Discovered the Notorious B.I.G.

Mr. Magic: Host of *Rap Attack* radio show. Founding member of the Juice Crew. Known as "Sir Juice."

Mo Ostin: CEO of Warner Bros./Reprise. Worked at Reprise and subsequently Warner Bros. between 1960–1994. Rock and Roll Hall of Fame inductee.

Peanut Butter Wolf: DJ/Producer. Owner of Stones Throw label.

Liz Rosenberg: Senior Executive Vice President of Publicity for Warner Bros. Records. Worked for Warner Bros. 1971–2010. Madonna's publicist 1982–2015.

Roxanne Shanté: MC. Member of the Juice Crew, recording artist for Pop Art 1984–1987, Cold Chillin' 1987–1991, Livin' Large 1992–1993.

Eugene Shelton: Vice-president of Media Relations, Warner Bros. Records 1988–1996. Publicist for Cold Chillin' recording artists, namely Big Daddy Kane.

Troy Shelton: Independent promotion man (Xpertz) starting in 1986. Worked many Juice Crew/Cold Chillin' records, and worked in promotion department at Warner Bros. Records starting in 1991.

Tom Silverman: Founder of Tommy Boy Records.

Jeff Smith: Product Manager at Warner Bros. Records 1988–1991. Assigned to handle Cold Chillin'.

TJ Swan: Hip-Hop singer. Member of the Juice Crew. Sang hooks for many Cold Chillin'/Prism artists 1986–1991, namely Biz Markie.

SHOUT OUTS

First and foremost I'd like to thank my Moms (Judy Moore), my own Big Daddy (Bob Merlis), my brothers Alex and Dr. Tim Merlis, Florence Gan, Mama Bear & Drew P., Scott B. Bomar at BMG for taking a chance on me and putting me on, David Manning for editorial suggestions, Jamillah Abdul-Kareem (Glamorous), Bill Adler, Arthur Baker, Bill Bentley, Big Daddy Kane, Andre Booth, Ced Gee, Dan Charnas, Stu Cohen, Brian Coleman, Cutmaster Cool V, Craig G, Cut Chemist, DJ Steve1der & The Questions Posse, Dr. Butcher, George DuBose, Easy Mo Bee, Geoff Edgers, Fly Ty, Kenneth Freundlich, Aaron Fuchs, Jeff Gold, Grand Daddy I.U., William "Miami" Hernandez, Robin Hurley, Ife Kiara, Jam Master Jae & The Noah's Bagels Posse, Dee Joseph, Kool G Rap, Koolie Koo, Ramon Limon & The Aron's Posse, Gene Lee, Monica Lynch, Marley Marl, Born King Mathematics Allah, Milky Wayne McCoy (the source of *The Source*), Mister Cee, Mr. C (Joe McEwen), Catherine McGann, Havelock Nelson, Al Pereira, Prime Minster Pete Nice, Mo Ostin, Bob Perry, Jay Quan, Liz Rosenberg, Shawn Setaro, Eugene Shelton, Troy Shelton, Tom Silverman, Graham Smith, Jeff Smith, TJ Swan, Noah Uman, Will C, Peanut Butter Wolf, anyone who was ever in the Juice Crew, anyone who was ever on Cold Chillin'—this is your story, thank you for the inspiration

Extra Special Thanks

Masta Ace, DJ King David Haze

SELECTED DISCOGRAPHY

Juice Crew Non-LP Singles

1983

Dimples D.—"Sucker D.J.'s (I Will Survive)" (Partytime) (Marley Marl's first production credit)

1984

Mr. Magic—"Magic's Message" (Posse Records)

Roxanne Shanté—"Roxanne's Revenge" (Pop Art)

1985

N.Y.C. Cutter—"D.J. Cuttin" (Pop Art) (this is Marley Marl)

M.C. Craig "G"—"Shout" (Pop Art)

M.C. Craig "G"—"Transformer" (Pop Art)

M.C. Shan—"Feed The World" (MCA)

Marley Marl Featuring McShan—"Marley Marl Scratch" (NIA)

Roxanne Shanté—"Queen Of Rox (Shanté Rox On)" (Pop Art)

Roxanne Shanté—"Runaway" (Pop Art)

Roxanne Shanté—"Bite This" (Pop Art)

1986

Abdul Tariq—"Education" (Sutra) (not Juice Crew, but features DJ work by Cutmaster Cool V)

Biz Markie "The Inhuman Orchestra" Featuring T.J. Swan—"Make The Music With Your Mouth, Biz"/"The Biz Dance"/"They're Coming To Take Me Away Ha-Haa"/"A One, Two" (Prism)

D.J. Polo & Kool G. Rap—"It's A Demo"/"I'm Fly" (Cold Chillin') (remix of "It's A Demo" appears on first LP)

Glamour Girls Featuring M.C. Craig "G"—"Oh! Veronica" (Pop Art) (Glamour Girls = Glamorous, Sweet Tee, Sin Ski)

M. C. Shan—"Beat Biter"/"The Bridge" (Bridge Records)

M.C. Shan—"Jane, Stop This Crazy Thing"/"Cocaine" (Cold Chillin') (first Cold Chillin' release)

Marley Marl—"The Man Marley Marl" (Smokin') (on Smokin' Beats compilation)

Roxanne Shanté—"The Def Fresh Crew"/"Biz Beat" (Pop Art)

Roxanne (Fly) Shanté Featuring Steady B—"I'm Fly Shanté (Pop Art)

Roxanne Shanté vs. Sparky Dee—*Round 1* 12" (Spin Records)

Super Kids—"The Tragedy (Don't Do It)" (NIA)

The Terminators—"Forever Dis"/"Polo" (Snowflake) (DJ Polo's group before Kool G Rap & DJ Polo)

1987

Big Daddy Kane—"Get Into It"/"Somethin' Funky"/"Just Rhymin' With Biz" (Prism)
("Just Rhymin' With Biz" appears on first LP)

Biz Markie Featuring T.J. Swan—"Nobody Beats The Biz" (Prism)
(remix appears on first LP)

D.J. Polo & Kool G. Rapp—"Rikers Island"/"Rhyme Tyme" (Cold Chillin')
("Rikers Island" is tacked to the end of CD version of *Wanted: Dead Or Alive*)

Hot Day/Super Kids—"Hot Day Master Mix"/"The Super Kids Live At Hip Hop U.S.A."/"Go Queensbridge" (Hot Day Records)

Juice Crew All Stars—"Evolution"/"Juice Crew All Stars" (Cold Chillin')
("Evolution" = M.C. Shan, Debby Dee, Kool G. Rap, Glamorous, T.J. Swan; "Juice Crew All Stars" = Roxanne Shanté, Craig G, MC Percy, M.C. Shan, Kool G Rap, Glamorous)

Marley Marl Featuring M.C. Shan—"He Cuts So Fresh" (MCA)
(b-side of Finesse & Synquis—"Bass Game" and also on *Uptown Is Kickin' It* compilation)

Roxanne (Fly) Shanté—"Pay Back"/"Freestyle Live" Featuring Biz Markie (Pop Art)

Roxanne Shanté—“Have A Nice Day” (Cold Chillin’) (abridged version appears on her first album without verse dissing Boogie Down Productions)

1988

Glamorous—“Good To Go”/”I Know You Want Me” (Prism)

Cold Chillin’ Juice Crew—“Cold Chillin’ Christmas” (Warner Bros.) (on *Winter Warnerland* compilation)

1989

Ace & Action—“Together”/”Letter To The Better” (Prism) (Remix of “Letter To The Better” appears on Master Ace’s *Take a Look Around* LP)

1990

Master Ace—“Movin’ On”/”Go Where I Send Thee” (Cold Chillin’) (a-side appears on his LP, b-side is exclusive to this single. B-side produced by Unique, but credited to Mister Cee)

1992

Scoob & Scrap—“Non Stop”/”Who’s In Da House” (Livin’ Large)

MC Shan—“Hip Hop Roughneck”/”Watchin’ My Style” (Livin’ Large)

1993

MC Shan—“Pee-Nile Reunion”/”Don’t Call It A Comeback” (Livin’ Large)

1994

Big Scoob—“Suckaz Can’t Hang”/”Big Booty Bandit” (Cold Chillin’)

1996

Big Scoob—“Champagne On The Block” (Cold Chillin’)

Roxanne Shanté—“Queen Pin” (Cold Chillin’, promo only)

Guest Appearances from Cold Chillin' Era

1988

Rick James—"Loosey's Rap" (Reprise) (single, and from Rick James' *Wonderful* LP, featuring Roxanne Shanté, Big Daddy Kane—some versions don't feature Kane)

Paul Simon—"Me and Julio Down by the Schoolyard" (Warner Bros.) (from *Negotiations and Love Songs* best of collection, originally released on *Paul Simon* LP, Columbia Records, 1972, music video features Big Daddy Kane rapping and Biz Markie beatboxing—this does not appear on any album)

1989

Quincy Jones—"Back On The Block" (Qwest) (from *Back On The Block* LP, featuring Big Daddy Kane, Ice-T, Kool Moe Dee, Melle Mel)

1990

Public Enemy—"Burn Hollywood Burn" (Def Jam) (from *Fear of a Black Planet* LP, featuring Big Daddy Kane, Ice Cube)

1991

Heavy D—"Don't Curse" (Uptown/MCA) (from *Peaceful Journey* LP, featuring Big Daddy Kane, CL Smooth, Grand Puba, Kool G Rap, Q-Tip)

Patti LaBelle—"Feels Like Another One" (MCA) (featuring Big Daddy Kane; also on Patti LaBelle's *Burnin'* LP)

1992

Beastie Boys—"The Biz Vs. The Nuge" (Capitol) (from *Check Your Head* LP, featuring Biz Markie)

Cold Chillin' LPs

1987

MC Shan—*Down By Law* (reissued on Cold Chillin'/Warner Bros. that year)*

1988

Biz Markie—*Goin' Off*+
Big Daddy Kane—*Long Live The Kane*+
Marley Marl—*In Control, Volume* 1+
MC Shan—*Born To Be Wild*+

1989

Kool G Rap & DJ Polo—*Road To The Riches*+
Big Daddy Kane—*It's A Big Daddy Thing*#
The Diabolical Biz Markie—*The Biz Never Sleeps*+
Roxanne Shanté—*Bad Sister*#

1990

2 Deep—*Honey, That's Show Biz*#
MC Shan—*Play It Again, Shan*+
Master Ace—*Take A Look Around*#
Kool G Rap & DJ Polo—*Wanted: Dead Or Alive*+
Grand Daddy I.U.—*Smooth Assassin*#
Big Daddy Kane—*Taste Of Chocolate*#

1991

Kid Capri—*The Tape*+
The Genius—*Words From The Genius*#
Big Daddy Kane—*Prince Of Darkness*#
Marley Marl—*In Control Volume II (For Your Steering Pleasure)*+

Diamond Shell—*The Grand Imperial Diamond Shell*#
Biz Markie—*I Need A Haircut*+

1992
Nubian M.O.B.—*Nubian M.O.B.*#
Shanté—*The Bitch Is Back*@
Kool G Rap & DJ Polo—*Live And Let Die**

1993
Big Daddy Kane—*Looks Like A Job For . . .* #
TBTBT—*Too Bad To Be True*+
TCF Crew—*Come And Play With Me*+
Biz Markie—*All Samples Cleared!*+
YZ—*The Ghetto's Been Good To Me*@

1994
Grand Daddy I.U.—*Lead Pipe*%
King Sun—*Strictly Ghetto** *(technically an EP)*

1995
Kool G Rap—*4, 5, 6*%
*Cold Chillin'
+Cold Chillin'/Warner Bros.
#Cold Chillin'/Reprise
%Cold Chillin'/Epic Street
@Livin' Large Records

BIBLIOGRAPHY

Author Interviews
Arthur Baker, February 24, 2018
Bill Bentley, August 8, 2018
Big Daddy Kane, November 28, 2017
Andre Booth, March 2, 2018
Ced Gee, February 25, 2018
Stu Cohen, April 5, 2018
Craig G, April 6, 2018
Cut Chemist, November 9, 2017
Dr. Butcher, January 23, 2018
George DuBose, December 29, 2017
Easy Mo Bee, July 19, 2018
Fly Ty, November 26, 2017
Kenneth David Freundlich, September 25, 2018
Aaron Fuchs, November 16, 2017
Dee Joseph, February 13, 2018
Glamorous, March 5, 2018
Grand Daddy I.U., January 9, 2018
Grand Dragon KD, April 1, 2018
Ife Kiara, January 19, 2018
Jay Quan, November 22, 2017
Kool G Rap, May 6, 2018
Marley Marl, March 16, 2018
Bob Merlis, September 17, 2018
Monica Lynch, November 7, 2017
Masta Ace, January 6, 2018 and August 11, 2018
Mister Cee, July 13, 2018

Mo Ostin, March 9, 2018
Peanut Butter Wolf, December 3, 2017
Liz Rosenberg, September 5, 2018
Eugene Shelton, January 28, 2018
Troy Shelton, October 29, 2017
Tom Silverman, February 2, 2018
Jeff Smith, November 2, 2017
TJ Swan, April 29, 2018

Books

Coleman, Brian. *Check the Technique: Liner Notes For Hip-Hop Junkies*. New York: Villard, 2007.

Lee, V., Dutch, L. *DJ Cool V Never Sleeps*. New York: Hip Hop Hands Foundation, 2017.

Slagel, Brian. *For the Sake of Heaviness: The History of Metal Blade Records*. New York/Los Angeles/Nashville: BMG, 2017.

Articles

Arnold, Paul. "MC Shan Recalls Laughing At Rakim And Squabbin' With LL Cool J, And Exposes The Label And Producer Profiting From His Classic Material," *HipHopDX*, February 23, 2012. https://hiphopdx.com/interviews/id.1859/title.mc-shan-recalls-laughing-at-rakim-and-squabbin-with-11 -cool-j-and-exposes-the-label-and-producer-profiting-from-his-classic-material#

Atco. "Record Report: Big Daddy Kane *Prince of Darkness*," *The Source*, January 1992.

Benatar, Giselle. "'Sex' and Money," *Entertainment Weekly*, November 6, 1992. https://ew.com/article/1992/11/06/sex-and-money/

Davidson, T., Biz Markie. "Tommy meets The Biz," *The Source*, February 1992.

Disco. "Record Report: Big Daddy Kane *A Taste Of Chocolate*," *The Source*, December 1990.

Erictb. "The Roxanne War: Complete Chronology of Hip Hop's Greatest Saga," *Ericpedia,* January 1, 2013. https://erictb.wordpress.com/2013/01/01/the-roxanne-war-complete-chronology-of-Hip-Hops-greatest-saga/

Ettelson, Robbie. "Interview: MC Shan Talks Juice Crew Legends, Little Known Beefs, and His Fallout With Marley Marl," *Complex,* January 12, 2013. https://www.complex.com/music/2013/01/mc-shan

Ettelson, Robbie. "The New Music Seminar Battle For World Supremacy: An Oral History," *Red Bull Music Academy,* July 24, 2015. http://daily.redbullmusicacademy.com/2015/07/new-music-seminar-oral-history

French, Howard W. "Drug Deaths After Arrests Draw Scrutiny," *New York Times,* June 14, 1989. https://www.nytimes.com/1989/06/14/nyregion/drug-deaths-after-arrests-draw-scrutiny.html

Jay Quan. "Interview w/ MC Shan," *Tha Foundation,* September 3, 2002. http://www.thafoundation.com/shan.htm

Mao, Jeff. "Lectures: Marley Marl," *Red Bull Music Academy,* November 25, 2014. http://www.redbullmusicacademy.com/lectures/marley-marl-tokyo-2014

Nelson, Havelock. "Soul Controller, Sole Survivor," *The Source,* October 1991.

peinti. "Roxanne Wars," *Discogs,* May 2018. https://www.discogs.com/lists/Roxanne-Wars/26904?page=1

Schwartz, Zach. "Talking to Tragedy Khadafi, New York's Most Slept-On Rapper," *Vice,* January 5, 2015. https://www.vice.com/en_us/article/5gk8bb/tragedy-khadafi-is-still-queensbridges-realest-456

Shecter, Jon. "Cop Killer Won't Die," *The Source,* November 1992.

Sorcinelli, Gino. "Biz Markie's 'Just a Friend' Started Out As 'You Must Be On Speed,'" Medium, October 19, 2016. https://medium.com/micro-chop/biz-markies-just-a-friend-started-out-as-you-must-be-on-speed-ab88ed69fa2c

Wilkinson, Dan. "The story of the first ever rap beef," *Red Bull,* August 13, 2015. https://www.redbull.com/gb-en/roxanne-shante-and-the-first-rap-beef

Films

Time Is Illmatic. Directed by One9, Kino Lorber, 2004.

Podcasts

Combat Jack. "The Bowlegged Lou Episode." *The Combat Jack Show*. Podcast audio, February 23, 2016. http://loudspeakersnetwork.com/show/the-bowlegged-lou-episode/#.W9tYLXpKii4

Combat Jack. "The Chuck D Episode Featuring Keith Shocklee." *The Combat Jack Show*. Podcast audio, July 15, 2014. http://loudspeakersnetwork.com/show/the-chuck-d-episode-featuring-keith-shocklee/#.W9tZ8XpKii4

Combat Jack. "The DJ D-Nice Episode." *The Combat Jack Show*. Podcast audio, May 20, 2014. https://soundcloud.com/thecombatjackshow/the-dj-d-nice-episode

Combat Jack. "The Marley Marl Episode." *The Combat Jack Show*. Podcast audio, May 27, 2014. https://soundcloud.com/thecombatjackshow/the-marley-marl-episode

Ice-T. "Episode 27: Battle Rapping with Roxanne Shante." *Final Level Podcast*. Podcast audio, January 20, 2015. https://podtail.com/podcast/ice-t-final-level/episode-27-battle-rapping-with-roxanne-shante/

Nardwuar. "Nardwuar Vs. Ab-Soul, Schoolboy Q & Kendrick Lamar." *Nardwuar*. Podcast audio, November 15, 2014. http://nardwuar.com/rad/kendrick-lamar/

Philaflava. "Take It Personal (KRS-One Interview)." *Take It Personal*. Podcast audio, April 25, 2018. https://www.takeitpersonalradio.com/krs-one-interview

Premium Pete. "Roxanne Shante." *The Premium Pete Show*. Podcast audio, March 22, 2018. http://thepremiumpeteshow.com/2018/podcast/03/22/roxanne-shante/

Setaro, Shawn. "Episode 150: Fat Joe & Remy Ma." The Cipher. Podcast audio, April 11, 2016. http://theciphershow.com/episode/150/

Stretch Armstrong and Bobbito Garcia. "The Roots' Black Thought On How Art Saved His Life." *What's Good With Stretch & Bobbito*. Podcast audio, September 19, 2018. http://thepremiumpeteshow.com/2018/podcast/03/22/roxanne-shante/

Videos

Buchanan, Gabriel. "Biz Markie vs. Gilbert O'Sullivan." Online video clip. YouTube, November 17, 2014. https://www.youtube.com/watch?v=08N719T_Me0

Clapa01. "Sweet Tee / Big Daddy Kane / Craig G / Lazy Laz—Freestyle (In Control Show)." Online video clip. Youtube, September 19, 2011. https://www.youtube.com/watch?v=JSTU2sn5Rq8

Dotvisionfilms. "Charlie Stettler Tells About 1st Black Show @ Radio City Music Hall with Fat Boys." Online video clip. YouTube, February 11, 2013. https://www.youtube.com/watch?v=zxGYGbuPWxE

KangK. "Big Daddy Kane—I Get The Job Done(Arsenio Hall Show)." Online video clip. YouTube. YouTube, March 2, 2006. https://www.youtube.com/watch?v=_R8hvjpdw54

mcshan1. Online video clip. Instagram, 2018.

Recording Academy / GRAMMYs. "Eminem accepting the GRAMMY for Best Rap Album at the 45th GRAMMY Awards | GRAMMYs." Online video clip. YouTube, January 29, 2010. https://www.youtube.com/watch?v=h_y2F8KjMTg

Sway's Universe. "Roxanne Shanté Talks 'Roxanne Roxanne,' Big Daddy Kane, Nas, Nicki Minaj and More." Online video clip. YouTube, March 22, 2018. https://swaysuniverse.com/roxanne-shante-talks-roxanne-roxanne-big-daddy-kane-nas-nicki-minaj-and-more/

VladTV. "MC Shan Talks About Being Molested as a Child." Online video clip. YouTube, December 8, 2016. https://www.youtube.com/watch?v=WZe0dCrk2yY

Audio Recordings

Will C. "WHBI Rewind & Classic Sign Off 1981," 2008. *Down The Dial*. Perf. Mr. Magic. Double You Productions, 2008. CD.

Court Cases

Grand Upright Music v. Warner Brothers Rec, et al. 1:91-cv-07648-KTD. U.S. District Court, Southern District of New York (Foley Square). 1992.

INDEX

Note: P indicates a picture in the photo insert

M

N

O

P

Q

R

S